CHAPTER 1
HEALTH CARE ETHICS

Chapter 1 introduces the reader to the nature of ethics and the place of medical ethics within this discipline.

- The medical and nursing professions have always prided themselves on maintaining high standards of morality. In modern times, this can be seen in various codes of ethics, such as those drawn up by the AMA and ANA.

- The chief theme through the ages is that medicine is for the people. Indeed, when the needs of the patient are the focus of health care, the ethical issues are fewer. One might then conclude that good medicine is good ethics.

- However, over the past 60 years, advances in medical treatment and technology have produced problems that did not exist in the past (eg, should we use treatments to keep dying patients alive when there is little hope the patient will benefit from the procedures?).

CHAPTER 2
ENCOUNTERING AN ETHICAL DILEMMA

Considerations when encountering a potential ethical dilemma:

- Does an ethical dilemma exist?
- What are the known elements of the situation?
- What additional information is necessary to understand the dilemma?
- What ethical framework(s) might help to understand and resolve the dilemma?
- Who should be involved in making and implementing the decision?
- All things considered, what ought to be done?
- How should the situation be evaluated?

Factors to explore when people disagree about how to resolve a dilemma:

- Are there differing views about the value of the proposed goal of care or treatment?
- Are there differing views about the ethical priorities?
- Are there communication problems among health care providers, family, and patient?
- Are there unresolved family issues?

CHAPTER 1
HEALTH CARE ETHICS

Methods of moral decision-making:

- Decision-making methods come in various forms and reflect different historical schools of thought.

- Induction is decision-making that depends on one's experience. This method is popular with some philosophers.

- Teleological systems are based on consideration of the ends, the goals, or the purposes of an action.

- Other methods favor principles that are derived from authority, religion, or reason itself. One example would be the deontological writers, who are inspired by Kant, whose basic tenet of behavior was to do one's duty.

- All of these methods can be helpful in reaching a decision on how best to deal with a problem. Ultimately the goal of any discussion is how best to serve the patient.

This card refers to the following book:
Perrin KO, McGhee J. *Ethics and Conflict*. Thorofare, NJ: SLACK Incorporated; 2001.

 **SLACK** INCORPORATED   6900 Grove Road • Thorofare, NJ 08086 • 856-848-1000
An innovative information, education and management company

CHAPTER 2
ENCOUNTERING AN ETHICAL DILEMMA

What a nurse can do to enhance group decision-making and resolution of an ethical dilemma:

- Actively listen to the concerns of the patient, family, and other health care providers
- Clarify the meanings of the words and phrases that others are using
- Summarize the facts to obtain a base for further discussion
- Attempt to understand the ethical perspectives of the other people involved
- Assist with development of a group statement of the clinical problems and the moral issues involved in the dilemma

When a nurse does not agree with an ethical decision, one possible option is conscientious refusal. A nurse might ponder the following questions before engaging in conscientious refusal:

- Is the decision to refuse based on personal moral standards? Is it motivated by personal rather than external sanctions?
- Has the nurse made a prior determination of moral rightness or wrongness of the proposed course of action?
- What are the attitudes of the institutional administration toward conscientious refusal and what state laws are in effect concerning conscientious refusal?

This card refers to the following book:
Perrin KO, McGhee J. *Ethics and Conflict*. Thorofare, NJ: SLACK Incorporated; 2001.

 SLACK INCORPORATED   6900 Grove Road • Thorofare, NJ 08086 • 856-848-1000
An innovative information, education and management company

CHAPTER 3
BEGINNING OF LIFE ISSUES

Problems arising at the beginning of life:

An initial question might be asked: When does life begin? Parents are fascinated by the role they play in transmitting life, and health care practitioners, from the nature of their profession, are involved in posing such queries.

Historically, the two main positions that attempted to answer this question were: (1) life begins at conception (instantaneous hominization) (2) life begins sometime later in the course of human gestation. There is no consensus on the matter, but how one answers the question influences how one will deal with later dilemmas.

Problems are usually divided into two sections:

BIRTH CONTROL

People have always attempted to control the size of their families or the population in general. Methods have included everything from contraception to abortion to infanticide. While the last method mentioned is not acceptable in modern society, recent advances in contraception have popularized such procedures during the past half century. In the area of birth control, churches have expressed strong opinions, and abortion has become a political issue.

CHAPTER 4
HEALTH MAINTENANCE ACROSS THE LIFE SPAN

Questions to consider when reviewing a patient's competence[1]:

- Does the patient understand her or his medical condition?

- Does the patient understand the options and consequences of her or his decision?

IF THE PATIENT IS REFUSING TREATMENT:

- Is the refusal based on rational reasons?

- If the refusal is based on religious beliefs, are the beliefs acceptable and entitled to First Amendment protection?

Additional information a nurse admitting a patient to a health care facility might wish to consider about a patient's advance directive:

- Has the patient spoken to anyone about the terms of the directive?

- Who has the patient spoken with?

- What was discussed?

- How does the patient express her or his wishes in her or his own words?

1. Chell B. Competency: what it is, what it isn't, and why it matters. In: Monagle JF, Thomasma DC, eds. *Health Care Ethics: Critical Issues for the 21st Century.* Gaithersburg, Md: Aspen Publications; 1998:116-127.
2. Harrison C, Kenny NP. Bioethics for clinicians: 9 involving children in medical ethics. *CMAJ.* 1997;156:825-829.

CHAPTER 3
BEGINNING OF LIFE ISSUES

INFERTILITY

While most people are trying to control their fertility, some 20% of the population have a different problem: they wish to have children but cannot do so because they are infertile.

Older methods for infertile couples were usually based on some kind of artificial insemination, but new procedures such as in vitro fertilization have raised new questions and problems. For instance, what are the limits of manipulation to enhance fertility? Does the bond of marriage become strained if a woman becomes pregnant when there is a donor or third party involved? What does one do with the embryos that are not implanted and are left in the clinic?

Many people seem to consider helping married people to have children very different morally from using the gamete of some known or unknown donor. The use of donor gametes can raise the issue, "Whose baby is it?"

This card refers to the following book:
Perrin KO, McGhee J. *Ethics and Conflict*. Thorofare, NJ: SLACK Incorporated; 2001.

 6900 Grove Road • Thorofare, NJ 08086 • 856-848-1000
An innovative information, education and management company

CHAPTER 4
HEALTH MAINTENANCE ACROSS THE LIFE SPAN

To ensure a patient has received sufficient information to understand the proposed treatment and consent to treatment, the nurse might ask the patient the following:

- What did the physician (or other health care provider) tell you about the treatment?
- Do you have any questions about your prognosis or expected recovery after treatment?
- What problems do you anticipate during the treatment?
- Do you understand the alternatives to the proposed treatment and know their consequences?

Harrison and Kenny[2] recommend the decision-making capacity of an adolescent be examined in light of the adolescent's:

- Ability to understand and communicate relevant information
- Ability to think and choose with some independence
- Ability to assess the potential for risks and harms as well as to consider consequences and multiple options
- Achievement of a fairly stable set of values

This card refers to the following book:
Perrin KO, McGhee J. *Ethics and Conflict*. Thorofare, NJ: SLACK Incorporated; 2001.

 6900 Grove Road • Thorofare, NJ 08086 • 856-848-1000
An innovative information, education and management company

CHAPTER 5
HOW SHOULD HEALTH CARE RESOURCES BE ALLOCATED?

As health care consumes increasingly more of the gross domestic product (GDP), people have begun to wonder if there ought to be a limit to how much money is allocated to it.

Economists, ethicists, politicians, insurers, and health care providers have begun to ask such questions as:

- Is health care rationing ever justifiable?
- If rationing is acceptable, what procedures should be rationed or which people should have their health care choices limited?
- Are there limits to the amount of health care an individual has a right to receive?
- How should rationing decisions be made?
- Who should make decisions about access to and allocation of health care?
- How should expensive or scarce resources be allocated?

CHAPTER 6
ENCOUNTERING UNJUST, INCOMPETENT, OR ILLEGAL BEHAVIOR

Nurses who are considering whether to report an error might contemplate the following:

- Are current or future patients likely to be harmed if the error is not disclosed?
- Will failing to disclose this error lead to additional errors for this patient or other patients?
- Would a recurrent problem be more likely to be rectified if this error is identified as one in a pattern of errors by various health care providers?
- What are the nurse's personal interests in the situation? Is failure to report a problem an egoistic decision?
- Does the nurse believe it is important to be known as a person who is truthful and trustworthy?
- Should the patient be notified of the untoward event?

CHAPTER 5
HOW SHOULD HEALTH CARE RESOURCES BE ALLOCATED?

Since there is currently a shortage of organs for transplant in the United States, health care ethicists and activists have raised the following questions about the just distribution of donor organs:

- Should the United States change to a presumed consent system for donation (one in which it is assumed that the person would want to donate her or his organs unless she or he had previously indicated an objection)?

- Should directed donation (when the donor or family can identify the recipient) be considered as a means of increasing cadaver donations?

- Should donors or families be paid for the organs, or should we continue to expect donation to be a voluntary, altruistic process?

- What is the fairest way to allocate an organ when there are several compatible matches: by region of the country, by severity of illness, likelihood of success of the transplant, or some other criterion?

This card refers to the following book:
Perrin KO, McGhee J. *Ethics and Conflict*. Thorofare, NJ: SLACK Incorporated; 2001.

SLACK INCORPORATED   6900 Grove Road • Thorofare, NJ 08086 • 856-848-1000
An innovative information, education and management company

CHAPTER 6
ENCOUNTERING UNJUST, INCOMPETENT, OR ILLEGAL BEHAVIOR

Nurses ought to consider carefully before committing to any collective action, particularly a strike.

Questions that a nurse might want to answer before joining a strike include:

- Is there sufficient cause for this strike?

- Is the quality of patient care or reimbursement for nursing services so poor that a strike would be the most effective way to improve them?

- Have all provisions of the collective bargaining agreement been maintained?

- Have all alternatives to a strike been attempted and found ineffective?

- Have all provisions of the law been met and is this a legally defensible strike?

- Have provisions been made to maintain safe patient care during the strike?

- Are there any damages that might occur as the result of a strike?

- How will this strike affect me and my family?

- Can I afford financially, physically, emotionally, and ethically to strike?

This card refers to the following book:
Perrin KO, McGhee J. *Ethics and Conflict*. Thorofare, NJ: SLACK Incorporated; 2001.

SLACK INCORPORATED   6900 Grove Road • Thorofare, NJ 08086 • 856-848-1000
An innovative information, education and management company

When caring for a patient whose family is considering a do-not-resuscitate order (DNR), the nurse might want to consider emphasizing to the patient and family that:

- Consent to a DNR order does NOT imply consent to withdraw other medical interventions, or a decision to switch to a goal of comfort rather than cure.

- Consent to a DNR does NOT imply the patient will receive less care. Patients with DNR orders in ICUs frequently receive more nursing time and nursing care than patients who do not have DNR orders.

Patients and families may request unrealistically aggressive care at the end of life because:

- They have falsely high expectations of modern medicine.

- They do not trust their health care providers or insurers to act in the patient's best interests.

- They have unresolved issues with the dying person.

- They believe a miracle may occur.

- The patient is afraid to die or not prepared to die.

CHAPTER 7
ETHICAL ISSUES AT THE END OF LIFE

The traditional ethical principle, double effect, is sometimes invoked in the discussion of pain management for the dying person. The Principle of Double Effect states that when an action has two effects, one good (relieving pain) and one bad (hastening death), it has been considered morally permissible to take the action if certain conditions are met.

These conditions include:

- The act itself (giving pain medication to relieve pain) is either good or morally neutral

- Only the good effect (pain relief) is intended

- The good effect is not achieved through the bad effect (the patient's pain is not relieved because the patient dies)

- There is no other means of attaining the good effect (other alternatives for pain relief are not possible or are ineffective)

- There is a good reason for assuming the risk of the bad effect (relief of severe pain)

This card refers to the following book:
Perrin KO, McGhee J. *Ethics and Conflict*. Thorofare, NJ: SLACK Incorporated; 2001.

SLACK
INCORPORATED

6900 Grove Road • Thorofare, NJ 08086 • 856-848-1000
An innovative information, education and management company

Ethics
and Conflict

Ethics
and Conflict

Kathleen Ouimet Perrin, RN, CCRN, PhD(c)
Saint Anselm College
Manchester, NH

James McGhee, PhD
Saint Anselm College
Manchester, NH

SLACK
INCORPORATED

an innovative information, education, and management company
6900 Grove Road • Thorofare, NJ 08086

Cover illustration by Thom Sevalrud
Copyright © 2001 by SLACK Incorporated

The procedures and practices described in this book should be implemented in a manner consistent
with the professional standards set for the circumstances that apply in each specific situation. Every
effort has been made to confirm the accuracy of the information presented and to correctly relate gener-
ally accepted practices. The author, editor, and publisher cannot accept responsibility for errors or exclu-
sions or for the outcome of the application of the material presented herein. There is no expressed or
implied warranty of this book or information imparted by it. Any review or mention of specific companies or products is not intended as an endorsement by the author or the publisher.

The work SLACK publishes is peer reviewed. Prior to publication, recognized leaders in the field,
educators, and clinicians provide important feedback on the concepts and content that we publish. We
welcome feedback on this work.

Perrin, Kathleen Ouimet.
    Nursing concepts : ethics and conflict / Kathleen Ouimet Perrin, James McGhee.
        p. ; cm. -- (Nursing concepts series)
    Includes bibliographical references and index.
    ISBN 1-55642-517-1 (alk. paper)
    1. Nursing ethics. 2. Nurse and patient. I. Perrin, Kathleen Ouimet. II. McGhee, James,
1937 - . III. Title. IV. Series.
    [DNLM: 1. Ethics, Nursing. 2. Nurse-Patient Relations. WY 85 P458n 2001]
    RT85 .P47 2001
    174'.2--dc21

                                                                                    2001042606

Printed in the United States of America
Published by: SLACK Incorporated
                 6900 Grove Road
                 Thorofare, NJ 08086 USA
                 Telephone: 856-848-1000
                 Fax: 856-853-5991
                 www.slackbooks.com

Last digit is print number: 10 9 8 7 6 5 4 3 2 1

DEDICATION

To my husband, Robin; our son, Scott; and my parents, Charles and Marie Ouimet, for being available when I needed them. To my doctoral committee members, especially Dr. H. Ira Fritz, and my peers at my entry colloquium at The Union Institute for insisting that I could and should write this book.
Kathleen Ouimet Perrin, RN, CCRN, PhD(c)

To my wife Mary and our children Kathleen, Jamie, and Fiona.
James McGhee, PhD

Contents

ACKNOWLEDGMENTS

Despite the passage of many years, I would like to acknowledge the 1983 National Endowment for the Humanities Summer Institute in Moral Philosophy and Nursing Ethics for beginning my formal education in nursing ethics.
Kathleen Ouimet Perrin, RN, CCRN, PhD(c)

I would like to recognize the help given to me by my students, without whom books like this would never be written; and also to express my gratitude to my fellow faculty colleagues, who are a continual source of encouragement in such endeavors.
James McGhee, PhD

ABOUT THE AUTHORS

Kathleen Ouimet Perrin, RN, CCRN, PhD(c) is an associate professor of nursing at Saint Anselm College, Manchester, NH, where she teaches critical care nursing to senior nursing students. She received her bachelor of science degree from the University of Massachusetts, Boston, her master of science degree from Boston College, and is currently enrolled in a doctoral program at The Union Institute, Cincinnati, Ohio. Her primary areas of publication and interest are critical care nursing (especially cardiovascular and neuroscience nursing), ethical issues at the end of life, and managing conflict in the health care system.

James McGhee, PhD was born and educated in Scotland. He received a doctorate in Christian ethics from the Gregorian University in Italy in 1974. After teaching in Britain and Canada, he came to New Hampshire, where he has been a member of the Theology Department at Saint Anselm College for 25 years, 11 of which serving as chairman. He has published in his field. He teaches courses in medical ethics and marriage and humanities; and serves on ethics committees for local hospitals, hospice, and other health care facilities. He acts as consultant to religious organizations and, on occasion, the state legislature. He is married and resides in Manchester, NH with his wife Mary and their three children.

PREFACE

This book is the result of many years of teaching, both in the classroom and in the clinical setting. Both authors, one a nurse and the other an ethician, are college professors who have served as members of hospital ethics committees for over 25 years. Thus, we bring to the book a combination of theory and practice. Knowledge of how ethical decisions are made is complemented by much experience with how health care is delivered and the principal problems associated with that delivery in our society.

This text presents bioethical issues and case studies from nurses' perspectives. What should a nurse do when patients, family, physicians, and other health care providers have varying perspectives on how to provide care for a patient? Should a nurse break confidentiality and tell a daughter that her mother is actively dying? When and how should a nurse intervene to protect an elderly person from a hazardous living situation?

Nurses have a compelling interest in bioethics because of their unique position in the health care system. They are strategically positioned between the patient, family, and physician. They listen to the medical, legal, and ethical concerns of the people involved, while taking responsibility for delivering the care in question. In their clinical practice, nurses must consider the ethical question, "What ought to be done for this person?"

It is our hope that the insights provided here will be of help to the reader in dealing with the moral problems that occur in the course of their professional work. After studying the case studies in this book, the reader will be prepared to encounter ethical dilemmas in the health care setting and participate in the debate about how health care should be delivered in the 21st century.

Kathleen Ouimet Perrin, RN, CCRN, PhD(c)
James McGhee, PhD

Chapter 1

Health Care Ethics

James McGhee, PhD

Mr. Paul Lazenby is in his late 70s. He is in the hospital intensive care unit, having suffered several strokes, which have partially destroyed his brain functioning. He is unconscious, on a ventilator, and is being fed by tubes. The doctor in consultation with others is sure that he is in the dying process. However, Mr. Lazenby lingers on, causing grief and anxiety to his family. What can be done? The physician calls for a consultation, and the ethics committee meets to advise her and the family about the best course to follow.

How would such a meeting proceed? What would be the method of discussion and possible argument that the committee members would follow?

Although we are in a hospital, we have now also entered into the world of moral decision-making or ethics.

WHAT IS ETHICS ALL ABOUT?

Ethics attempts to answer the question, "What should I do?" or "What ought I to do?" These two little English words, *should* and *ought,* lie at the heart of ethical decision-making. To pursue this line of thinking, one might further ask, "What is the goal of my action?" The standard answer would be to act well! Or, to meet the basic needs of myself and others. To whom does this task belong? To everyone, of course. We are all in our own

> Ethics is about making decisions in order to act well. We all are faced with such dilemmas every day.

way *ethicians* trying to act the best possible way and solve our ethical dilemmas. Such is indicative of ethics—showing us the direction in which we should act. In a hospital, as in other institutions, an official ethics committee is often established. Made up of health care workers from various departments of the hospital, as well as others from the general community (say someone trained as an ethician), its tasks can vary from advising when consulted, as in the case of Mr. Lazenby, to assuming an educational role or reviewing policy statements.

Beyond such indicative ethics, there is another level of thinking called *metaethics*, in which people search for values or standards that will help them in their decision-making. A fine example of this would be the principle called *the golden rule*—to treat others as you yourself would like to be treated. It is found in every system and every culture from as far back as we can go in our history.

MEDICAL ETHICS

Sometimes a group of problems crop up in a particular area of life. If we put these related ethical questions together; we call the manner of dealing with them *applied ethics*. Such is medical ethics: it attempts to discuss those moral problems that occur in the practice of medicine from the viewpoint of the patient and the physician, nurse, or other health care workers.

> Medical ethics deals with moral problems that arise in the practice of medicine both from the viewpoint of the medical care provider and the client.
>
> Bioethics expands the concept to include problems coming from the life sciences (eg, cloning).

Sometimes this discipline is called *bioethics*, a word that seeks to extend the scope of the subject to include problems coming from all the life sciences. The case presented at the beginning of this chapter with Mr. Lazenby clearly falls into the category of medical ethics.

Probably no branch of applied ethics has grown in popularity more than medical ethics over the past 40 years or so. You can scarcely pick up a reputable newspaper or journal without some ethical situation being presented to you. Think of the human genome project where we are discovering more and more about the fundamental structure of our bodies and life in general, and increasing our ability to manipulate them.

A LITTLE HISTORY

Ancient Times

Among the ancient Greeks and in the study of "Western civilization," we find that the practice of medicine has always entailed a high moral standard. Originally, sickness and health were associated with religious belief. The ancient god of medicine, Aesclepius, known as the mild god, had shrines built to him where the sick and dying went to have their dreams interpreted and to die peacefully in the presence of the god. Such a good death was known as *euthanasia*, a term which takes on several shades of meaning in our society today. Gradually, however, the priests of Aesclepius found themselves in contention with the followers of a philosopher and physician called Hippocrates (c.460 - c.377 BC). He followed a much more practical approach to illness, trying through observation and treatment to cure or comfort the sick; in other words, this is the start of what we now call *clinical medicine*. Both groups had something in common—the care of the patient.

Hippocrates laid down a code of behavior for physicians, whose principal rule was that a physician should do no harm to his patients. This standard has become the guide for Western medicine ever since. If you go to a medical school graduation ceremony, listen for the part when the new doctors will stand and take what is called the Hippocratic oath. The welfare of their patients will be their first concern. In the course of this centu-

> If we trace the origins of medicine to ancient Greece, we find that from the beginning there was always a high standard of morality associated with its practice. The priests of the god Aesclepius linked sickness to religion, while the followers of Hippocrates were more secular and analytical in their approach. The patient was always the focus of attention.

ry, professional organizations such as the American Medical Association (AMA) and the American Nurses Association (ANA) have set forth modern codes of ethics. These codes reflect the ancient and traditional focus on the needs of the patients.

The Medieval World

With the creation of universities in the 12th and 13th centuries in Europe, added impulse was given to the study of medicine; likewise, new ethical questions arose. A couple of authors will suffice to illustrate the times. Moses Maimonides (1138-1204), a Jewish rabbi and scholar who lived in North Africa and Spain, drew up a code of standards for medical practitioners. While it addresses his own cultural group, he clearly relied on the values of Hippocrates. It is patient-centered and is usually the basis of the ceremonial oath taken at graduations in medical schools within the Jewish tradition. Another writer from Europe was Albert the Great, a philosopher, Catholic bishop, and scientist (1200-1280). He contributed to a trend that continues today with religious moralists. This trend investigates questions about the beginning and end of life and draws up principles to justify medical interventions into peoples' bodies in order to promote their well-being. One example is the principle of totality, which was used to justify sacrificing part of one's body for the sake of the whole. Another common trend to-

> In the Middle Ages, interest centered on ethical-based principles, often based on Greek philosophies. These principles continue what is now called the Hippocratic oath tradition. Principles of behavior were developed by such writers as Maimonides and Albert the Great.

day is to acknowledge that one does not have to use extraordinary means to preserve life. Ordinary means of supporting life were defined as those which did not cause excessive burdens on the patient and family. They offered definite hope of recovery. On the contrary, extraordinary means of life support would not, and thus one would not be obliged to employ them. The Catholic tradition today still provides a rich source for decision-making in the medical-moral field.

The 20th Century

In reality, apart from these theologians, few writers were interested in medical ethics. The reasons were many, but probably the main one was that because the goals of both medicine and ethics were the same, namely to promote the good of the patient, few ethical dilemmas arose. Physicians would visit the sick in their homes, developing a kindly bedside manner. The competent doctor would be able to diagnose the malady and describe its prognosis, advising on the best known way to keep the patient from harm. If the patient recovered, then it was well and good; and if the patient died, the physician would assume a traditional role of helping the person die as well as possible. When the Scotsman Sir Alexander Fleming discovered penicillin from molds in 1928, a new era arrived. We could now place in the patient's hand a pill that would cure an infection. The development of antibiotics, alpha drugs, new machines such as dialysis, and other technologies, coupled with ever-increasing knowledge about our bodies, not only saved lives but produced ethical situations that could not have existed in the past. Without modern techniques, Mr. Lazenby would have died. Now the question is whether or not to let him die

> Recent interest in medical ethics has grown because of advances made in medical science and technology. For instance, we can now keep people alive who in the past would have died. Ethical systems and historical principles are often incorporated into codes by professional organizations. The needs of the patient are still the center of concern in medical care.

or to continue to make heroic efforts to keep him alive. The members of the committee, reflecting a whole variety of systems and principles of behavior common in medical ethics, will make questions and comments. Let's look now at some of the more popular schools of thought or methods that may help us to decide on the right course of action.

METHODS

Induction

When deciding on what to do, many people reflect on what they have done in similar circumstances in the past. Over time they have amassed a series of behavioral patterns that they and others whom they have consulted considered to be right. From experience, they have developed a system on which they can lean when making decisions. The Jesuit educators of the past developed a method of teaching through cases to help in moral decision-making.

Deduction

Most of today's ethicians prefer methods that are more deductive in style, moving along some logical path toward decision-making. Let's look at two main deductive theories of ethics: deontology and teleology.

Deontology

This approach stems from Immanuel Kant, a German philosopher. Although he was a devout Lutheran, he wanted to establish a basis for ethical thinking that was not religious but autonomous and philosophical. He struck upon the idea of *duty* (in Greek *deon*) as the source of ethics. If we all did what we ought to

> *Deontology*: a popular and influential method of moral decision-making derived from the German philosopher Kant. The key to acting well is doing one's duty. They employ principles that they claim should be used universally (eg, autonomy, justice, nonmaleficence, and beneficence).

do, namely our duty, then our communities would be better places. How do we get direction? For Kant there were certain principles from reason, such as truth telling, that should be universal. He called this the *categorical imperative*. For instance, everyone should avoid lying. Truth telling becomes the maxim for all in society. Sometimes the appeal to authority, religious or otherwise, enters the field. It is the voice of the leader, the church, the law, or simply the boss that is the basis for all. Christians, Moslems, and Jews all had their deontological expressions. At the Watergate hearings in the 1970s, Senator Sam Ervin warned the witnesses that he was not interested in their attempts to justify their actions by appealing to the good ends or results they intended. His simple but telling query was: "Did you obey the Constitution or not?" Let us look at some different versions of the deontological approach.

1. **Formalist.** A group of American authors (Rawls, Ramsey, Frankenna) who adopted the deontological method, and are thus called neo-Kantians, have been most influential in medical ethics by drawing up a series of principles that relate directly to our topic. Writer James Childress stresses principles of autonomy (letting the patient decide), nonmaleficence (the Hippocratic standard of not harming), beneficence (doing good), and justice (giving to each what is their due). Using this framework, he and others discuss cases that cover most aspects of health care. You can imagine in Paul Lazenby's case, members of the ethics committee will use many of these principles in their discussions.

2. **Existentialist.** Although they may not like rules, they do produce in their literature an attractive ethic for many. Camus and Sartre stress freedom, responsibility for themselves and those around them, and the duty to promote the lives (sweet existence, in fact) of all. Buber makes an authentic relationship the heart of his ethical approach. All of these writers, whether they are believers or not, empha-

> *Existentialism*: a 20th century philosophical movement that emphasizes personal responsibility for one's own actions and promotes the well-being of others. This principle places great value on life, personal freedom, and opposes any form of suicide.

size that life is precious and should not be violated. Thus, they would raise a strident voice against such movements as physician-assisted suicide.

Teleology

The word *teleology* comes from the Greek *telos*, which means end, consequence, or purpose. Teleologists come in several forms, but they criticize the deontologists for not paying sufficient attention to what happens after you act. There are some popular teleological models employed by writers in medical ethics.

1. **Situationism.** In 1953 Joseph Fletcher published his groundbreaking work on medical ethics. What was new was that he was a Protestant theologian entering an area where only Catholic authors were writing. His methodology, while it was concise and clear, was controversial. He held that each time we make a moral decision, it is a unique situation,

> *Teleology* is the foundation of systems that are interested in producing good consequences.

never quite the same as others; thus the name *situationist*. All you need is a couple of rules of thumb to help in this kind of decision-making. First, and most importantly, the consequence of your action must be good; if that is so, then the whole action is good. Secondly, since our author is Christian, one should always act out of love and with charity. Many are attracted to this system's simplicity and practicality. Critics, however, see it as a version of pure consequentialism where the end clearly justifies the means. Assassination, theft, prostitution, you name it, all could be sanctioned within this method.

2. **Utilitarianism**. This well-known method comes from 19th century Britain. Jeremy Bentham proposed that an action is good when it promotes more utility, namely value over disvalue in a society. Sometimes it is stated as the greatest good for the greatest number, but such a description is not completely accurate. Utilitarianism has different expressions. If the value is for the good of society, as Bentham intended, then we might talk of altruism. However, if the purpose is solely to promote one's own interest, then it becomes a selfish or egoistic exercise. Such, perhaps, was the enlightened selfishness of the 1980s, encouraged by author Ayn Rand and possibly by her admirer, Alan Greenspan, and his laissez-faire interpretation of economics. The cost-benefit analysis of a situation is attractive to many, and beneficial rules can emerge from this method. But if such a method is employed rigorously, there will always be a group who will be left out or suffer. Suppose, for instance, we were to introduce a national care system based on utilitarian thinking, which would cover the needs of the majority of the people. How large a minority would be excluded from such a scheme?

3. **Proportionalism**. As we have seen, religious thinkers are to be found among both deontologists and teleologists. Recently, a group of German Catholic moralists proposed a method that is principally teleological. It goes by the nickname of *proportionalism*, because one of its main tenets is to always maintain a proportion between the good and the evil effects of one's action. Relying on the medieval principle of double effect, they summarize all moral actions being

> *Proportionalism* is a recent methodology concentrating on weighing the circumstances, the intention of the doer, and the consequences to produce the least harmful result of your action. Most of its adherents are Roman Catholic moralists.

made up from the intention of the doer (which must be good), and the circumstances of the action (where the end never justifies the means). There must always be that balance between an evil effect, which is tolerated, and the good effect, which is desired. Like all moral rules or principles, they should appeal to our common sense. Suppose a mother is awakened in the night by a restless child. She decides to remain awake and sooth her upset infant, knowing that in the morning she will not be able to fulfill all her work obligations. Her intention is not to avoid working the next day. Performing poorly at her job is not the means to calming her fussing infant. There is a proportion between the good and evil effect: the welfare of the child and her efficiency at work on the following day.

Natural Law

This is an ancient theory subscribed to by such pagan thinkers as Aristotle and Cicero, and then by Christian writers like Thomas Aquinas. It is based on the idea that by use of our right reason, we have the means to work out values, standards, or principles by which we

> *Natural law* is an ancient theory that maintains that by the use of our "right reason" (Cicero), we can deduce standards by which to live well.

should live properly. These values, as Jefferson would say, are self-evident. It is a system that can be used both by deontologists and by teleologists, and is occasionally introduced into arguments from church bodies.

Principles and Virtues

Principles are standards that have developed over the years or even centuries that people have used as guides to their actions. They have been tried and examined in different circumstances and have achieved universal recognition (eg, the golden rule). In our present case with Mr. Lazenby, over the past 20 years or so, there has been a growing agreement that in some cases it is correct to withdraw treatment when there is no hope of benefit from what is available.

Virtues, on the other hand, are qualities that people develop in the course of their life and that become part of their character. If we say that someone is a good person, then we expect her or him to exhibit certain traits such as compassion, honesty, tolerance, a sense of justice, etc. A good person is expected to act well. Among educators there is a debate about whether such qualities can be learned through the example of others.

Conscience

It is appropriate to mention conscience. When all is considered in a possible situation and we are left to decide what ought to be done, if asked, most people would say that they try to act in accord with their conscience. What is it? While most confess to having a conscience and can even describe the effects of it (feelings of guilt or well-being), they find it difficult to define. Some call it the voice of God within them, others a call to compassion, a guide, the superego (Freud), or a summons to be. It seems that we have an obligation as we go through life to form our conscience with prudence and make it as mature as possible so that when we are faced with making a moral decision, we can rely on it for assistance. It is the best we can do. "Conscience doth make cowards of us all," said Shakespeare.

> *Conscience* is looked on by many as the basic subjective tool in moral decision-making. To act well is to follow one's conscience. Feelings of remorse or well-being are said to stem from our conscience after we have acted. It is hard to define, but the obligation to form this guiding force within us is a continual task throughout our lives.

CONCLUSION

In the course of the consultation concerning Paul Lazenby, many topics will be raised before any advice is given or decision is made. Here is a sample of how the committee might approach the case, bearing in mind the various ethical methods we have covered in this chapter:

1. A clear statement should be made about the patient's medical condition. This can come from two principal sources: the doctor and the nurse. The physician may describe the diagnosis and the prognosis. The nurse, often in the role of advocate, can provide some of the most insightful observations about both the physical and mental state of the person.

2. Questions may then arise from members of the committee as they broaden their picture and understanding of who Mr. Lazenby is. Let's look at a couple of areas that are of utmost importance:

- **Family**. Mr. Lazenby's story may emerge from the presence of a family member, perhaps his wife, daughter, or son. Their involvement, if they wish to be there, gives very poignant testimony to the person whom the committee is discussing. They would play a major role in the decision-making process. If there is no family member present, then perhaps social affairs may fill in the gap and build up the biography of Paul Lazenby.

- **Religion.** From the point of view of the terminally ill, this may be the most important aspect of their lives. The hospice movement has emphasized how spiritual care should be integrated into the total care of the patient. For instance, Presbyterians may wish the chaplain to read the Bible to them, Roman Catholics may like to receive the sacraments of the church, and Jehovah's Witnesses could request a visit from an elder and be assured that no blood products are involved in their treatment. Whether Greek, Jewish, Muslim, or Russian Orthodox, individuals are entitled to the consolations of their faith and cultural traditions—and the ethics committee might confirm if this has happened.

- **Ethical considerations.** Although we have been discussing ethical methods in the course of the chapter, people will not describe themselves in terms of deontology or teleology, yet questions will emerge from just such approaches. For instance, a deontological view might give rise to the following: Does Mr. Lazenby have a living will or advance directive in health care? The query is trying to protect his autonomy, his ability to give consent for what is happening. How did we deal with a similar case last year? Are all his needs being met? Is he being kept pain free? Are there legal issues to be raised? On the other hand, someone more interested in teleology might ask, "What will happen if we pursue this approach?

> Ethical consultations within the hospital setting are common occurrences today. In the tradition of Hippocrates, the focus of concern still centers on the patient, meeting their needs and promoting their well-being.

What is the benefit to continuing the use of these life support machines? Will this continued treatment place an excessive burden on Mr. Lazenby, his family, and the staff of the hospital?" Irrespective of the approach, or whatever school the member of the group favors, they all could arrive at the identical conclusion.

Finally, it should be said that beyond individual cases, there are situations that call for a reply from the community. Is the idea of the common good consistent with the good of the individual? For instance, in the United States today there is much turmoil about access to and the cost of health care. The United States is the only country in the industrialized world that does not have some national health care system in place which guarantees basic care to those living within its boundaries. Is the principle of justice involved here?

BIBLIOGRAPHY

Ashley BM, O'Rourke KD. *Healthcare Ethics: A Theological Analysis.* St. Louis, Mo: Catholic Health Association of the United States; 1989.

Beauchamp TL, Childress JF. *Principles of Biomedical Ethics.* New York, NY: Oxford University Press; 2001.

Bonhoeffer D. *Ethik.* Smith H, trans-ed. New York, NY: McMillan; 1995.

Cassidy S. *Sharing the Darkness: The Spirituality of Caring.* London, England: Darton, Longman and Todd; 1988.

DeVries R, Subedi J, eds. *Bioethics and Society: Constructing the Ethical Enterprise.* Upper Saddle River, NJ: Prentice Hall; 1998.

Frankl VE. *Man's Search for Meaning*. Boston, Mass: Beacon Press; 1959.

Kuhse H, Singer P, eds. *Bioethics: An Anthology*. Oxford, England: Blackwell Publishers Ltd; 1999.

Lammers SE, Verhey A, eds. *On Moral Medicine: Theological Perspectives in Medical Ethics*. Grand Rapids, Mich: Eerdmans Publishing Co; 1989.

Mahoney J. *The Making of Moral Theology*. Oxford, England: Oxford University Press; 1987.

McCabe H. *What Is Ethics All About*? Washington, DC: Corpus Books; 1969.

McGrew RE. *Encyclopedia of Medical History*. New York, NY: McGraw-Hill; 1985.

Munson R. *Intervention and Reflection: Basic Issues in Medical Ethics*. Belmont, Calif: Wadsworth Publishing Co; 2000.

Nelson CE. *Conscience: Theological and Psychological Perspectives*. New York, NY: Newman Press; 1973.

Ramsey P. *The Patient As a Person*. New Haven, Conn: Yale University Press; 1970.

Veatch RM. *Medical Ethics*. 2nd ed. Sudbury, Mass: Jones and Bartlett; 1997.

MULTIPLE-CHOICE QUESTIONS

1. Which of the following questions does ethics attempt to answer?
    A. How can I help this patient?
    B. What are the legal implications of this action?
    C. What does this patient need or want?
    D. What should I do?

2. Who is responsible for developing the best possible way to solve bio-ethical dilemmas?
    A. Clergy
    B. Ethician
    C. Everyone
    D. Philosophers

3. To which of the following fields of ethics does bioethics belong?
    A. Aesthetics
    B. Applied ethics
    C. Utilitarianism
    D. Meta-ethics

4. Which of the following precepts is of primary importance in both the Hippocratic oath and the principle of nonmaleficence?
    A. Do no harm
    B. Do to others as you would have them do to you
    C. Do what promotes the greatest good for the most people
    D. Let the patient decide what should be done

5. Which of the following methods of ethical inquiry would advocate a balance between the evil effect that is tolerated and the good effect that is desired?
    A. Existentialism
    B. Formalism
    C. Proportionalism
    D. Situationism

6. Which of the following methods of ethical inquiry is based on the notion that each moral decision is never exactly the same as any other moral choice we have encountered?
    A. Existentialism
    B. Formalism
    C. Proportionalism
    D. Situationism

CHAPTER 1 ANSWERS

1. D
2. C
3. B
4. A
5. C
6. D

Chapter 2

Encountering an Ethical Dilemma

Kathleen Ouimet Perrin, RN, CCRN, PhD(c)

While caring for Mr. Jones after his abdominal surgery, his nurse realizes that his respiratory rate and oxygen saturation are dropping. Normally, the nurse would awaken the patient, encourage him to deep breathe, recheck him frequently, and perhaps administer either naloxone hydrochloride or flumazenil to reverse any previous medications. However, should the nurse behave the same way if Mr. Jones is terminally ill with cancer, has a living will, a do-not-resuscitate (DNR) order, and his surgery was intended to be palliative in nature? Should the nurse allow Mr. Jones to gently slide off to sleep possibly to die, or should the nurse treat him just as aggressively as any other patient, maybe causing him more pain by reversing his narcotic with naloxone hydrochloride? When situations like this occur, normal nursing behaviors and judgments may not be sufficient to guide nursing decisions and actions, and the nurse may have to carefully consider how to intervene.

Nurses are usually able to respond quickly and instinctively to a variety of situations with predetermined interventions. However, at times the ordinary patterns of behavior may not be satisfactory for a variety of reasons. The behavior, which normally has appropriate consequences (eg, keeping a person alive) may result in less acceptable consequences in the particular case (eg, prolonging a person's painful death). There may not be any obvious right choice about how to proceed (eg, to increase the person's pain or to ignore a decreasing respiratory rate). When the nurse identifies a situation where she or he asks the question, "What should I do now?" then she or he has most likely encountered an ethical dilemma. In such a dilemma, there may be a conflict between how different ethical reasoning systems, religious perspectives, legal considerations, or personal values motivate the nurse to respond.

DOES AN ETHICAL DILEMMA EXIST?

When a nurse encounters such a situation, the first question she or he might ask is, "Is this an ethical dilemma?" Ethical dilemmas may exist when there is a conflict between the rights or values of the people involved in the situation. They may occur when those involved believe that different principles ought to motivate their behavior or when they believe that considerations of the consequences of their actions should drive their decision-making. An ethical dilemma might be defined as a situation that gives rise to conflicting moral claims, resulting in disagreements about choices for action. A cue that a nurse is dealing with an ethical dilemma is the language used to describe the situation. Ethical dilemmas are usually described in terms of right or wrong, duty or obligation, rights or responsibilities, and good or bad. Ethical dilemmas are commonly identified by the question, "What should be done?"

> Cues to an ethical dilemma are the uses of terms such as right and wrong, duty and obligation; and questions such as "What should I do?"

Nurses often have difficulty identifying ethical dilemmas. They may fail to note the ethical elements of a situation and proceed according to their usual pattern of behavior. Or, they may misinterpret the problem as a communication, legal, or institutional one and never recognize the ethical component. Failing to identify and respond to the ethical elements of a situation may be associated with an increase in a nurse's frustration and burnout.

At other times, nurses confound ethical dilemmas with tragic circumstances. A tragic circumstance is one when nothing can be done to alleviate the situation. In this case, a good choice or solution may be lacking. The sadness of the situation may make the nurse wish that there was something that could be done, but there are often no further options for treatment. For example, several years ago, a 10-year-old boy with leukemia was being considered for a bone marrow transplant. Just as a donor was found, he developed an infection that would not respond to the most potent antibiotics, and donation was no longer a possibility. He died within a few days.

> The sadness inherent in a tragic circumstance may cause the nurse to experience emotional turmoil and wish there was some way she or he could intervene to improve the situation.

Another example of confounding a moral dilemma with a tragic circumstance occurred when a 16-year-old girl was severely injured in a motor vehicle accident. She was brought to an emergency department where she went into cardiac arrest. After resuscitation, she was found to have a fracture of her second cervical vertebrae and a severe head injury. Within hours she was pronounced brain dead. Her parents were located and they requested that she be an organ donor. Then they added, "She's 6 weeks pregnant. We're losing both our child and our grandchild." The hospital staff was emotionally devastated. Although they knew that the fetus was not viable and the mother could not survive more than a few more hours, even with the most extensive medical support, they felt uncomfortable about

> It is the conflict between rights, duties, values, and principles that is the hallmark of an ethical dilemma.

the organ donation. After discussion with an ethicist and the local organ donor bank, they proceeded with the donation of the mother's organs but decided with the family against donation of the fetal tissue.

In each of these tragic circumstances, although they were very sad and distressing situations, there was no conflict between rights, principles, values, theories, or duties. It is conflict between these moral considerations that identifies an ethical dilemma. Is the situation with Mr. Jones, whose respiratory rate is dropping following palliative surgery, an ethical dilemma? Could there be a conflict between Mr. Jones' right to life and right to a death with dignity? Could the nurse consider principles? What might the nurse envision as doing no harm for Mr. Jones? What would be doing good? Does Mr. Jones have a voice in this situation?

WHAT INFORMATION IS NECESSARY TO MAKE AN INFORMED DECISION?

Once it seems apparent that an ethical dilemma exists, the first essential step is the identification of significant information. It is the specifics of Mr. Jones' situation, his terminal cancer, palliative surgery, and DNR status that might cause the nurse to reconsider her or his intuitive response to the situation. Without a clear understanding of the particulars of the situation, the nurse will not be able to fully understand the dilemma or choose an action wisely.

It is important that the nurse understand the person's medical condition. In order to limit potential confusion, it is helpful if the person, family, and all health care providers share an understanding of both the person's disease state and the goals for her or his treatment. Disagreement about a person's prognosis, disease progression, and likely outcome is frequently the reason health care providers, the patient, and family members are unable to agree on a treatment plan.

The nurse should gather data from a wide variety of sources and perspectives, not just medical information. For example, Mr. Jones' nurse might want to learn if Mr. Jones had any responsibilities he needed to attend to or if he had indicated that he was prepared to die. If the nurse was working in a postanesthesia care

> Although accurate information about a patient's medical status is essential, the nurse should gather information about the patient's psychological and interpersonal resources, as well as her or his sociocultural background, values, and religion.

unit (PACU), she or he might consider if the hospital had a policy that all patients in surgery and PACU have their DNR status rescinded from the beginning of surgery until they were discharged from PACU. The nurse would also want to discover if there were any laws that governed her or his action in the situation. The more accurate and complete the picture, the more clearly the dilemma can be described and appropriate decisions can be reached.

It is also important that the nurse consider the time frame for making a decision. Many situations allow time for adequate reflection and consideration. However, others such as the case of Mr. Jones, need more immediate assessment and decision-making. The amount of information it is possible to gather may be dependent on the immediacy of the decision.

WHO SHOULD BE INVOLVED IN MAKING THE DECISION?

Next, the nurse might consider who should be involved in making the decision. Does the patient have a voice? In Mr. Jones' case, should his living will speak for him? Should the family or primary health care provider be involved? Are there any reasons why an administrator or lawyer might be needed? The nurse should determine her or his role in the decision-making process.

> The nurse should identify who should be involved in making the decision and identify if she or he has a role, as well as what that role is.

Nurses may be represented in the decision-making process in several ways. First, they may represent their ethical perspective on the situation, carefully explaining their rationale. More commonly, nurses serve as the intermediary between patients, families, and health care providers, helping each group to understand the concerns of the others. Nurses often translate the ethical perspectives of their patients for other health care providers and clarify what the providers are saying to patients and families. Less frequently, nurses may act independently on their own moral decisions.

> If a nurse realizes she would not want the results of her ethical deliberation publicized, then the nurse ought to reconsider the decision.

In the case of Mr. Jones, the decision-making and action could be unusually private, quick, and unmonitored. By including others in the process, the nurse is required to publicize the reasons for her or his decision. The publicity helps to assure that the nurse's rationale for her or his decisions and actions is sound. If it is not possible to include others in the decision-making, one initial test of the appropriateness of the decision-making process is for the nurse to consider if she would want her decisions and actions to be widely publicized.

> Ethical decision-making theories can assist the nurse to choose what information is relevant to a situation and to identify the most ethically defensible action.

WHAT ETHICAL FRAMEWORKS WOULD HELP THE NURSE TO UNDERSTAND AND RESOLVE THE DILEMMA?

Utilizing ethical frameworks or perspectives is rather like using a filter. It helps the nurse to sort the material and identify what information is important when making her or his decision. It also assists in identifying appropriate alternatives for action. Ethical decision-making theories were described in Chapter 1, but brief discussions and questions for the nurse to consider when making a decision will be reviewed here.

Individual health care providers, including nurses, tend to use the same ethical reasoning systems repeatedly. For example, nurses often approach a dilemma using the principle of beneficence by asking, "What action would do the patient the greatest good?" On the other hand, financial agents for hospitals and insurance groups might consider the consequences to the patient and institution, and ask, "What is the cost-benefit ratio?" If a nurse consistently examines dilemmas from a variety of ethical perspectives, it may allow the nurse to articulate alternative solutions, to clearly understand the positions of the other people involved in the decision-making process, and to voice convincing ethical arguments.

Egoistic Approach

It is important that the nurse recognize what ethical reasoning system she or he is using as well as to appreciate the ethical viewpoints of others. One viewpoint that health care providers and families rarely acknowledge they are using is the *egoist* framework. In an egoist framework, the reasoner often asks, "What will do me the most good?" "What action will cause me the least discomfort?"

Often without being aware they are using an egoistic approach, families, nurses, and physicians utilize this system to make decisions that affect another person. For example, a niece had a durable power of attorney for health care purposes for her aunt, a wealthy woman with early Alzheimer's disease. The niece had consented to her aunt's cholecystectomy. But when the aunt, who had a considerable fortune, was going to require intubation and ventilation for an additional 8 to 24 hours, the niece demanded her aunt be extubated immediately and allowed to die. The

> When people use egoistic reasoning to make a decision for a patient, their choices should be subject to careful examination, since they are choosing to act in their own best interests rather than the best interests of the patient.

aunt, who was awake and coherent enough to write, clearly printed she wanted to stay alive. Nursing students are often afraid to deep breathe, cough, and ambulate postoperative patients because the students don't want to make their patients experience any additional discomfort. Some physicians are uncomfortable initiating end-of-life care discussions with their patients, so they defer the discussion until it is too late and the patient is unresponsive. When a nurse recognizes another health care provider or family member is using egoist reasoning to make a decision for a patient, the nurse should closely scrutinize the decision.

Utilitarian Approach

Another perspective that health care providers might use to make an ethical decision is *consequentialism* or *utilitarianism*. Using this framework, a person would ask, "What will bring the greatest good to the greatest number of people?" "What will bring about the best consequences to all those directly or indirectly involved?" This system is not concerned with the good of the individual person, but rather what action will benefit the most people.

Health care providers argue from a utilitarian perspective when they announce that more money should be spent on prenatal care because for every dollar spent, it saves between $3 and $9 of high-risk infant care. Nurses act from this perspective when they consistently cough, deep breathe, and ambulate their postoperative patients because it prevents pneumonia and other complications, thus decreasing the financial, physical, and emotional costs of surgery. In these examples, there are clear and obvious benefits to the greater good, despite possible temporary inconvenience or discomfort to an individual.

One difficulty of this approach is that the consequences of an action are not always as obvious as one might imagine. To return to the situation of Mr. Jones, two different consequences were envisioned: that he drifted asleep and died, or that he awoke and experienced more pain if the narcotics were reversed. Other consequences are also possible: Mr. Jones might drift off to sleep, occlude his airway because no one was observing him, suffer brain damage, and neither die nor awaken. He might awaken once the medication was slightly

> Consequentialist approaches are often utilized when politicians and health care providers attempt to develop ways to distribute health care resources.

reversed but not experience pain. Disagreements about the projected consequences of an action can cause conflict among health care providers when utilitarianism is used as an ethical framework.

Sometimes, consequentialist arguments are presented as quality of life discussions. In these discussions, a health care provider might argue that a patient's probable future quality of life would not warrant providing certain, usually aggressive, interventions. The underlying implication is that the cost of care required to maintain a patient at a certain quality of life, which the provider usually feels is undesirable, should not be borne by society.

In Mr. Jones' situation, if the nurse had decided not to awaken him but let him sleep, she or he might have justified the action by saying that Mr. Jones was dying anyway, that his dying would only have been longer, more painful, and costly to society if she or he roused him to breathe. The niece of the woman with Alzheimer's disease, who had had abdominal surgery, insisted that it would be too costly to pay for the care her aunt required as she slowly deteriorated with Alzheimer's disease. Thus, her soon to be deteriorating quality of life did not warrant the cost of additional care.

Principled Approach

Many health care providers employ a principled approach when examining ethical dilemmas. This method arises from deontology, an ethical theory that emphasizes duties and obligations based on rules and principles. The major principles identified in nursing literature include respect for persons with an emphasis on patient autonomy, non-maleficence often incorporated with beneficence, and justice.

The principled approach, as stressed in respect for persons, stands in opposition to a utilitarian approach because it is concerned with what will benefit each individual person rather than what will bring the greatest good to the most people. This approach emphasizes that people should be treated with empathy and consideration, and never approached as

> The principles most consistently identified by health care ethicists are autonomy, beneficence, and justice.

a means to an end. Thus, an action is to be chosen based on a principle or rule rather than on the likely consequences. Unfortunately, this system does not identify which of the principles should receive priority when two or more are in conflict.

Respect for Persons

The first principle, respect for persons, implies that each individual matters. Further, that each individual should receive full consideration of her or his concerns. It follows that these needs and concerns should be important factors when decisions are made about health care. In fact, if the individual is to be autonomous, the individual should be the primary decision-maker when decisions are made about her or his health care.

It is appropriate for persons to be autonomous in their health care decisions for several reasons. First, people who are autonomous and take responsibility for their lives and actions on a daily basis should not become subservient only because they are ill. Also, according to Benjamin and Curtis, there are both technical and conscience elements of any medical decision. An example of a technical element of a medical decision would be what specific antibiotics are likely to cure a particular infection. For this technical element of the decision, the health care provider would most likely be the expert.[1] However, it is the patient who must live with the effects of the treatment. Perhaps one of the antibiotics is too costly for the patient to afford, while another causes the patient severe diarrhea. Thus, the decision of whether it is possible to live with the effects and side effects of the treatment is a decision of conscience and should be made by the person most affected, the patient. According to this principle, it is the patient who should decide what action is most likely to offer her or him the most benefit and to choose not to accept treatments that do not appear to be in her or his best interest.

In the United States, a competent adult has the legal right to decline treatments, even those treatments that are deemed to be medically necessary, unless the refusal to accept treatment affects the health and welfare of others. In addition, patient autonomy in decision-making has had a major emphasis in health

> Physicians are usually assumed to be the experts regarding the most appropriate medical treatment. However, it is for patients to decide whether or not they can endure the suggested treatment.

care ethics for the past 20 years. Thus, many health care providers are guided by the principle of autonomy.

When approaching an ethical dilemma, health care providers guided by the principle of autonomy might ask themselves the following questions:

- Does the person have the capacity to make a personal decision about health care?
- Has the person stated a preference for the management of her or his care either in the past (advance directive) or currently?
- To whom or how was the preference stated?
- What is the person's expressed preference?

How might a nurse (who supported the principle of patient autonomy) reason in Mr. Jones' situation? The nurse might recognize that although Mr. Jones was not currently competent, at one time while competent, he had consented to a DNR order and signed a living will. The nurse might learn that in these directives, he had requested not to have his dying process interfered with by medical measures. Thus, the nurse might reason that Mr. Jones had expressed his desire not to be treated should his respiratory rate decrease and not to be awakened and encouraged to breathe.

Beneficence

A second principle commonly discussed in health care ethics is the principle of *beneficence*. Some ethicists consider *nonmaleficence* to be a part of beneficence; others consider it a separate principle. In either case, nonmaleficence, the principle of avoiding or preventing harm, is thought to take precedence over the principle of beneficence, attempting to do good for others. Ethicists would argue that it is more important to avoid doing harm to patients than it is to attempt to benefit them. For example, a nurse might be preparing to administer a dose of digoxin to a patient. After noting the patient's apical heart rate is 52 and the patient is complaining of nausea, the nurse might recognize the symptoms of digitalis toxicity and hold the medication while consulting with the physician. The potential benefit of the administration of the digoxin was avoided until the likely physical harm to the patient from digitalis toxicity was ruled out.

Often, the harm inferred is a moral harm rather than a physical one. So, the principle of nonmaleficence is influential in debates about physical and chemical restraints. When a person is physically or chemically restrained, she or he is deprived of a moral good, autonomy, and thus is harmed. Usually restraints are utilized to benefit the person by keeping

> Most ethicists argue that there is a stronger moral duty to remove or prevent harm than to do good.

her or him safe and preventing her or him from falling. The argument may be developed that since avoiding the moral harm of loss of autonomy is more important than potentially benefitting the patient by keeping her or him safe, the patient should not be restrained.

One concern about the principle of beneficence is this: Who should decide what is in a patient's best interests? If the answer was the patient, then the principle being applied would be that of autonomy. Therefore, the principle of beneficence may be most appropriate when dealing with vulnerable people who do not have the capacity to make reasoned decisions for themselves. This group of people might include young children, unconscious individuals, some mentally ill people, and others temporarily without the capacity to make a rational, reflective decision for themselves. A person with a health care proxy or durable power of attorney for a patient might act out of the principle of beneficence.

Questions an individual utilizing the principle of nonmaleficence or beneficence might ask include:

- Would the proposed action or actions result in physical, emotional, or moral harm to the patient?
- What action would result in the least harm to the patient?
- If none of the actions were likely to result in foreseeable harm, what action would offer this patient the most benefit or would be in this patient's best interests?

Deciding what would benefit another person or be in that person's best interests can be very difficult. Health care providers and family members may hold different conceptions of what would benefit the patient most or what moral values are most important. For example, there may be a disagreement about whether a longer, perhaps more painful life, or a shorter, perhaps higher quality of life, would be the greater good.

If Mr. Jones' nurse was utilizing the principle of beneficence, the nurse might develop the following argument: Mr. Jones is currently incapacitated and unable to reason and decide for himself following his palliative surgery. To allow him to stop breathing is to deny him his life, causing him irreversible moral and physical harm. There is every indication he wanted routine interventions performed since he consented to palliative surgery. Awakening him and encouraging him to breathe is not an aggressive intervention and would be in his best interests because it would allow him to continue to live.

Justice

Justice may be approached as either one of the cardinal principles of health care ethics or as an ethical theory. Usually the type of justice discussed in health care ethics is *distributive justice*. Distributive justice deals with the fair distribution of goods and services, in this case medical and nursing services. This distribution occurs at several levels, the amount of national funds that should be allocated to health care; the allocation within health care of the funds for research, prevention, or illness care; and the allocation of care to individual people. Discussion of the first two topics will be delayed until the chapter on Health Maintenance Across the Life Span.

The question of how to distribute a good justly is often described as a concern with what is due or what is owed to a person. But how should one decide what is due to an individual? What criteria should identify fair allocation of resources? Jameton describes seven different ways that benefits might be distributed:[2]

1.   To each equally
2.   To each according to merit
3.   To each according to past or social contribution
4.   To each according to what can be acquired in a free market
5.   To each according to need
6.   To each according to ability
7.   To each according to… (to be supplied by the reader)

He argues that to each according to need is most applicable to health care because health care is good only as long as it is needed, and it should be distributed in accordance with the benefit it can provide. Unfortunately, according to Callahan, Americans have developed an increasing number of health care needs and are no longer able to distinguish between a need and a desire.[3] For example, does an individual need to have his

> The just distribution of health care resources may be discussed at several levels: the amount of governmental resources to be allocated to health care, the amount of available health care resources to be allotted to various health care services, and the allocation of health care services among individual patients.

health care plan pay for his Viagra prescription or to have knee surgery so he can play competitive tennis at his country club?

Nurses may be faced with the question of just distribution of their services on a daily basis. In this time of reductions in the professional nurse staff and increases in unlicensed assistant personnel, how should the nurse justly distribute her or his time? A home health nurse from one agency must see six patients each day; she or he has 110 miles to travel over the course of the day and must consider the travel time as well as the patient and family time. Each of the six patients requires attention, but three have significant needs. One is dying from a brain tumor, is in severe pain, and his medications need readjusting. Another is recently diagnosed with amyotrophic lateral sclerosis, is very frightened, and his wife must learn to suction his secretions. The third is a diabetic who is unable to control her blood sugars and has an infected wound on her foot. In this example, each of the patients has a justifiable need for a nurse. How should the nurse fairly allocate her or his time?

When considering allocation of care to the individual person, the nurse might ask:

* What is due to this person?
* Is this action fair?
* Does it treat this person like every other and show neither favoritism nor discrimination?

If there are more justifiable needs than there are resources available (such as in the situation described above), additional criteria to guide resource allocation must be identified. Some nurses rely on triage principles and utilitarian strategies to review who might benefit the most from their interventions. Other nurses try to divide the resources or time evenly between their patients (to each equally), or try to determine which of the people deserves care the most (to each according to merit).

Rights-Based Approaches

In rights-based theories, actions are deemed to be appropriate or not based on selected rights. Hospitalized patients in the United States have rights to privacy, confidentiality, and to know their caregivers according to the American Hospital Association. These rights are enforceable, even if the person cannot ask to have them enforced. Thus, even while unresponsive, Mr. Jones retains his ethical right to personal respect and to private, confidential care.

> Legal rights, such as the right to privacy, may be protected by law. But moral rights, such as the right to dignified, humane care, are only protected by social sanction.

Rights may be justified on legal or ethical grounds. Both types of rights can serve as social sanctions and action guides, but only legal rights are enforceable with punishment by the law. Thus, Mr. Jones, while unresponsive, retains his ethical right to dignified, humane care and his legal right to safe, competent care. Negligent medical or nursing care may be punished by law, but not inconsiderate or apathetic care.

A competent person may choose to exercise her or his rights or forgo them. However, only the holder of the right or his designee can choose to renounce a right. Thus, only Mr. Jones or his designate could decide that he no longer wanted to receive CPR, one type of urgent medical care to which Americans have a right.

There is no universal right to health care in the United States, yet there is a right to emergent and urgent care, such as CPR. Rights entail duties and since Americans have a right to urgent health care, then society or health care providers have the duty to provide it. Thus, hospitals cannot legally turn away someone who is urgently in need of medical care.

Americans are often confused about their rights to health care, and people frequently demand care to which they have no clear moral or legal right. For example, one woman arrived at the emergency department (ED) triage desk, announced that she was 6 weeks pregnant, and needed prenatal care. After the triage nurse assessed the woman and determined that she was experiencing a normal pregnancy, she provided the woman with an appointment at the hospital's prenatal clinic for the following week. A few minutes later the woman returned to the triage area with her significant other and demanded that she be given an ultrasound so that they could

> A key understanding concerning rights is that if a patient has a right to some aspect of health care, then a health care provider, an institution, or a government agency has the duty to provide that care.

determine the sex of their child. The couple insisted the woman had a right to prenatal care, specifically an ultrasound, and they would not leave the ED until the woman had the procedure. The triage nurse contacted her supervisor, who responded that the hospital had a duty to deliver urgent medical care and was prepared to provide appropriate prenatal care. However, an ultrasound did not fit in either of those categories. A security guard was required to escort the couple from the premises.

One of many problems with the language of rights is that it tends to be confrontational and divisive, as in the previous situation. The language of competing rights often leads to conflict rather than compromise. The use of slogans, such as the "right to prenatal care," can actually be misleading. In the previous example, the woman claimed a right to prenatal care but actually insisted on a right to an ultrasound, a procedure not necessarily part of prenatal care. In other situations, such as when competing rights are projected in the same situation, the use of slogans and the language of rights can be explosive. Consider the abortion debate with the slogans "Right to Life" and "Women's Right to Choose."

It is also possible for health care providers to identify differing rights for the same individual in the same situation. Consider the example of Mr. Jones. One nurse might argue that Mr. Jones had the right to life and therefore ought to be awakened, encouraged to breathe, and have his pain medication reversed. Another health care provider might insist that Mr. Jones had the right to a death with dignity, and he should be allowed to drift off to sleep and die. Since there is no agreed upon method to prioritize rights, there is no current way to resolve this impasse in rights-based approaches to ethical decision-making.

When utilizing a rights-based approach, a nurse might ask the following questions:

- Does the patient have any legal rights in the situation?
- Has she or he chosen to exercise them?
- What is the corresponding duty and whose duty is it?
- Does the patient have any moral rights in the situation?
- What action would best protect the patient's moral and legal rights?

Care-Based Approaches

Benner and Wrubel have proposed a system of nursing ethics based on care and responsibility.[4] By being "connected" and caring about the patient, the nurse is able to discern that certain aspects of a situation are relevant. The nurse is able to understand the meaning of the experience to the patient, while the patient feels cared for by the nurse and develops trust in the nurse. This discernment enables the nurse to identify problems, describe possible solutions, and take action. The process may not be an intellectual activity; rather it may be a rapid, nonreflective understanding of the situation, which Benner calls "embodied intelligence."

> Nurses who utilize a caring approach may develop an intuitive understanding of their patient's needs and desires.

Benner states an ethic of care is learned only through experience because it requires an understanding of the ethical practices of the community. The culture of the community and family supplies background meaning. Without an understanding of the background meaning, chosen actions may be culturally insensitive or completely objectionable. According to Benner, abstract reasoning using universal principles is of no use if the reasoner cannot identify pertinent situations or does not have the skill to act ethically.

Despite an interest by many nurses and ethicists in an ethic of care, there are some problems with its implementation. Since it is a nonreflective, subjective process, it may be difficult to convey a rationale for the action chosen to other health care providers or family. In the current health care arena, it is usually necessary to convince other providers of the appropriateness of a decision before proceeding. Most other health care providers will not be convinced by an argument that begins, "I feel the patient wants or does not want."

Different individuals in the same situation may have varying "embodied intelligences" and different decisions about actions. There is no way to resolve a discussion about such a difference. When each person argues that she or he "knows in their bones" what the right thing is to do, the argument will reach an impasse.

Finally, it will not be possible for all nurses and all patients to have such intense, connected, and caring relationships. Both patients and nurses will have reasons why they are not able or willing to have such close encounters. As some nurses state, "You can't develop a rapport with everyone." If the connection does not occur, then how are the patients' concerns understood, nursing care delivered, and moral decisions made? Olsen argues that because caring can be based on individual relationships, ethical decision-making can be influenced by such morally irrelevant factors as whether or not the nurse likes the patient.[5]

A nurse using the caring approach might not need to question how to proceed; rather she or he might simply know what the patient needs to have done. If, however, a nurse were considering the caring approach, the following questions may arise:

- Have I formed a human connection with this patient?
- Do I know what this experience means to her or him?
- Do I know the culture and family of the person and appreciate the background meaning?
- Do I know what ought to be done?

To return to Mr. Jones' situation, perhaps his nurse had cared for him during previous hospitalizations for cancer. During those hospitalizations, the nurse had developed a warm, close relationship with both Mr. Jones and his family. The health team had recommended the palliative surgery to Mr. Jones to extend his life several months. Mr. Jones had consented to the surgery because he desperately wanted to live until Christmas when his daughter, whom he had not seen for 20 years, and her family would be visiting from overseas. In this situation, the nurse would hurry to reawaken Mr. Jones and encourage him to breathe. The nurse would probably even reverse Mr. Jones' pain medication if it were necessary to keep him breathing.

These are just a few of the ethical approaches that a person might utilize to explore an ethical dilemma. Each of the approaches guides the person to seek out particular types of information and suggests certain guidelines for choosing an appropriate action. The nurse should recognize what ethical reasoning approach both she or he and any other people involved in the situation are employing. Then the nurse should consider the shortcomings of each of the approaches when preparing to make a decision.

All Things Considered, What Ought to be Done?

How should one make a decision and choose a course of action? Most people will state that making any decision should involve clear thinking and consideration of the implications of each of the alternatives. Kuhse writes that making an ethical decision is at least "reflective, a social activity, a matter of

> When nurses make ethical decisions, they should consider their decisions carefully, discuss their decisions with other health care providers to identify flaws in their reasoning, and be as impartial as possible.

sound reasoning, impartial, and universal."[6] Moreover, according to Kuhse, making such a decision should not be "a matter of religion, a matter of obedience to authority, what comes naturally, social practice, or just a matter of feelings."

Unfortunately, many people view resolving a dilemma as choosing between two options. Consider how the phrase "on the horns of a dilemma" captures the feeling of being caught between two impossible choices. An alternative would be to view moral decision-making as exploring a maze. Both experiences involve considering many possibilities, exploring a variety of pathways, being open to various possibilities, and remaining flexible. In a maze, as in health care decision-making, the consequences of each choice are not always readily apparent, and there are usually at least several alternatives and often a series of decisions to be made. Using the analogy of the maze reminds people that the choice of a direction (or an ethical viewpoint) is only the beginning of the process. The progression through the maze will necessitate action (actual movement) and possible future decisions, especially if the consequences are different than those envisioned.

> Tracing one's path through a maze, like making an ethical decision, involves considering multiple choices, exploring various pathways, and being open to numerous possibilities.

Exploring a maze has a defined goal: finding a path out of the maze. Sometimes health care decision-making focuses on choosing a particular action and neglects deciding on a goal. For example, the goal of Mr. Jones' care might be keeping him alive until his daughter arrived, while the action was awakening him from the medications. Identifying both the goal of health care and proposed actions to meet that goal helps to clarify the decision-making.

When preparing to enter the maze of ethical decision-making, the nurse might ask herself or himself the following questions:

- What ethically justified goals can be identified?
- What are the ethically justified alternatives for action?
- Are there any practical constraints to following any of them?
- What arguments can be constructed in favor of these alternatives (this includes considering the probable consequences)?
- How can these arguments be evaluated?
- What ought to be done?
- Is this decision reflective of sound thinking, or is it based on pressures from society, authority, religion, or purely on emotions and feelings?

When the nurse has made a decision that she or he feels prepared to defend, presenting the decision to health care colleagues will allow others to evaluate the decision. This publicity and scrutiny will help to assure all those involved of the soundness of the decision. Most health care decision-making is a group process. The difficulties occasionally encountered in reaching consensus on an ethical decision will be discussed later in the chapter.

What should the nurse do for Mr. Jones? While he lies sleeping with his respiratory rate and oxygen saturation dropping, should the nurse awaken him and encourage him to breathe or allow him to continue to sleep and possibly die? Although he has expressed a desire not to be resuscitated, awakening him from sleep and resuscitation are two very different interventions. There is every reason to believe he has expressed a competent wish to live until his daughter arrives and no reason to assume that he is currently prepared to die. Awakening him would be in his best interests since it preserves a moral and physical good—his life—and would be treating him fairly, as postoperative patients are usually treated. Additionally, Mr. Jones has a legal right to competent nursing care. Identifying and treating respiratory depression postoperatively is considered normal nursing practice. Therefore, shouldn't the nurse awaken Mr. Jones and encourage him to breathe?

How Can the Nurse Best Carry Out the Decision?

Most philosophers and ethicists assume that once the decision has been made, the process is complete. However, that is rarely the case for nurses involved in ethical decision-making. First, as mentioned earlier, nurses rarely act alone, so making a personal decision may be only a preparatory step for the nurse before convincing others of the soundness of the choice. Also, it is usually the nurse, patient, and family who must implement and live, or die, with the decision. As Jameton says, this phase is often full of surprises.[2] Or to return to the analogy of the maze, the pathway does not always lead in the direction that was envisioned, and the decision may have to be reconsidered.

For example, a 90-year-old independent woman with chronic obstructive pulmonary disease (COPD) and a living will developed pneumonia following a mastectomy. Anticipating the woman's death within 24 hours, her physician recommended that antibiotics and mechanical ventilation be withheld and she be allowed to die peacefully. The family agreed. However, the woman, a stubborn New

> Just as a path in a maze does not always lead in the direction anticipated, so too a health care intervention does not always have the intended consequences. Thus, carrying out the decision can have surprising, occasionally disturbing results.

Englander with a strong constitution, survived. Several months later when the family was placing her in a long-term care facility because of her severe respiratory involvement, they wondered if they should have treated her more aggressively. They wished that they had reconsidered the treatment strategy when it became apparent that she was going to survive.

During the intervention phase, the nurse might wish to consider:

- Are the needs of the patient being met by this course of action?
- Is this proceeding as envisioned or does this course of action need to be reconsidered?
- What else could be done to meet the goal?

Despite the best possible medical and nursing care, Mr. Jones' condition deteriorated rapidly after his surgery. As it became apparent that he would not survive until Christmas for his daughter's visit, his family considered other options. His daughter left her family overseas and was able to spend several days with her father while he was conscious before he died peacefully.

How Should the Situation be Evaluated?

The nurse should evaluate what she or he learned from the situation. By systematically evaluating all phases of the decision-making process, future decision-making might be less complicated. The nurse should consider the following:

- Did an ethical dilemma really exist, or had the nurse been caught up in a difficult or tragic circumstance?
- Was the nurse able to obtain necessary information in a timely fashion?
- If additional information would have been useful, how could the nurse obtain that information for future decisions?
- Were any legal or policy issues involved?
- Was the nurse able to obtain the appropriate policies or legal consultations in a timely manner?

- Do any of the policies need reconsideration or revision?
- Were the appropriate people involved in the decision-making? Were there others who should have been consulted?
- Was the nurse able to use ethical theories to develop alternatives for action and explain the rationale for her or his chosen intervention? Was this helpful?
- Would the nurse advocate the same action again in a similar situation, or were there unforeseen issues that would cause the nurse to recommend another course of action in similar cases in the future?

The nurses, who had cared for Mr. Jones, evaluated the situation after Mr. Jones' death. The nurse who had encouraged him to breathe was satisfied he had had an opportunity to be reunited with his daughter and he had not suffered unnecessarily before his death. The family and health care providers agreed that all things considered, they had cared for Mr. Jones as compassionately and as ethically as they could. However, the institution did decide to reconsider its policy that all surgical patients have their DNR orders rescinded during surgery.

Group Decision-Making: Why Do Reasonable People Disagree About How to Make a Decision?

Although the situation with Mr. Jones portrayed a circumstance in which the nurse could make a decision on her or his own, this is rarely the case in health care. Most often, ethical decision-making is a group process, in which the voices of those affected by the decision are

> Ethical decision-making in health care is usually an exercise in group process. People affected by the decision ought to be included in the decision-making process.

heard. Typically, the group includes the patient, family member(s), physician(s), and nurse(s). It may also include a social worker, an ombudsperson from the institution, chaplains or religious advisers, health care administrators, and lawyers. The more complex the decision, the more likely it is that numerous people will be involved.

The following is an example of a complex decision-making process in which multiple people are involved. Mr. Williams is a 52-year-old paraplegic who had injured his spine while racing motorcycles at the age of 20. He is currently hospitalized for initiation of amiodarone therapy to control cardiac dysrhythmia. His care is complex; he requires dialysis three times weekly for renal failure that resulted from recurrent urinary tract infections. He has a bowel regimen that takes an hour each morning, yet he still is incontinent of feces during the day. He has two decubiti that reach to his pelvis and has chronic osteomyelitis from E. coli that has not responded well to intravenous antibiotics. His 76-year-old mother has been caring for him at home. After completing his morning care about 11 AM each day, she volunteers at a local hospital so she can obtain his medications at minimal cost. Mr. Williams states that he "has had enough." He wants to die and wishes to discontinue all treatment including dialysis during this hospitalization. His mother is begging him to continue living. She has encouraged his minister to support her in her entreaties.

When a situation is as complex as Mr. Williams' care and there are a number of people involved, the people will often disagree about the course of action. The reasons for possible disagreement are extensive. A few of the more common reasons are described in the following section. Some of the reasons are moral in nature, while others are not.

Differing Opinions About Outcomes of Medical Treatment

When encountering such a complex situation, the people involved may envision very different outcomes. For example, hospital nurses and physicians see different subsets and different phases of the illnesses of the same groups of patients. The hospital nurse may see only the sickest of a group of patients,

> Because physicians have experience with patients in various stages of their illnesses, they may be more optimistic about a patient's prognosis than hospital nurses, who only see patients when they are very ill.

where only half of the patients survive to hospital discharge. These patients may be severely debilitated at the time of discharge, and the nurse may worry about their ability to survive. The physician or home health nurse, in contrast, may see the same subset of patients on a longer term basis, realize how infrequently these people need hospitalization, and how well they do following it. Thus, the physician may realize that the actual outcomes of care are better than the hospital nurse envisions them to be.[7]

When the prognosis is unclear, there is some indication that nurses and physicians use different types of cues to determine what they believe will be the outcome. According to Anspach, physicians are more likely to rely on technological cues, such as lab tests or findings from a physical examination, to determine prognosis; while nurses tend to attach more significance to interactive cues, such as when a patient appears depressed, cannot be comforted, or appears to be suffering.[8] Anspach suggests that nurses' reliance on the in-

> Physicians and nurses often use different types of cues to determine a patient's prognosis.

teractive cues is related to the time that they spend caring for and interacting with their patients. There is no current indication that one type of cue is more likely to predict a patient's outcome than the other.

One thing is clear: When health care providers, patients, and families envision different outcomes from the same situation, they tend to weigh the benefits and burdens differently. Sometimes this is because they have had previous experiences with different subsets of patients. Sometimes this is because they view different types of cues as important, and other times it is because they are looking at different pieces of a complex illness puzzle. Anticipating different outcomes, benefits, or burdens from treatments results in differing opinions of the value of the treatments for the individual.

The people involved in Mr. Williams' care saw very different likely outcomes of his medical care. His hospital nurses and cardiologist believed that his existence, even with the best medical and nursing care, would be short. Even with amiodarone therapy, he had occasional ventricular tachycardia, a lethal dysrhythmia.

> When health care providers, patients, and families anticipate different benefits and burdens from a treatment, they may have very different opinions about the value of the treatment.

Since Mr. Williams was refusing defibrillation or an implanted defibrillator, the dysrhythmia was likely to be fatal. In addition, the chronic osteomyelitis was not responding well to treatment, and they were concerned about worsening infection. The home care and dialysis nurses insisted that Mr. Williams functioned well at home, and he should be able to return to home care and continue as before. His nephrologist and orthopedic physicians both stated that there was little more they could do for him. The orthopedic surgeon had already performed several pelvic resections to remove infected and necrotic bone. Further surgery would prevent Mr. Williams from sitting, which could drastically change his quality of life. Mr. Williams' mother and minister believed he had benefited from the sophisticated medical care available to him until this point, and he could continue to do well with high-tech care. Each of these groups saw different pieces of his health care needs and anticipated different outcomes from his medical care.

Differing Beliefs About Ethical Priorities

Health care providers, family members, patients, and others may disagree about a course of action because they have different beliefs about what ethical values should receive priority in a particular situation. Some members of the health care team may argue that patient autonomy is a primary principle that should always be respected. Others may state that preventing harm to the

> Because words have cultural, emotional, and literal significance, in order to understand the ethical perspectives of other people, it is often necessary to inquire about the meaning of the words they are using.

patient (beneficence) is the most essential concern of nursing of health care. According to MacIntyre, when people argue from differing ethical perspectives, it can be very difficult for them to understand one another, rather like communicating with someone who is speaking another language.[9]

People from different cultural and religious heritages may reason from different ethical perspectives. For example, people of Jewish or Hindu heritages are more likely to reason from a duty-based perspective than a rights-based perspective. People of traditional Chinese culture may place greater meaning on the patient's place in the family and community and less emphasis on patient autonomy. People of Islamic tradition may emphasize prevention as well as respect and compassion for the physical, mental, and spiritual components of the illness when making an ethical decision.

The people affected by Mr. Williams' stand quickly took different positions about what ought to be done, developing their opinions from varying ethical perspectives. A group of hospital nurses and his cardiologist were convinced Mr. Williams had made an autonomous choice, and it ought to be respected. His home care and dialysis nurses noted he seemed more depressed than usual and doubted his plan to discontinue treatment represented an authentic choice. They believed they should protect the patient from harm, act in his best interests, and continue treatment until his depression cleared and he was able to make an authentic decision. The nephrologist argued from a justice perspective, saying that Mr. Williams' dialysis needs were becoming greater due to the infection. By continuing Mr. Williams' dialysis when he no longer desired it, others could be deprived of an essential resource. Mr. Williams' mother was clear in her egoist position, "He can't leave me, I need him." When consulted, the hospital lawyer was equally certain, "If he is competent, than he has a legal right to discontinue treatment."

Differing Information Gathering and Communication Styles

There may be difficulties in communication between health care providers, patients, and families. In a health care crisis, the patient and family members may need to have the same information repeated several times before they can understand even the basic pathophysiology of the patient's illness and the usual treatment. It may take some time before they can begin to weigh the risks and benefits of any treatment alternatives. Health care providers need to be prepared to offer repeated explanations of the same information and, if possible, to allow those involved to gather information from several sources before requiring a decision.

Health care providers and families may have different understandings of the same terms. A once common problem was for the physician to ask the family of a dying patient if they "wanted everything done." The physician was actually asking if the patient died, did the family want cardiopulmonary resuscitation per-

> People in crisis need to have information repeated multiple times before they are able to comprehend it. Therefore, health care providers cannot assume that because a patient or family has had a treatment explained to them once, that they understand and are prepared to make a decision.

formed. However, the family usually believed the physician was inquiring if they wanted the patient to be cared for, turned, comforted, or fed. They responded, "Of course, we want everything done." It is essential that health care providers and families reach a common understanding of the terms they are using.

Health care providers may also experience problems communicating among themselves. Shannon states that physicians and nurses are taught to gather information and communicate it in very different ways. Physicians are taught from medical rounds to present diagnostic information in a succinct format with an emphasis on pathophysiology

> A common cause for miscommunication between health care providers and families is misunderstanding of health care terminology.

and treatment of the disease in an attempt to arrive quickly at an appropriate diagnosis. The depersonalized nature and brevity of the information gathered and presented may give the impression that the physician is "too busy, uninterested, or unaware of the larger picture." In contrast, nurses are urged to attend to the idiosyncrasies of the patient's response to the disease. They consistently report and record detailed information in the patient's chart and in the change-of-shift report, with the goal of providing individualized care to each patient. Shannon believes that from this style of communication, other professionals may believe that a nurse is "disorganized, unfocused in his or her thinking, concerned with relatively trivial matters, or disrespectful of other professionals' time."[7]

While physicians often rely on diagnostic information and lab data for cues, the nurse may rely on the ways in which the patient responds to the interventions for her or his cues. This focus on different information can be worsened if a male physician defends his position using a rational argument,

> Variations in how health care providers are encouraged to collect, classify, and communicate information about patients may lead to misunderstandings between types of professionals.

while a female nurse supports hers with a caring base or feelings argument. Grundstein initially found some indication that this type of reasoning dispute was a substantial problem in health care communication.[10] However, further research has not indicated it is as significant as originally believed. Still, the emphasis on different styles of information gathering and communication can lead to misunderstandings and impaired interactions between different members of the health care team.

In Mr. Williams' situation, the hospital nurses argued from a caring perspective. They believed that they were the only people, other than Mr. Williams and his mother, who understood the enormity of what the experience meant to him and why his daily life felt so intolerable to him. The hospital nurses argued that although his physicians, home care nurses, and dialysis nurses had known him for a longer time, they only saw selected aspects of his care. For example, the home care nurses became involved in his care to teach his mother to care for the central venous access and administer antibiotics. They had never assisted with his bowel regimen, seen his decubiti, or watched his exhaustion after dialysis. In this situation, it was the home care and dialysis nurses who responded with what was often the physician's argument. They stated that Mr. Williams was doing well, and the dialysis was preventing any severe uremia or electrolyte imbalance. His central line was functioning well, and his antibiotics were preventing the infection from getting any worse. Neither of the two groups of nurses could understand the position of the other.

Family Issues

Frequently, family issues affect the patient's and family's ability to make a rational decision. Family communication and dynamics are far more complex than this chapter can address. However, there are some minimal factors the nurse should consider when dealing with each patient and family. The nurse should examine what factors, such as guilt or greed, might be influencing the family's decision.

> Nurses should review the family's decision-making process to identify any egoistic reasoning that might be influencing their decision.

Sometimes, the family will readily identify an issue likely to cloud their judgment. For example, one large family relocated their 90-year-old father from Canada to the United States, despite his protests that he would die if they made him leave his home. Three weeks after arriving in this country, the father had a huge myocardial infarction, became unresponsive, and appeared to be dying. The family, feeling guilty and distraught, insisted on every possible medical and surgical intervention and would not consent to a do-not-resuscitate order because they felt directly responsible for his heart attack.

At other times, the issue affecting the family's decision-making ability may be a family secret, which members disclose only with difficulty. One woman, who had an abortion as a teenager, had never told anyone. When her only daughter developed leukemia, the woman believed it was divine punishment for her abortion. At first, she would not consent to treatment for her daughter, saying it would result in no benefit. Until she consulted with the chaplain, the woman believed that her daughter was the replacement for the aborted fetus, and that since she had deprived that fetus of life, God could deprive her daughter of life.

The nurse and social worker also need to examine the patient's role in her or his family structure. A few of the questions they might want to consider include:

- Does the person have a specific role in the family? What is that role?
- How necessary is the person for continued family functioning?
- What are the likely consequences to the family if the person's role is altered by the illness?

Mr. Williams' family consisted of himself and his mother. His mother's life revolved around delivering and obtaining the means to deliver his care. She spent her morning hours providing his physical care, then volunteered at a hospital to obtain his medications for lower cost. Her volunteer hours, visits to the dialysis center with him, and visits from the home care nursing staff represented all her social interactions. For 30 years, Mr. Williams had been the sole focus of his mother's life; she could not imagine what she would do with her life if he died.

Expectation of a Miracle

According to Rushton and Russel, both families and health care providers may use the language of miracles.[11] However, since religion, worldview, and culture define the meaning, the two groups may mean very different things when using the same words. For example, health care providers have been known to describe patients who survived extreme illness with high technology care as "miracles." The use of the word in this context places an emphasis on faith in medical technology

> Families may make health care decisions based on their expectation of a miracle. Although the decision may appear irrational to members of the health care team, the family may believe that only by awaiting a miracle can they keep faith and not abandon their loved, ill family member.

and human ingenuity, rather than faith in divine intervention. These cases of survival may be publicized and sensationalized in the news media, raising public expectation of cures against all odds.

"Traditionally, however, miracles are linked with faith in God rather than faith in humanity or technology."[11] Expecting a miracle may be a profound expression of the family's belief in their God's ability to heal all human ills. The family may believe that by keeping faith in their God's ability to heal, they are offering hope to their suffering family member. Abandoning the hope for a miracle means acknowledging there is little or no hope, and the family member probably will not survive.

The language of miracles is usually an emotional rather than a rational one, according to Rushton and Russel.[11] Appeals to reason and medical facts are unlikely to have any effect on the family. In fact, continued emphasis and repetition of the same facts may only entrench the family in their belief a miracle is possible. Rushton and Russel suggest it may be more appropriate to see the claims for a miracle as expressions of the family's faith and to use the strength of the faith to assist with family coping.[11] They also recommend examining the family dynamics to determine if the expectation of a miracle may be masking underlying family problems.

The expectation of a miracle does not mean the family expects a total cure. They may only desire an amelioration of the current situation. Mr. Williams' mother had long ago stopped believing her son would walk again. But she was praying, with her minister, for her son's osteomyelitis

> Moral as well as nonmoral reasons for disagreement must be resolved before a group can proceed to determine the most appropriate solution to an ethical dilemma.

to respond to the antibiotics, so that he could have plastic surgery for his decubiti. He would then be able to sit for longer periods each day, enjoy more mobility, and possibly return to work. As long as she believed that such an improvement in his life was possible, she could not allow him to terminate treatment.

It is clear that numerous factors may influence why different members of a group form different opinions and reach varying decisions about what ought to be done in an ethical dilemma. Some of the reasons for advocating different approaches are moral in nature. For example, without a clear understanding of and agreement on the medical events and likely consequences of the illness, it is difficult to weigh the benefits and burdens of any proposed treatment to the patient. It can also be very difficult to come to an agreement when group members are developing their stance using different ethical perspectives. Other reasons for group disagreement are nonmoral concerns, such as problems in communication or underlying family issues. Still, these interests must also be addressed and resolved if a satisfactory and ethical solution to the dilemma is to be reached.

What Can the Nurse Do to Enhance Group Decision-Making and Resolution of the Dilemma?

Both the moral and nonmoral concerns contributing to group disagreements are often based on poor communication, lack of understanding of others' terminology, and disagreement about anticipated outcomes. Therefore, an initial step in enhancing the decision-making process is improving group communication and understanding. It is important that the people involved listen to each other and attempt to understand the true meaning of the others' words. Slogans should be avoided because of the possibility that they will further cloud the issue, and the people involved should describe their concerns in their own words.

> Slogans should be avoided in moral discourse because they usually obscure the real issue and inflame emotions.

Active listening can help the nurse to understand more accurately what other members of the team, the family, and the patient are saying. Active listening encompasses such techniques as the following:

- Encouraging the person to continue to speak (Tell me more.)
- Clarifying what the person is saying (What does... mean to you?)
- Restating what the speaker said to check meaning (So,... is that right?)
- Summarizing the facts to establish a basis for further discussion (These seem to be the main concerns you have mentioned.)

The nurse should not be listening only for the meaning of the words; she or he should also be attempting to understand the ethical perspective of the other person. As the person is speaking, the nurse should attempt to understand the meaning of the person's words and ethical values. The nurse should also review her or his own moral arguments in light of the other person's position.

> Only by attempting to put her or himself in the position of someone arguing from another ethical perspective can the nurse truly understand the person's concerns and develop an acceptable compromise.

MacIntyre cautions that it is very difficult for supporters of one moral tradition to understand the arguments and concepts of a rival tradition.[9] He suggests that to resolve a controversy between rival moral traditions, the reasoner must be able to characterize her or himself from the perspective of the rival tradition. Once that occurs, the nurse may be able to envision a neutral way of characterizing data that is acceptable to both traditions.

Once an understanding of their words and moral traditions has been reached, it is important for the group to develop a statement of the clinical problem and the moral issue. This can serve as a basis for further discussion. Any interpersonal issues, whether between patient and family or health care providers, should be resolved before an attempt is made to reach a decision, for these issues will only obscure the decision-making process.

One of the advantages of group decision-making is the opportunity for ethical consultation. It is possible for any group member to present her or his thoughts to others in order to identify flaws in the logic. In such a circumstance, the group member might abandon her original decision and be open to other possibilities. Another advantage is the potential for the group, after defining the problem, to develop innovative, ethically acceptable alternatives that had not been previously considered.

Informal group decision-making situations may resolve in a variety of ways. The group may come to consensus, one powerful member may announce her or his decision and take action, or members of the group may develop a compromise solution. Rarely does such informal discussion

> The people required to implement the planned action to a dilemma in health care should be in agreement with the decision and should not be coerced into participation.

involve a vote, since not all of the individuals involved may have to institute the action. They may not even all agree with the plan. However, the people taking direct action, the patient and family, should be in agreement with the decision.

In Mr. Williams' situation, it was active listening, attention to family issues, acknowledgment of Mr. Williams' plea for autonomy, and some innovative planning by a dialysis nurse that resulted in Mr. Williams making a decision to continue treatment. Mr. Williams' mother and minister spoke with him for several hours one morning, both trying to convince him to continue treatment. He agreed to dialysis for that day only. During dialysis, he confided to the nurse that he wanted to discontinue treatment and die in the hospital. Mr. Williams believed he was dying from his infection and his uncontrolled dysrhythmia, perhaps not this week but surely this year. He did not want his mother to be alone when she found him dead. The nurse acknowledged Mr. Williams' right to discontinue treatment if he chose but also explained that his dysrhythmia was now more controlled and only occurred during dialysis. Mr. Williams entered into an agreement with the nephrologist and dialysis nurse that he would continue to accept treatment if he could be assured he would not be resuscitated during dialysis. He also asked that the dialysis nursing staff stay with his mother and offer her support if he cardiac arrested during dialysis.

What if the Group Remains Unable to Make a Decision or to Take Action?

Ombudsperson

There is a variety of possibilities for appeal if group members are unable to come to an acceptable decision. One common approach is for the institution's ombudsperson to become involved. Although this person is rarely an expert in ethics, she or he is usually very experienced in dealing with interpersonal conflict. Sometimes, this neutral person is able to translate the concerns of the health care providers to the family or vice versa. The ombudsperson may be aware of any cultural concerns that are affecting the decision and may be able to encourage greater cultural sensitivity. Although these are nonmoral concerns, they are often the stumbling blocks to reaching a decision and taking action in an ethical dilemma.

Ethics Committees

Most institutions, hospitals, medical centers, long-term care facilities, and home care agencies have or have had ethics committees. Ethics committees are usually composed of the following: physicians, nurses, administrators, members of the clergy, a psychiatrist, an attorney, a consumer or patient advocate, and an ethicist. The qualifications of the ethicist may vary. She or he may be a moral theologian, a philosopher, or a member of a health care profession with an advanced degree in ethics.

The ethicist or philosopher may serve a variety of functions on the committee and as a consultant to employees within the institution. The ethicist brings formal education in ethical reasoning to assist both the ethics committee and individual employees to clarify and articulate their thoughts. According to Jameton, a nurse might want to consult an ethicist when she or he has:[2]

- Conflicting ideas about what to do because of different values or principles
- No idea about what to do
- Clear ideas of what to do but no idea about why
- Ideas of what to do that conflict with those of others
- A need for critical review of her or his thinking

Ethics committees usually recognize that the presence of one ethicist will not provide sufficient grounding in ethics for the entire committee to engage in ethical deliberation. Therefore, most ethics committees begin their existence with some preparation in ethical theory for all members of the committee. The education may involve sending members away for formal study or group research and presentations of ethics content. This preparatory period lasts as long as a year for some committees.

Following the preparatory period, the committee usually attempts to set a climate conducive to ethical discussion and problem-solving within the institution. The committee usually assumes at least four functions:

- Legitimizing the importance of ethical practice by presenting ethical conferences and issues to the institution
- Assisting with the development of appropriate policies and procedures
- Developing a consistent framework for making ethical decisions
- Providing a neutral environment for problem-solving in "hard cases."

The issues facing ethics committees have shifted since they came into existence approximately 30 years ago. In the early 1970s, committees often dealt with end-of-life decision-making, outlining policies for use, and withdrawal of high-technology care. The committees discussed such issues as do-not-resuscitate orders, policies of life support withdrawal, and the definition of brain death as it relates to organ donation. By the mid 1980s, committees were focusing on issues related to fiscal and technologic capabilities.[12] Since the mid to late 1990s, ethics committees have been asked to review the ethical implications of managed care, focus on fraud prevention, and determine compliance with payer requirements.

Since the beginning of the 1990s, ethics committees in many institutions have been meeting much less frequently. In part, this is because they are being overshadowed by federally required corporate integrity programs and ethics hotlines directly linked to an integrity officer. Most calls to the hotline involve such practices as unfair billing and upcoding rather than

> Institutional ethics committees may serve as neutral, educated sounding boards to aid in the resolution of difficult cases.

patient care issues. Still, these programs are an attempt to create an ethical culture within the institution, once a function of the ethics committee. An ethics committee may appear redundant in such an environment.[13]

However, there is also some discontent with the way in which some ethics committees carry out their fourth function, the deliberation and resolution of hard cases. Despite attempts to prepare all members of the committee to have common preparation in ethical reasoning, some members may be unwilling to participate in the preparatory phase. At one institution, none of the eight physicians on the ethics committee chose to participate in the discussions and programs during the introductory period.[14] An ineffective ethics committee without strong leadership and administrative support may merely debate hard cases, never come to any resolution, and never offer any practical recommendations. Some institutions relegate strongly opinionated staff to positions on the ethics committee. This can condemn the committee to highly inflammatory debates without possibility of resolution.[13]

Yet health care providers, families, or a patient might want to ask for an ethics committee consultation in a "hard case." When those intimately involved in the situation cannot agree on a solution, it is possible that the more neutral and distanced ethics committee may provide assistance. Most ethics committees deliberate carefully, considering the views of all those directly involved, and make practical, ethically justified recommendations for the care of the patient and family concerned. Still, their recommendations are only suggestions, and they are not enforceable either by law or by institution policy. Thus, those immediately involved with the patient are not required to follow the recommendation of the ethics committee. They have little to lose in requesting a consultation and potentially much to gain.

Referral to the Court System

When disagreements become highly charged and there does not appear to be any possibility to arrive at a mutually acceptable decision, any of the parties involved in the dispute may bring the issue to the court system. Frequently cited examples of such a situation involve the Karen Quinlan[15] and Nancy Cruzan[16] cases. In both of these situations, family members argued for withdrawal of life-sustaining technologies from an incompetent family member, while health care providers advocated that the care be continued. In contrast, a family in Massachusetts has argued unsuccessfully that their family member ought to be allowed to continue with care that the health care team deemed futile.[17] When the court renders decisions, they become legally enforceable and set precedents for determination of similar cases within that jurisdiction.

There are several reasons why health care providers, families, and patients might want to avoid appealing to the legal system. The process of decision and appeal can consume several months to years, as it did in the Cruzan case.[16] The patient may remain in limbo, with caretakers and family divided on how to care for her or him during that time

> When health care providers or patients and families desire to expand a health care obligation to a legal right, they must utilize the legal system. However, in other circumstances, bringing a health care ethical issue to the courts may delay the resolution of the issue and solidify opposition to any compromise solution.

period. The tension between the opposing sides can become intense, and this may affect patient care. Finally, some people argue that although an appeal to the court system will result in a legally defensible course of action, it will not necessarily result in a morally appropriate course of action.

However, there may be an advantage to appealing to the court system. If the family or health care team wishes to establish a legally enforceable right, not only for this particular person but for other people as well, they will need to bring a legal suit. The Quinlan case established the right to terminate ventilator treatment from people who were not actively dying and did not have written preferences for their care.[15] The Cruzan case established similar rights for people whose lives were being prolonged through the use of enteral nutrition, also known as tube feeding.[16] The Massachusetts case recognized that an individual did not have a right to all possible health care, rather only to health care that would appear to offer a demonstrable benefit.[17]

In any case, appeals to the court system usually represent a last resort and signal failure of all other methods to resolve the dilemma. The adversarial relationship that is essential to the legal process often heightens the contentiousness of the situation. Lawyers and judges are not experts in medical, nursing, or health care, and they often have misconceptions and misunderstandings about the type of care that is being delivered. Avoiding involvement of the legal system, if possible, is probably the most prudent course of action if the goal is to reach a fairly prompt and ethically acceptable solution to the particular case in question.

What Should the Nurse Do If She or He is Unable to Agree With the Group's Decision?

It is perhaps easiest to begin with what the nurse ought not to do if she or he does not agree with the group's decision about how to proceed. If the nurse is going to be the person who will put the decision into action, it appears fairly clear that she or he ought not to just go along with the decision and carry out the plan. Numerous authors have noted that just going along and implementing the plan when a nurse does not agree with the decision is associated with an increased likelihood of burnout.

> Nurses experience moral distress if they recognize what ought to be done but are unable to respond as they believe they should.

Jameton describes a circumstance that he calls "moral distress."[2] In this situation, the nurse may believe she or he knows the right thing to do, yet institutional constraints prevent her or him from doing it. In the past, experiencing moral distress has been correlated with burnout in nurses. Shindul-Rothschild, as quoted in Joel's editorial[18], describes a similar circumstance, moral compromise, as "when nurses are in situations where they feel obligated to commit acts that can be justified, but they know are morally wrong." Joel characterizes the nurses' response to moral compromise as worse than what might have been called burnout in another era. She says it "results from a personal attack on our integrity, a matter of conscience, a moral imperative, and ultimately for many, a moral compromise."[18] It seems that just going along with a decision the nurse believes is morally wrong can be hazardous to the nurse both personally and professionally.

Compromise

Sometimes, even when an action is about to take place, it is possible to reconsider what is about to occur and achieve a compromise. The ideal compromise follows renewed discussion of the situation and involves a third choice that is acceptable to the parties directly involved. This spares the people involved in carrying out an action that they believe is morally wrong.

The wealthy woman with Alzheimer's disease, who required continuing intubation and mechanical ventilation postabdominal surgery, is an example of such a compromise.

The niece wanted her extubated immediately; the aunt was aware enough to signal she did not want to die but wanted to be "off the machine," and the nurse clearly opposed extubation at that time. A compromise was reached. The woman would continue to be ventilated for 24 hours and then be extubated whether or not she appeared fully ready. As the nurse had predicted, she did well over the next day and was fully prepared to be extubated the following morning.

Reaching such a compromise may consume a considerable amount of nursing time. Although the compromise described appears simple and obvious, the nurse spent most of her morning conferring with the niece, physician, ombudsperson, and patient. She also obtained the support of the unit director and hospital administration for her actions. The nurse believed that her time was well-spent. She had been distressed about the initial decision to extubate the woman immediately and believed she had facilitated an appropriate compromise.

> Compromise may result when another choice that is mutually acceptable to all is identified, when people recognize outcomes other than those originally anticipated are possible, or when they realize they had been missing important pieces of information.

Compromise may also occur when people recognize there may be other outcomes than they had postulated. The health care provider, family member, or patient may review the situation and realize that the difference of opinion has less to do with differences in the moral sense and more to do with a different view of the possible consequences of the action. Once the person realizes this, she or he may consent to a different course of action. When Mr. Williams realized that he was more likely to experience dysrhythmia and die during dialysis than while he was at home alone with his mother, he consented to continue treatment. However, he insisted that he not be resuscitated if he died during dialysis, and he asked for emotional support for his mother.

Occasionally, a member of the health care team may recognize that she or he was missing a vital piece of information. Once the person has a more complete understanding of the situation, she or he may be willing to give up the previous position and carry out the plan of action. When the nurse experiences moral distress, it is important that she or he ask for additional information, and to indicate her or his distress and confusion about the current course of action.

For example, an 88-year-old woman had abdominal surgery the previous day. At 4 AM, she became suddenly hypoxic and hypotensive and deteriorated quickly. Aggressive medical therapy was instituted, but by 7 AM it was evident she was dying. Her blood pressure was extremely low, despite maximum use of intravenous agents to

> Policy revisions following a difficult case can limit future dilemmas.

increase it; she was in considerable discomfort, since her blood pressure dropped dramatically if she was given pain medication. The nurse wanted the physician to institute comfort measures and cease aggressive therapy. However, the physician would not call the family to obtain permission, which was the policy at the institution at that time.

The nurse approached the physician and explained her frustration and distress about being unable to relieve the pain of a woman who was clearly dying. The physician recognized the nurse's distress and stated he was uncomfortable with the situation also. Unfortunately, the woman's only living relative, a son, was having minor surgery that morning and been premedicated the night before. As soon as the son was finished with the minor procedure and was fully awake, the physician intended to speak with him. Although the nurse did not approve of the situation, she could at least understand the problem now and was able to continue with the patient's care. Five minutes later, the son arrived; his EKG had showed minor changes and his procedure had been postponed. He was immediately apprised of the situation, and he consented to the discontinuation of aggressive therapy. His mother, adequately medicated for pain, died 2 hours later with her son at her side.

Policy Revision

One way in which nurses may have an effect on the ethical structure of the entire institution is to be involved in policy formulation and revision. Following the incident of the dying woman described above, the policy regarding notification of next of kin was revised and

> Nurses involved in developing policies they believe are ethically justifiable experience less moral distress.

a provision was made for what ought to occur when a patient's durable power of attorney for health care or next of kin is unavailable for consultation.

Nurses who are involved in formulating agency policies have been identified to be more autonomous in their ethical practice. Wurzbach noted nurses in long-term care who were involved in policy development for tube feeding withdrawal identified fewer situations when they experienced ethical distress.[19] The morally certain nurses involved in writing policy were also determined to be more action oriented. If they could not support or change policies to which they were morally opposed, they would seek another place of employment.

Conscientious Refusal

When a nurse believes she or he cannot ethically perform an action she or he is being asked to, she or he may utilize conscientious refusal and ask to be excused from participating in or assisting with the action. Conscientious refusal or objection is similar to civil disobedience, when people refuse to comply with an unjust law. However, in conscientious refusal the nurse refuses to comply with a policy or physician's order that she believes does not comply with her personal moral code.[1] Conscientious refusal might be used when the nurse believes the action is immoral or illegal, but that often requires stronger action, as described in Chapter 6. Instead, con-

> A nurse might utilize conscientious refusal when she or he cannot personally support an action planned by a health care provider or team. The suggested action, although justifiable, would be in violation of the nurse's personal code and she or he would therefore refuse to participate.

scientious refusal is often used when the supporters of an action can offer a justification for their action, but the nurse does not find their reasoning convincing. Nurses have utilized conscientious objection to express their concerns since the beginning of the century. A common statement of an individual using conscientious refusal would be, "I could not live with myself if I had done that. My conscience would have bothered me too much."

Benjamin and Curtis state that it is nurses who are highly principled, thoughtful providers of nursing care, who are most likely to request to be excused from care they believe they cannot condone.[1] They suggest that when certain characteristics are met, the administrators of the institution should honor the nurse's conscientious refusal. These characteristics identify the moral nature of the nurse's concern. According to

Benjamin and Curtis, a thoughtful nurse would identify her or his conscientious refusal to participate as:[1]

- Based on personal moral standards
- Determined by a prior judgment of rightness or wrongness
- Motivated by personal sanction and not external control

Conscientious refusal is not an option to be chosen without very careful consideration. There are a number of possible consequences for the nurse and patient. The first is that the nurse-patient relationship will be disrupted. If the patient and family have developed a relationship with the nurse; they may wish the nurse to remain with them beyond the decision-making phase to see the planned action accomplished and help them cope with the consequences of their decision. On the one hand, the nurse must consider the effect that disrupting the nurse-patient relationship will have on the patient and family. On the other hand, the nurse must consider what effect her disapproval of the planned action will have on her ability to deliver quality nursing care to this patient and subsequent similar patients.

One nurse had been caring for a patient who was a Jehovah's Witness. The woman began to bleed from a rectal tear, and her hematocrit dropped drastically and quickly. Although the patient consented to surgery, she would not consent to blood administration. The nurse realized she could not support the patient's ability to refuse a simple lifesaving intervention while requesting expensive, invasive life-prolonging technologies. When the patient continued to refuse the blood transfusion and request other extraordinary care, the nurse asked to be relieved from caring for the patient. The nurse realized her attempts to persuade the patient to receive blood were preventing her from providing the necessary nursing care nonjudgmentally and communicating therapeutically with the patient and family.

> Conscientious refusal may result in a variety of consequences to the nurse from disruption of the nurse-patient relationship to termination of employment.

The nurse must also consider the amount of support she or he will receive from her supervisor and the administration of the institution. The personal repercussions of employing conscientious refusal may range from nonexistent to dismissal from her or his nursing position. Institutions vary from being supportive of conscientious refusal and changing their institutional policies to support it, to being legally required by some states to allow nurses to utilize it, to being able to dismiss the nurse who utilizes conscientious refusal. It is important that the nurse know the legal ramifications in her or his state as well as the likely administrative support for such actions. The following situations will describe a series of nurses who utilized conscientious refusal, and the responses of the administration.

The first circumstance describes the response of a supportive administration in a morally difficult situation. A 67-year-old woman had incurred a fracture of her fourth cervical vertebrae, with subsequent damage to her spinal cord. She was paralyzed below her shoulders and unable to breath without a ventilator but awake, alert, and able to signal her wishes with a letter board and blinking. The woman asked to be extubated and allowed to die. The ethics committee of the institution was convened and concurred with her request. The nurse caring for the patient could not fully understand or support the decision, so she conveyed her concerns to the unit director, also a nurse. The unit director had been present during the ethics committee deliberations and supported the decision. She immediately suggested that since the patient's nurse was experiencing some moral distress, she should remove herself from the situation, and the unit director would care for the woman as she was extubated and died.

In the second situation, nurses gained the right to conscientious refusal at their hospital through mediation. Nurses in a newborn nursery opposed the practice of physicians routinely asking parents if they wanted their child circumcised, in effect soliciting what the nurses believed was unnecessary surgery. Eventually 54% of the nursing staff on the newborn unit was refusing to assist in obtaining consent, setting up equipment, or preparing the babies for routine circumcisions. When the nurses were ordered to assist, they continued to refuse. Following mediation, their hospital became the first in the country to recognize RN Conscientious Objectors to Infant Circumcision.[20]

The final example illustrates the severity of the consequences that can follow a nurse's utilization of conscientious refusal. A nurse employed by a New Jersey hospital refused to participate in the dialysis of a patient who was terminally ill and suffering during dialysis. The nurse requested to be removed from the patient's care. The hospital warned the nurse she could be fired and insisted the nurse perform the procedure. When the nurse continued to refuse to dialyze the patient, she was fired. The nurse's dismissal from her position was upheld by the New Jersey court system.[21]

Conscientious refusal is an avenue that is available for nurses to employ when they are encountering moral distress. The nurse wishing to utilize conscientious refusal should assure her- or himself that she or he has tried other possibilities before attempting conscientious refusal. The nurse should review the criteria suggested by Benjamin and Curtis to determine if she or he meets those criteria.[1] Is the decision:

- Based on personal moral standards?
- Determined by a prior judgment of rightness or wrongness?
- Motivated by personal sanction and not external control?

Finally, the nurse should familiarize her- or himself with the attitude of the administration toward conscientious refusal and the state laws in effect.

Finding an External Advocate

When the nurse finds her- or himself in a position that she or he believes is morally compromising and the nurse is not able to establish a compromise or utilize conscientious refusal without excessive penalties, Joel recommends the nurse seek out the counsel of an external advocate.[18] Joel suggests that the nurse might find such an advocate through her or his state nurses association or by networking with colleagues. The external advocate might enable the nurse to identify options and choices that the nurse had not previously considered in response to the dilemma.

SUMMARY

Decision-making in nursing ethics takes time, an understanding of the language and concepts of ethics, and an ability to make appropriate distinctions. It takes an appreciation of what it is to be human, and of the successes and limits of medicine. Further, decision-making in nursing ethics takes an ability to communicate with people who are in distress, an awareness of cultural and religious values, and an ability to compromise. Nurses, because they are intimately involved with patients and families, may have strong feelings or beliefs about what should be done. It is important that nurses learn to translate these feelings and beliefs into ethical discourse so that they can participate in the discussion of what ought to be done for their patients. Since nurses are often the people who carry out the interventions, they ought to believe that acceptable resolutions to the dilemmas have been identified. Nurses should search for morally acceptable alternatives, such as compromise, so that they have an alternative to participating in the action if they believe it is not morally justifiable.

REFERENCES

1. Benjamin M, Curtis J. *Ethics in Nursing.* 3rd ed. New York, NY: Oxford University Press; 1992: 11-21,112-113.

2. Jameton A. *Nursing Practice: The Ethical Issues.* Englewood Cliffs, NJ: Prentice Hall; 1984:6.

3. Callahan D. *Setting Limits: Medical Goods in an Aging Society.* New York, NY: Simon and Schuster; 1987.

4. Benner P, Wrubel J. *The Primacy of Caring.* Menlo Park, Calif: Addison-Wesley Publishing; 1989: 1-11.

5. Olsen DP. Controversies in nursing ethics: a historical view. *J Adv Nurs.* 1992;17:1020-1027.

6. Kuhse H. *Caring: Nurses, Women, and Ethics.* Oxford, England: Blackwell Publications; 1997.

7. Shannon SE. The roots of interdisciplinary conflict around ethical issues. *Critical Care Nursing Clinics of North America.* 1997;9:13-28.

8. Anspach RR. Prognostic conflict in life and death decisions. *J Health Soc Behav.* 1987;28:215-231.

9. MacIntyre A. *Whose Justice? Which Rationality?* Notre Dame, Ind: University of Notre Dame Press; 1988.

10. Grundstein AR. Differences in ethical decision making among nurses and doctors. *J Adv Nurs.* 1992;17:129-137.

11. Rushton CH, Russel K. The language of miracles: ethical challenges. *J Pediatr Nurs.* 1996;22:64-67.

12. Abel PE. Ethics committees in home health care. *Public Health Nurs.* 1990;7:256-259,1190.

13. Pastin M. The medical ethics committee: dinosaur or phoenix? *Health Systems Review.* 1996; 29:1-5.

14. Dalgo JT, Anderson F. Developing a hospital ethics committee. *Nursing Management.* 1995;26: 104-107.

15. *In re Quinlan,* 70 NJ 10, 355 A2d 647 (1976).

16. *Cruzan v Director, Missouri Department of Health,* 497 US 261 (1990).

17. *Gilgunn v Massachusetts General Hospital.* No 92-4820 (Mass. Sup. Ct. Civ. Action Suffolk Co. 22 Apr 1995).

18. Joel L. Moral compromise: burnout revisited [editorial]. *Am J Nurs.* 1997;97:7.

19. Wurzbach ME. Long term care nurses' moral convictions. *J Adv Nurs.* 1995;21:6,1059-1064.

20. Sperlich BK, Conant M, Hodges F. Conscientious objectors to infant circumcision: a model for nurse empowerment. *Revolution: The Journal of Nurse Empowerment.* 1996; Spring:86-89.

21. *Warthen v. Toms River Community Memorial Hospital,* 199 NJ Super 18, 488 A2d 229 (1985).

MULTIPLE-CHOICE QUESTIONS

1. The posing of which of the following questions would most likely indicate that the nurse has encountered an ethical dilemma?
   A. What should I do?
   B. What will the consequences of this action be?
   C. Who will be responsible for this action?
   D. Who will pay for this procedure?

2. If a nurse posed the question, "Which action would do the patient the most good?" she or he would most likely be reasoning from which of the following ethical perspectives?
   A. Beneficence
   B. Egoistic
   C. Justice
   D. Rights-based
   E. Utilitarian

3. If a nurse posed the question, "What would bring the greatest good to the greatest number of people?" she or he would most likely be reasoning from which of the following ethical perspectives?
   A. Beneficence
   B. Egoistic
   C. Justice
   D. Rights-based
   E. Utilitarian

4. Which of the following ways does Jameton say that health care benefits might be distributed?
   A. To each equally
   B. To each according to merit
   C. To each according to what can be acquired
   D. To each according to need
   E. All of the above

5. Which of the following types of cues is a physician more likely to rely on when determining a patient's prognosis?
   A. Development of depression by the patient
   B. Findings from the physical examination
   C. That the patient appears to be suffering
   D. When the patient cannot be comforted
   E. None of the above

6. According to MacIntyre, when people argue from differing ethical perspectives:
   A. It is usually easy for them to appreciate each others' values
   B. It can be difficult for them to understand each other, like speaking two different languages
   C. They frequently develop and use jargon as a short-hand means of communication
   D. All of the above
   E. None of the above

7. Shannon believes that health care providers infer which of the following about nurses from their style of communication? That nurses are:
   A. Concerned only with important patient issues
   B. Disorganized and unfocused in their thinking
   C. Respectful of other professionals' time
   D. All of the above
   E. None of the above

8. When a family refuses to believe a patient is dying and expects a miracle, Rushton and Russel suggest which of the following interventions?
   A. Appeals to reason and medical facts
   B. Examination of family dynamics
   C. Undermining of the family's faith with medical truth
   D. All of the above
   E. None of the above

9. Which of the following is true about conscientious refusal? It is:
   A. Based on personal moral standards
   B. Determined by a concurrent decision about the rightness or wrongness of the action
   C. Motivated by external sanction
   D. All of the above
   E. None of the above

10. According to Jameton, a nurse might want to consult an ethicist when she or he has which of the following:
    A. Conflicting ideas about what to do because of values or principles
    B. A clear idea about what to do but no idea why
    C. Ideas about what to do that conflict with those of others
    D. A need to critically review her or his thinking
    E. All of the above

CHAPTER 2 ANSWERS

1. A
2. A
3. E
4. E
5. B
6. B
7. B
8. B
9. A
10. E

Beginning of Life Issues

James McGhee, PhD

Mary Shaw, a married woman of 30, is 3 months pregnant. Regretfully, she has been diagnosed with cancer of the uterus. The physicians recommend an immediate hysterectomy to save her life. Such surgery will cause, albeit indirectly, an abortion, for the fetus is not viable. If one were to wait until the unborn had a chance of surviving, the mother and the fetus almost certainly would die from the original condition.

This is an old and somewhat classical case, but it still appears today and raises significant ethical questions. There are several problems associated with the start of life, and in order to deal with this kind of dilemma, some ideas must be explored.

When Does Life Begin?

Those of us who are parents are fascinated with the role we play in transmitting life to the next generation. The birth of our children ranks among the highest of personal experiences. Medical professionals, by reason of their calling, are naturally involved in this process.

Before delving into any possible problematic areas, such as the case offered above, let's ask the first fundamental question: When in the course of human reproduction does life actually begin? We know, of course, that some form of new life occurs with the meeting of the human gametes, normally within the mother's body. Is the fertilization of the female egg by the male seed the start of a new human being?

Two Basic Positions

One term, which is used for the beginning of the human person, is *hominization*, from the Latin *homo*, meaning a human being. There is no agreement when this happens. In the

Middle Ages there were two main opinions, both of which are expressed by modern writers:

1. **Instantaneous**. This opinion maintains that hominization occurs at the time of conception.
2. **Delayed hominization**. This opinion states that hominization happens sometime later in the pregnancy.

Only a few of the medieval thinkers, such as Albert the Great, supported the first position. The authority for the second was the famous Greek philosopher Aristotle, who held that the unborn went through various stages of ensoulment: vegetable, animal, and finally human. Male fetuses developed within this system

> The question of hominization underlies all the issues concerning the beginning of life. If, for instance, life begins in its entirety at conception or some other stage in a pregnancy, then what is our obligation to protect the unborn at that particular time?

much faster than females, thus explaining the superiority of men and the physical and mental inferiority of women! Such faulty thinking relied on mistaken biology: it was thought that the entirety of the species rested solely with the male, and that the male semen contained the entire new human being. The role of the mother was simply to house the seed in her womb and let it grow there. This was repeated by such intellectual giants as Augustine of Hippo and Thomas Aquinas, resulting of course in the prejudice against women.

Today, instantaneous hominization has many supporters, while the delayed hominization opinion is spread over the whole period of gestation, from implantation of the embryo, through the formation of the brain, to viability, and even birth. One can easily see that when conflicts arise, as with the case of Mary Shaw, this question occupies a key role in any solution.

In general, problems that center around human reproduction fall into two categories: those who wish to prevent birth, and those who want to have a child but are dealing with infertility. It is estimated that 20% of those who wish to have children cannot do so because of some fault in their reproductive organs. Infertility is equally divided among men and women.

BIRTH CONTROL

Contraception

Far back in history, societies have attempted to regulate birth. The unwitting and unwilling father of the modern movement is by common consent Thomas Malthus, the 18th century Anglican priest, who issued dire warnings about the dangers of overpopulation and subsequent starvation of the masses. During the industrial revolution, social reformers in both Britain and America (eg, Robert Owen)

> There is a long history of attempts at controlling birth. Contraception is the prevention of the meeting of the human gametes and should be carefully distinguished from abortion, both physically and morally.

used their findings to argue for a birth control movement to meet the needs of poor women in large cities. In this country, the movement did not receive official legal approval until the middle of the 20th century. Spearheading the drive for better, more efficient, and safer methods was Margaret Sanger, a nurse from New York, who worked in the slums of the city and who encouraged the development of the hormone-based pill in the 1950s. The pill popularized contraception more than any other method in history. It provoked a widespread debate on the morality of birth control and is held responsible for a change in family life and sexual mores in recent society. One aspect of the situation was the possible injurious side effects of these artificial methods. For instance, due to the scare of spreading the AIDS virus, then Surgeon General Admiral Koop would not endorse any artificial means of contraception except the condom. His first advice to the unmarried was abstinence. The Catholic Church and Pope Paul VI entered the fray in the 1960s, arguing that though the regulation of one's family size was legitimate in some cases, the use of artificial means of contraception is immoral because it is against the natural law. The only means the Pope agreed to was what is called natural family planning. However, especially in the United States, polls show that most Catholics, including theologians, respectfully disagree with the Roman Pontiff. Most moralists would agree that to introduce a foreign substance into one's body does involve risk, and such risk should be commensurate to any benefit gained.

Abortion

The debate over the direct interruption of pregnancy is one of the most heated in today's society. Direct abortion means precisely that—a pregnancy is brought to an end intentionally by an outside agent. In the case of Mrs. Shaw, the abortion would be indirect because the main intention

> Direct abortion is the interruption of a pregnancy by an outside agent. Indirect abortion is caused by some problem within the body itself; sometimes it is called a miscarriage.

is to save her life. The death of the fetus is tolerated because of the circumstances.

The principal means of abortions today depends on the stage of the pregnancy. Early abortions are brought about by drugs, such as RU-486, or by a surgical intervention such as a dilatation and curettage, and most popularly by vacuum aspiration. Later in the pregnancy, surgical or chemical interventions are more dangerous for the mother. The struggle to introduce RU-486 into the United States has been marked by rancorous politicking and emotional ethical debate typical of the past 25 years. This French pill may change the scene again because it is taken secretly in a doctor's office with none of the outward publicity of an abortion clinic. Immediately, one can see that the position taken on when life begins colors the tone as well as the content of the arguments used.

In 1973, the Supreme Court decision in two cases took the matter out of state control (*Roe v Wade, Doe v Boston*). The political and legal situation in the United States was most uneven at the time, differing greatly in different regions. This is what the court decided:

1. During the first trimester of a pregnancy (roughly the first 3 months), states cannot interfere in the decision of a woman to have an abortion.

2. During the second trimester, when such procedures are more hazardous for the mother, states may legislate where abortions may be performed. Beyond such procedural conditions, no one can interfere in this private decision between a woman and her physician.

3. In the third trimester, states may ban abortions except in the case where there is a threat to the life or well-being of the mother.

The principal argument given by the majority (7 to 3) was based on the right to privacy. The justices claimed that they did not consider the question of hominization, but since they withdrew all protection from the unborn prior to viability, that stage is often referred to as the Supreme Court position on the beginning of life. Thus, the country moved from being one of the most

> The Supreme Court of 1973 legalized abortion throughout the United States. The argument of the court was based on the right of privacy of the mother to control her own body.

restrictive in the world to one of the most permissive on this question. Many authors covering the topic conveniently divide the contestants into three groups, according to their mode of argument.

Those Who are Against Abortion

Those who hold this position refer to themselves as pro-life, since the principal argument used is that the right to life is fundamental to our society and it is the duty of all honest people to come to the aid of those who cannot help themselves. Such is the hallmark of all civilized communities. Further is the role of physicians to save and care for human life, never to take it. Thus, abortion makes the practice of both medicine and law something of a conundrum. Biology indicates that life begins at conception, for here the complete human genotype emerges in the meeting of the human gametes and from then on all that is needed is growth. To this group might be added those who would add one exception—when there is a threat to the life of the mother.

Abortion is Wrong, Except...

Most popular in today's pluralistic society are those who consider abortion to be undesirable but see the need for several exceptions to a general rule. Social indicators, such as a threat to the life or well-being of the mother, post-felonious assault such as rape or incest, and the danger of a handicapped child being born are examples of a list of valid reasons for allowing the interruption of pregnancies. Principal arguments might include the idea that laws in society come into being through compromise, and thus citizens with contending views might live at peace with each other. When life begins is not clear from science, religion, or philosophy, so it should be decided by each according to his or her own beliefs.

Abortion Upon Demand

This position, known as pro-choice, reflects the actual situation within many countries including the United States. Privacy seems to be the pivotal ethical, legal, and medical argument put forward. A woman has a right to privacy over her own body, her sexual activity, and her reproductive system. Abortion is thus an individual's right, a private decision between a woman and her doctor. While a large number of abortions is not desirable and probably should be used ideally as a backup to failed contraceptives, all women should have access to abortion if they wish. The middle position fails to meet the needs of the majority of women who have abortions (it is not convenient for me at this time to bear a child) and thus should be rejected along with the first group.

One's position on hominization often determines where one lands in the abortion debate. But it is reasonable to say that while the majority of people in this country would like to decrease the number of abortions performed, at the same time they would defend the present law, which allows abortion on request. Many would also like to see more protection given to the rights of fathers, grandparents, and underage teenagers in the general scene. In the case of Mary Shaw, some of these issues arise and add to the consideration of her case.

INFERTILITY

While great numbers of the population are trying to control birth, there is a sizeable number, possibly 20%, who sincerely wish to have children but because of one reason or another are unable to do so. Methods, some old and some recent, are available and raise provocative ethical questions.

Artificial Insemination

In this situation, the seed is extracted from the husband or a donor and placed in the uterus of the woman during her time of ovulation. If the husband is the donor, it is called *homologous artificial insemination* (AIH), and when the donor is another, it goes by the name of *heterologous artificial insemination* (AID). Most

> Infertility affects a large number of people. In the past, women were often "blamed" for a childless marriage, but the causes are many and are equally distributed among men and women.

ethical thinkers and the general public see little problem when the process takes place between a married couple but have reservations with heterologous artificial insemination. Here are a few:

- Artificial insemination could be argued to be adultery. An outsider is entering into the sacred and exclusive union between the spouses. Perhaps with maturity and clarity of intention, such a difficulty could be overcome, but this argument against AID has been used in such a manner in divorce cases.

- Psychological difficulties could arise. The mother's deep desire for a child has been fulfilled but the father's wish for paternity has not. This could be the basis of conflict within the marital relationship.

- The legal situation is strange. The mother's biological role is clear, but the father would have to adopt the child and perhaps make him or her his heir. It could become somewhat of a legal no-man's land.

- With widespread unknown paternity, there is a danger of incestuous relationships arising. It sounds somewhat far-fetched, but all authors point to the possibility, and there have been some very strange cases reported in this area. To deal with this problem, fertility clinics today attempt to document their clients as far as possible, but still a great deal of secrecy surrounds such procedures.

- What about the rights of the child who is born? Do we have a right to know our personal story, and our medical and genetic background? Do we have a right to know who our parents are?

Artificial insemination remains a key ingredient in the more sophisticated methods we will now review.

In Vitro Fertilization

The first test tube baby was born in Leeds, England in the summer of 1978. It was a little girl named Louise Brown. The method was to mingle the sperm of the father and the eggs of the mother in a laboratory dish and then transfer the new embryo(s) into the mother's womb. Its success was dependent on developing drugs, which would suppress the mother's immune system and allow her to implant the new conceptus. Further advances were made when it became possible to freeze embryos, just like male semen could be frozen. Over the past 20 years or so, fertility clinics have spread worldwide and are even covered by some medical insurers in the United States. Drawbacks would include the expense, the danger to the mother, and the rate of success (30% in the best of facilities). Other problems are raised. For instance, what does one do with those embryos that are not implanted and are left in the clinic? When does life begin anyway?

> Manipulation of human reproductive systems has increased with the spread of fertility clinics since the 1980s. The new technology gives rise to new ethical problems.

Surrogacy

A few years ago the American public was treated to a public squabble of "Whose baby is it?" in the struggle between two biological parents claiming exclusive right to have their own child. The case, *Mary Beth Whitehead v Stern*, played out in a courthouse in Hakensack, NJ. Mr. Stern, a rich man from the suburbs of New York, hired a poor woman, Mrs. Whitehead, to be artificially inseminated by his semen, bring the baby to term, and then hand the child over to him and his wife. The amount of money involved was fairly large. For him the total bill was $20,000; $10,000 going to the natural mother and the rest for medical and legal services. All went well until the baby was born. The mother, Mary Beth, fell in love with her daughter, refused to honor the deal, sent back the money, and fled with her child to her own mother in Florida. Mr. Stern sued for custody before Judge Slokum in Hakensack. An interested nation was treated to extensive coverage of the event by the media. During the lengthy spectacle, many came to give evidence and offer opinions. The spokesperson for the American Adoption Societies, for instance, stated that the child should be given to the care of the mother. The judge decided to give the baby to the Sterns, making Mrs. Stern the adopting mother in his chambers. He claimed that the case was unique, that he had no precedents to lean on, and that he did not wish his decision to be the basis of future laws. In fact, there had been similar cases in England and Germany where the sympathy of the courts and the public went to the natural mothers. In the appeal, Mrs. Whitehead was granted rights to visit her daughter, who was to be informed of the situation when she was older. Afterward, many expressed dissatisfaction with the event and several states, including New Jersey, banned what was termed commercial surrogacy—as had happened in Europe.

The subject of children, of course, raises problems at a different level from those confronting adults, and they cannot always be solved in entirely the same fashion. Remember there is a difference between pediatric and adult medicine. The subject of consent is challenging when we are dealing with children. It is presumed that parents will give

> The history of children presents us with a mixed picture. Many ancient civilizations, such as the Greeks and Romans, had a low opinion of children and abused them regularly. Today, we attempt to protect and treat our children as persons and are upset when they are not awarded the rights that all in our society possess.

consent to accepted treatment for their children. But here again, practical problems now exist that were not there in the past. Should a parent consent for a child in a transplant case? Parents do not own their children, although they have a duty to protect, raise, and educate them. Should surgery be performed on a baby to correct a grave malfunction, if the child will be severely retarded or physically deformed even if the surgery is successful? Sometimes the state may wish to intervene if the parents refuse standard treatment for their offspring. This would be the accepted procedure in the case of religious groups who refuse to give permission for blood transfusions. To solve such cases we could have recourse to some principles, such as the use of the terms "ordinary" and "extraordinary" means of life support.

As scientific knowledge and our ability to intervene in our bodies increases, more and more ethical questions will arise. Genetic manipulation has already made it possible to clone animals, such as sheep and cows. What can be done with animals can be done with humans. The human genome project has unraveled the secrets of our genetic makeup and marvels of nature in microcosm, which again gives us more power over our destinies. For instance, we now know how many diseases, including cancer, are caused without knowing the cures. It is something similar to the discoveries of the 19th century, when the causes of horrendous sicknesses, such as the bubonic plague, were discovered before the cure of penicillin. Clearly, advances in medicine will result, but there are pitfalls to be avoided.

Some dilemmas might even arise from knowledge of our own genetic screening. For example, if we were all genetically screened, such as the recent events in Iceland, who has a right to this knowledge: the government, the court, a school, or an insurance company? Some have

> The advance in knowledge acquired recently through the human genome project has presented society with new ethical questions.

expressed much concern over such questions. Some people do not want to know if they are genetically inclined to develop a certain disease at the age of 40 or 50.

Then there is the general problem of who controls research. Should scientists in this field, for instance, be forbidden to insert into the human genetic pool something completely new—say a gene from another species? In Europe, laws prohibit such research and many people in this country, including government officials, have urged for a similar moratorium in the United States. Such questions as, "Whose science is it, anyway?" are legitimately being raised.

The basic ethical question is the same. Does the fact that we *can* do something mean that we *should* do it?

Here again, some old principles might help. The underlying standard of respecting life is always advantageous to keep in mind, for the notion of the dignity of each individual life is well-rooted in our religious and philosophical heritage. The Jewish, Islamic, and Christian religions hold that God made the human being and entrusted each person with innate sacredness from creation itself. Most philosophical systems also maintain similar standards, so that if we enter into new terrain with regard to manipulating human life, this idea of respecting life at all levels in our world could or should be an overriding principle to observe.

What of Mrs. Shaw? Could we dig into our ethical methods and come up with some sort of common-sense answer? The principle of double effect might help, for if we refer back one could see that there are two possible evil results here: the death of the mother and the death of the fetus. According to this way of reasoning, the circumstances, intention, and consequences must be taken into consideration, while the action must not be judged to be evil. A hysterectomy is morally neutral—most surgery would be so. The circumstances are such that the evil effect, the death of the unborn, is not the means to saving the mother's life. It is the removal of her cancerous uterus. The intention of the agent, in this case the surgeon, is not to kill but to save the life of the mother. Finally, there is proportion between the good effect, the

> If an ethical consultation occurred about Mrs. Shaw, many of the issues in this chapter could be raised. It could be asked at such a meeting, "Which principles could be employed and whose rights might take precedence over all others?"

woman's life, and the death of the fetus, which is not intended but merely tolerated.

It is principles like these that should appeal to our common sense. These principles not only help us through the gray areas of life but also assist us in feeling good about ourselves when we act well.

BIBLIOGRAPHY

Alpern KD, ed. *The Ethics of Reproductive Technology.* New York, NY: Oxford University Press; 1992.

Crigger BJ, ed. *Cases in Bioethics.* New York, NY: St. Martin's Press; 1993.

Grisez G. *Abortion: The Myths, the Realities, and the Arguments.* New York, NY: Corpus Books; 1970.

Horgan J, ed. *Humanae Vitae and the Bishops.* Shannon, Ireland: Irish University Press; 1972.

Levine C, ed. *Taking Sides: Clashing Views on Controversial Bioethical Issues.* Guilford, Conn: McGraw-Hill College Division; 1993.

McGee G, ed. *The Human Cloning Debate.* 2nd ed. Berkeley, Calif: Berkley Hills Books; 2000.

Ministry of Health. ACT on a Health Sector Data Base. Reykjevak, Iceland; 1998:139-199.

Newman JT, ed. *The Morality of Abortion: Legal and Historical Perspectives.* Cambridge, Mass: Harvard University Press; 1970.

Shannon TA. *What Are They Saying About Genetic Engineering?* New York, NY: Paulist Press; 1985.

MULTIPLE-CHOICE QUESTIONS

1. The fundamental question about ethical issues at the beginning of life is which of the following:
    A.   Does hominization occur?
    B.   How should the rights of every fetus be protected?
    C.   What are the consequences of genetic screening?
    D.   When in the course of human reproduction does life begin?

2. What was the Supreme Court argument that favored allowing abortion upon demand?
    A.   A woman has a right to privacy over her own body.
    B.   Biology indicates that life begins at conception.
    C.   Women must be able to follow their own conscience.
    D.   None of the above.

3. Which of the following questions is/are raised about heterologous artificial insemination?
    A.   Does the child have a right to know her or his genetic background?
    B.   Is it a form of adultery?
    C.   Will conflict over the child's paternity damage the parent's relationship?
    D.   All of the above.

4. The basic ethical question underlying issues of genetic research is which of the following?
    A.   Does the fact that we can do something mean that we should do it?
    B.   How should genetic screening information be utilized by employers?
    C.   When should genetic screening be conducted?
    D.   Who has the right to information about an individual's genetic code?

CHAPTER 3 ANSWERS

1. D
2. A
3. D
4. A

Health Maintenance Across the Life Span

Kathleen Ouimet Perrin, RN, CCRN, PhD(c)

AUTONOMY: SHOULD THE PATIENT ALWAYS BE THE PRIMARY DECISION-MAKER ?

Mr. Stevens, a 67-year-old man, was admitted to the ICU of a community hospital with respiratory failure secondary to pneumonia. He was intubated and placed on a ventilator. As the pneumonia cleared, Mr. Stevens could not breathe. It became apparent Mr. Stevens was suffering from amyotrophic lateral sclerosis (ALS), a degenerative neurologic disease resulting in muscular failure. No one had been aware of this illness prior to Mr. Stevens' hospitalization. Although Mr. Stevens was able to communicate by computer and eye blink, he refused to communicate with anyone except a student nurse, and he repeatedly "told" her that he wanted all treatment to stop.

One month prior to his admission, Mr. Stevens' wife had died from cancer. His older son, who had durable power of attorney for health care, was in the process of a difficult divorce. Unable to wean Mr. Stevens from the ventilator, a decision had to be made about whether to remove the ventilator and allow him to die or to transfer him to a long-term care facility that specialized in the care of people on ventilators. Mr. Stevens would only "talk" with a student nurse, and his son would not allow the father to be taken off the ventilator. The son consistently repeated he could not lose his father too. The ICU staff, physicians, nurses, social workers, and clergy were unable to agree about what should be done.

Although this book is primarily concerned with ethical issues, there are often legal considerations that parallel ethical concerns. Should the patient always be the primary decision-maker concerning her or his care? Are there instances when the family, health care provider, or significant other ought to be making the decision? Most legal and ethical authorities will agree that the decision-maker ought to be someone other than the patient when the patient is no longer competent or lacks capacity.

Incompetent or Incapacitated Patients

Competence is a legal term and has specific legal meanings and ramifications. Americans over the age of 18 are assumed to be competent, unless it is demonstrated that they are not of sound mind and are unable to make reasoned, rational decisions. To determine a person's competency, the person's comprehension of reality, understanding, and ability to make

> An adult is presumed to be competent and retains the ability to make decisions about her or his medical care unless it is demonstrated otherwise.

rational decisions are tested. A person must be declared incompetent by a legal proceeding and a substitute decision-maker or guardian identified.

However, inability to reason in one area of a person's life does not necessarily mean that the person is unable to reach a rational decision about other issues. So, competence may be considered to be task specific. The individual may be unable to balance a checkbook but still be able to explain why she or he did not want to have her or his leg amputated. Even more importantly, a person's disagreement with the treatment plan proposed by the health care team does not mean that the person is incompetent. If the person has a rational reason for the disagreement, a level of competency may be demonstrated to make a medical decision.

Although the final determination of competency is a legal issue, it is important that the nurse be able to identify people who do not appear to be competent to make decisions concerning their medical care. Since people who are incompetent are not capable of making valid decisions, their consent for or refusal of treatment would not be valid. Chell recommends considering the following questions when reviewing whether a patient is competent to make a decision concerning medical care:[1]

- Does the patient understand her or his medical condition?
- Does the patient understand the options and the consequences of her or his decision?

In addition, if the patient is refusing to consent to recommended medical treatment, these extra questions should also be considered:

- Is the patient's refusal based on rational reasons?
- If the refusal is based on religious beliefs, are the beliefs acceptable and entitled to First Amendment protection? In other words, are these accepted beliefs, or are they part of a patient's irrational belief system and illness?

In contrast to incompetence, *incapacity* is a less restrictive term. A determination of incapacity does not require a legal proceeding; it merely requires a determination of the individual's capability to make decisions. The incapacity may be temporary. For example, a patient

> Incapacity often entails a temporary inability to make a reasoned, thoughtful decision.

might be incapacitated while unresponsive for the first few days following a head injury or while disoriented from ketoacidosis. During the period of incapacity, a predetermined proxy decision-maker might be used.

To return to the case study described previously, the recent death of Mr. Stevens' wife and his unwillingness to communicate or indicate any feeling except exhaustion caused the staff to question his capacity. It was clear he was still grieving the death of his wife, while trying to understand what was happening to him. No one was certain how clearly he understood his prognosis or the options for his care. He had made no effort to assist in his weaning from the ventilator. When the student nurse was available, he would indicate to her his disgust with the situation and his desire to have the ventilator removed. She was unable to determine if he understood that he would die soon after being extubated.

The staff members were clearly motivated by the ethical principle of autonomy, the ability of individuals to be self-governed, and to choose their own destiny. They had experience in preparing ALS patients for ventilator care at home or in long-term care but also in terminal weaning when the person requested no further treatment. The health care providers were willing to prepare their patient for either outcome but were very concerned that his depression made it difficult to determine his authentic choice. Most of this man's health care providers thought that his situational depression precluded his competency.

After consultation with a psychiatrist, the health care team decided to give their patient a trial of antidepressant to see if that would relieve his depression and make his authentic choice apparent. Mr. Stevens was so depressed that he was communicating with only one person, a student nurse. The health care team did not want to rely on such limited communication, which would probably be open to legal challenges. The patient was not consulted about the decision to initiate antidepressant therapy. Still, he was informed.

Advance Directives

Another way to approach the legal-ethical consideration of who should make the decision about Mr. Stevens' care during his incapacity is to review the use of advance directives. Since 1991, when the Patient Self-Determination Act took effect, people in all states are entitled to describe in advance the medical treatments they would desire should they become incapacitated. The act requires health care institutions (hospitals, long-term care facilities, home care agencies, and HMOs) to provide written information for clients describing their rights to make advance directives. Institutions must determine if a client has an advance directive and document the presence or absence of the directive in the client's record. Institutions may not discriminate in the care provided to the client based on the presence or absence of an advance directive.[2]

The intention of the legislation is that an individual, while competent, can indicate how she or he would like to be treated should she or he become incapacitated. Depending on the state, a person might delineate the desired types of treatment (instructional directives, such as a medical directive or living will) or identify someone to make decisions (health care proxy or durable power of attorney for health care). Since the majority of Americans

> Types of advance directives:
> - Instructional directives
>   - living wills
>   - medical directives
> - Designation of proxy decision-maker
>   - durable power of attorney for health care
>   - health care proxy

do not have advance directives, many states also have statutes that allow relatives to serve as proxy decision-makers when no advance directive exists.

Instructional directives specify a client's desire for medical treatment under specific circumstances. Living wills are an example of this type of directive. They are meant to reaffirm the patient's right to refuse life-prolonging intervention when the person is dying. Specific treatments that the person wishes to avoid, such as mechanical ventilation, are usually listed. One of the major problems with living wills is that it is not always apparent that the patient is dying. Ironically, Mr. Stevens had arrived at the hospital with a living will saying he did not desire intubation and CPR if he was terminally ill. However, on admission, no one suspected that he had ALS. His diagnosis was severe but treatable pneumonia, so he was immediately intubated and ventilated.

Another type of instructional advance directive is a medical directive. According to Emanuel and Emanuel, medical directives attempt to eliminate some of the problems of the living will such as vagueness in terminology, lack of ability to request an intervention, and poor communication.[3] By asking a person what interventions she or he would choose in various circumstances, medical directives make explicit the person's wishes for medical treatment in those situations. For example, a person might be asked if she or he would desire artificial feeding or mechanical ventilation should she or he develop ALS. In another situation, a person might be asked about desired interventions if she or he was in an irreversible coma.

One advantage of the medical directive is that a client may affirm a desire for aggressive intervention. In this era of health care cost containment, many people, especially members of minority groups, are fearful that they will not receive all necessary and appropriate health care. Medical directives allow people to request that all medically appropriate interventions be utilized.

However, there are significant disadvantages to the use of medical directives. According to Pellagrino, new therapeutic options might have been discovered, which the person might not have considered when preparing the medical directive.[4] Also, the person's interests might have changed since the directive was originally written, and she or he might no longer desire the specific interventions to be employed. More importantly, the situations described in the directive rarely match the specific clinical situation of the patient, so some discretion is required when determining if the medical directive is applicable.

Health care proxies or durable powers of attorney for medical purposes are the final type of advance directive. These directives allow an individual to designate an agent to make medical decisions for her or him should she or he become incapacitated or incompetent. Proxy directives have the advantage of greater flexibility, with more relevance to the actual clinical situation and more personal involvement of the decision-maker. However, for proxy decision-makers to express the authentic desires of the patient, the proxies and the patients must have discussed the patients' goals and desires for health care.

When the patient and proxy decision-maker have not discussed the patient's goals and desires for health care, there are two methods the proxy might use to assist in making the decision. The first, substituted judgment, means the proxy uses the information that she or he knows about the patient to make the decision that the proxy believes the patient would make if she or he were able. Suppose Mr. Stevens had been fiercely independent all his life, refusing help with even simple activities. A person with his health care proxy, using substituted judgment, might recognize that Mr. Stevens valued his independence above other factors and would not desire to be constrained to a ventilator for the remainder of his life.

If the proxy was unaware of the person's wishes or lacked information about how the patient might view the particular situation, the proxy might employ a best interests standard. The best interests standard directs the agent to choose the intervention that best promotes and protects the patient's interests. Usually, the agent selects the intervention that most reasonable people would select under the circumstances. If Mr. Stevens had directed his son to make a decision for him using best interests standards, he might have said something like, "I chose you to be my health care proxy because I trust you to know what is important to me in this life. I cannot foresee all the possible medical interventions or consequences, so I trust you to use your best judgment and act to protect my interests."

Many health care providers and ethicists are expressing concern about the use of advance directives because the current directives have not been nearly as effective as was anticipated. The reasons for the lack of effectiveness include:

- Only a small percentage of the American population has completed an advance directive.
- The preferences for health care stated in the advance directive have not been demonstrated to be stable over time.
- The signing of a directive represents only the completion of a process that should include discussion of health care goals and decisions with health care providers and family.

This last point is probably the most significant. It is only through discussion with health care providers and family that the patient becomes aware of the potential advantages and disadvantages of life-sustaining technologies for his or her condition. Through this discussion, the health care provider will better understand the patient's values. No signed document should ever substitute for such a discussion between patients, families, and health care providers. Unfortunately, although all three parties believe this discussion is important, they have been reluctant to initiate it.

The Nurse's Role in Advance Directives

It is the nurse's responsibility in health care institutions to know if each of her or his patients has completed an advance directive. If a patient has not completed a directive, then the patient must be asked during admission if she or he would like more information or to complete a directive. If the patient desires more information or wishes to complete a directive, then the responsible party in the institution should be contacted.

Although in many institutions the admission clerk is responsible for asking patients if they have advance directives, there are major advantages to the primary care provider being the person who discusses an advance directive with the patient. There is evidence that if a physician or nurse initiates the discussion, the patient is more likely to complete a directive. Also, the discussion required to prepare a directive usually results in a clear understanding of the patient's values and preferences for treatment. Physicians who clearly understand the reasons for patient treatment preferences are much more likely to honor them.

If a person admitted to a health care facility has an advance directive, a copy should be obtained for the patient's record. There are a few additional questions that are useful for the nurse to ask to clarify the wishes of the individual. The nurse might wish to know:[5]

- Has the patient spoken to anyone about the terms of the advance directive?
- With whom did she or he speak?
- What was discussed?
- What are the patient's wishes in her or his own words?

The nurse especially wants to determine if the patient has spoken with her or his health care proxy and primary health care provider. The nurse is identifying who has the legal authority to make a health care decision for the patient. Additionally, the nurse determines if the patient believes the proxy has the information necessary to make an appropriate decision. A few patients change their mind after completing a directive, usually requesting fewer interventions, so it is wise if the nurse also asks the patient if she or he still desires the directive to remain in effect.

Merely because a patient has completed a directive, explained her or his wishes, and designated a proxy does not mean that her or his wishes will be followed. Mr. Stevens had completed an advance directive, giving his son durable power of attorney for health care purposes. The son was adamantly opposed to stopping treatment for his father. He understood that his father would not improve, that his condition was degenerative, and that although he could not move, he could still feel and was often uncomfortable. He knew that his father was telling the student nurse that he wanted the ventilator removed. Yet, he

> Summary of benefits and problems of advance directives:
> - Living will
>   - affirms desire to avoid certain treatments if terminally ill
>   - not always clear when a patient is dying
> - Medical directive
>   - may request as well as decline treatment
>   - circumstances covered are broader than just terminal illness
>   - medical advances may not be considered
>   - patient's desires may change over time
>   - rare exact match between patient's circumstance and directive
> - Health care proxy
>   - greater flexibility relevant to actual situation
>   - personal involvement of decision-maker
>   - proxy may be unaware of patient's wishes
>   - proxy may be motivated by self-interest rather than the patient's best interests

repeatedly said, "I can't let my father die now."

Everyone involved in the situation doubted the son was making his decision using either of the accepted methods of proxy decision-making, patient's best interests, or substituted judgment. In this case, most people believed the patient's son was making a very egoistic decision. At times the son was heard to say, "My father can't leave me now."

The members of the health care team doubted either the patient or his son had the capacity to make a thoughtful decision. Staff members sincerely questioned the validity of the directive as well as the capacity of the patient. Yet, the procedure to remove a proxy is cumbersome, lengthy, and divisive so no one wanted to initiate the process. Instead, the previous decision to wait for the antidepressant to work was upheld. Everyone was hoping Mr. Stevens' depression would lift, so he would be able to make and convey his authentic choice.

> In the past, health care providers often acted paternalistically. These health care providers would decide what interventions they believed were in their patients' best interests and act on behalf of their patients, without the patients' consent.

Should Patients' Families Have Special Consideration in Medical Decision-Making?

Families have always had a major role in medical decision-making for very young children. In fact, most ethicists agree that for incapacitated adults and young children, families are usually the most appropriate decision-makers. Twenty-five years ago, physicians and families often made decisions for care of the patient without consulting the patient, even when the patient was competent. This approach, called paternalism or parentalism, meant that the patient was not allowed to exert her or his autonomy, and the health care provider or family member acted in what was presumed to be the patient's best interests.

The paternalistic approach to patient care often resulted in subterfuge and abuse of medical power. One common occurrence was that physicians and families, wanting to spare their patients the distress and knowledge of impending death, would not tell the patients that they were dying. This created major problems for patient care delivery, especially for nurses. The patients would frequently ask if they had been told the whole truth; they would wonder why palliative rather than curative care was being suggested, and they would be less likely to have their personal and financial affairs in order before dying. Clearly, this paternalistic approach to caring for dying patients did not work well. For the past 20 years, the emphasis has instead been on truth telling and patient autonomy.

However, some ethicists are now proposing a return to limited paternalism. They believe that families should be actively involved in making decisions for many chronically ill older adults and any family member whose care will require substantial family resources. To explain this viewpoint, the situation of a second man with ALS, Mr. Raymond, will be explored. Mr. Raymond was hospitalized because his second wife, and primary caregiver, was institutionalized for exhaustion and severe depression. Mr. Raymond had obtained custody of his children from his first marriage. He wanted desperately to remain at home with the children despite his complete inability to move and ventilator dependence. He required complete physical care, as well as someone available 24 hours a day to respond to his ventilator alarms and suction him if necessary. He was highly anxious, feared being alone, and rarely allowed his wife to be out of his sight for more than 5 minutes. His second wife had initially attempted, with the assistance of home health care, to keep him at home and raise the children.

However, as home health services were curtailed and the children became teenagers, the 24-hour responsibility became too much for his wife. Now, she was hospitalized, exhausted, and insistent that she could not return to the same situation. Both Mr. Raymond's sisters and children wanted him to return home but stated they were unable to provide any additional assistance with his care. Social services could identify no additional services for which he was eligible. Mr. Raymond refused to consider going anywhere but home. He requested a family member stay with him constantly while he was in the hospital, and he could not comprehend why his wife and family could not continue to care for him at home.

Hardwig argues that family conferences that are active decision-making forums should be required to plan appropriate care for all seriously ill family members.[6] He believes the self-absorption of many seriously ill individuals precludes their consideration of the effects of their illness on their family. By emphasizing the principle of patient autonomy and allowing the patient to make the decision unhampered by a discussion of family needs and concerns, "the lives of the family members may be dramatically affected by treatment decisions" in which they have no voice. Hardwig argues that the family should be actively involved in promoting and protecting its needs during a family conference to plan patient care.

Family conferences may be focused on a variety of issues. One of the most significant is the exhaustion of family resources and the consideration of long-term care placement or cessation of treatment. Sometimes respite care will provide temporary relief so that a family may continue giving care. However, years of care giving may be exhausting, especially if the ill member has increasing needs, such as a person with ALS or Alzheimer's disease, and less assistance with health care delivery is being provided to the family.

Families may also be concerned with issues of safety. The family of a patient with ALS might worry that no one would hear a ventilator alarm, and the patient might die because she or he became detached from the ventilator. The family of an Alzheimer's disease patient might fear the patient wandering off and getting lost or turning on a kitchen burner and starting a fire. While the patient is competent and aware of the risk she or he is assuming, such as the ALS patient preferring to be home even if someone might miss the alarm, patient autonomy would warrant allowing the person to assume the risk. However, when the risk could involve another's safety, such as the Alzheimer's patient starting a fire, then there may need to be limits placed on the patient's choices and autonomy.

Some ethicists and health care providers argue that if family members are to be involved in providing the care, they should have some voice in determining what care they can realistically deliver. However, a family conference with several members proclaiming family needs can be overwhelming for a sick and vulnerable patient. Many families

> Supporters of the current return to limited paternalism suggest that patients' families should have some role in medical decision-making.

are not fully functional, and allowing all members to vocalize their concerns may be counterproductive. Thus, the family members, invited to a care-planning conference, need to be carefully prepared. The patient should acknowledge that these people are involved in planning and providing her or his care. The health care provider facilitating the conference must be skilled in family mediation and group process and be familiar with a community's health care resources.

Are there times when the interests and needs of the family are more important than those of the patient? At such times, would paternalism be an appropriate principle? It would certainly be preferable that the patient would listen to the concerns of her or his family and consider their needs along with her or his own when deciding what the plan of care should be. Careful deliberation, accompanied by a realistic review of the situation, will often assist even the most depressed and vulnerable person to consider her or his family's needs. However, when family caregivers are exhausted, when the safety of others is imperiled, or when the patient's decisional capacity is in doubt, the needs of the family might need to be given precedence over patient autonomy.

Returning to the case of the first patient with ALS will reveal how family considerations may influence a patient's decision. Mr. Stevens remained in the ICU for several days after beginning antidepressant therapy. Although he was stable enough for transfer, he had finally developed trust in the staff. During this time, the subject of his future was only broached when he initiated the "conversation." When he was willing to communicate with the psychiatrist, he was determined to be competent. He informed the staff that although he really felt ready to die, he could not "abandon" his son, who obviously needed him. During his life, he had valued his family above everything else. He chose to be transferred to a long-term care facility on a ventilator until his son's divorce proceedings were complete and his son no longer needed him so desperately.

Truthfulness: Should the Nurse Always Convey the Full Truth to Patients?

The divorced mother of a 13-year-old boy without a pediatrician brought her son to the nearest emergency department (ED) because of severe headaches. After a CT scan, the ED physician realized the boy, Jeff, needed specialized services that the community hospital was unable to provide and referred him to a tertiary children's hospital 100 miles away. His father and grandmother transported him there so a biopsy could be performed and a ventriculovenous shunt inserted. The mother, the custodial parent, did not have a car and remained home but in phone contact with the physicians at the children's hospital. She requested that Jeff and her former husband be given limited information about the boy's prognosis. After surgery, the neurosurgeon informed Jeff, his father (the noncustodial parent), and father's mother that there was no reason for further surgery. Jeff would have the shunt for the remainder of his life, and he would begin radiation treatment in a few weeks.

For the next 7 months, Jeff's father and grandmother continued to provide the transportation to the children's hospital radiation service. The boy and his relatives asked few questions about the treatment until 6 months after initiation of radiation, when Jeff began to loose strength and sensation in his right hand. Shortly after that, his right leg became weaker and he could no longer walk the half-mile to school without falling. At each of the last few visits, Jeff asked the nurse at the radiation clinic, "Why aren't I getting any better? Why couldn't they just remove the tumor? What is going to happen to me?" The nurse at the clinic had developed a close relationship with Jeff, his father, and grandmother, who she had seen on a regular basis. The physicians continued to have phone contact with the mother, who insisted that her former husband and her son be given minimal information about the boy's treatment and prognosis. What should the nurse do?

Most ethicists and health care providers will argue that "the covenant of trust between physician and patient is central to the practice of medicine" and "the candid disclosure of information fosters and helps to maintain that trust."[7] Telling the truth, especially when it means providing bad news to a patient, has only become the professional standard within the past 30 years. In a study conducted in 1961, 90% of American physicians would not disclose a diagnosis of cancer to their adult patients.[8] When a similar study was conducted in 1979, a complete reversal had occurred and 97% of American physicians stated they would inform their patients of their disease.[7] During that time period, ethicists began to emphasize the importance of truth telling and full disclosure so that patients could make autonomous decisions about their care.

The reliance on truth telling and full disclosure appears to have a cultural bias. American physicians are somewhat more likely than European physicians to say they will reveal the entire truth. Patients from some cultural backgrounds have indicated preferences not to be fully informed. Studies indicate Hispanic women and Korean families are less likely to want to know the full truth. However, these cultural norms are changing. In Japan, traditionally known for physicians withholding bad news, physicians are now calling for full disclosure, and 97% of patients ask to be given complete and truthful information about their condition.[9]

Some families still request that information about serious illnesses be withheld from patients. The family may fear how the patient will respond to the bad news and may wish to protect the patient from pain. However, there are numerous reasons in favor of telling the patient the truth. If the patient does not understand his or her prognosis, she or he may fail to continue appropriate treatment for the disease, or may make life choices that she or he would not have made if she or he had been fully informed. Moreover, most adult patients insist that they, not their family members, should receive the bad news and that they should be able to determine who else is told. Adult patients have a clear legal right to full information about their diagnosis and prognosis. Finally, since it is usually not possible to keep the patient from suspecting the bad news, withholding information damages the communication and relationship between patient, family, and health care providers. Jameton suggests the nurse ask the following questions, when requested by either the family or another health care provider to withhold bad news:[10]

- Is the staff (family) successfully hiding things?
- Is the information really harmful?
- Does the harm of disclosure outweigh the good?
- For whom is this bad news?

Additionally, the nurse will need to ask the following: Do I have the authority to hide or divulge this information? What are the likely consequences if the bad news is divulged? The decision to withhold bad news from adults should never be made lightly and should be a joint decision of health care team members and family.

In contrast to adults, parents and health care providers often make health care decisions for children without the child's consent since the ethical principles utilized to guide decision-making for adults are not as applicable with children. For example, children are not considered to be legally competent and may be incapable of giving fully reasoned consent that is not coerced. Young children in particular often have limited understandings of illness and death and may engage in magical thinking.

However, "over the past 30 years... new ways of thinking about children in medical decision-making have evolved."[11] Bandman and Bandman stress that there should be "an open, shared decision-making process, in which children's growing autonomy is supported by each child's cognitive maturity, personality, and thought process."[12] Preschool children are usually assumed to lack decision-making capacity and their parents are usually required to make decisions for them based on the best interests standard. As children enter elementary school, many ethicists recommend that the child be provided with information about her or his condition to the extent that she or he is able to comprehend it. Although the child may express a preference, parents and health care providers continue to be the primary decision-makers. Once a child enters adolescence, she or he may have the decision-making capacity of an adult. Harrison and Kenny recommend that the decision-making capacity of the adolescent be examined in the light of the following:[11]

- Ability to understand and communicate relevant information
- Ability to think and choose with some independence
- Ability to assess the potential for benefit, risk, or harm, as well as to consider consequences and multiple options
- Achievement of a fairly stable set of values

Ethicists recommend that decision-making for the child should acknowledge the parents' concerns and wishes while recognizing that the primary duty of the health care provider is to the child. Although most parents attempt to make decisions in their sick child's best interests, the parents are often juggling many competing concerns. The parents may be worried about providing for the needs of their other children. They may be emotionally, financially, or physically exhausted by giving care and unable to think clearly. Or, the parents may be separated or divorced, and unable to agree on treatment for the child.

Thus, the health care provider should affirm the parents' responsibility for care of the child, while allowing the child to exercise choice appropriate to her or his level of development and experience with illness and treatment.[13] Allowing the child's participation in the decision-making encourages the development of the child's autonomous decision-making and develops the child's sense of responsibility for self-management of the disease process. This is especially important for the child with a chronic illness.

Obviously, if the child is to be included in the decision-making process, then the child needs to have an understanding of the truth about her or his illness. Jeff, because he had been told only a portion of the truth, did not have an accurate understanding of his illness. Jeff's neurosurgeon had told him that there was no reason to operate and he would have a shunt and radiation therapy. These carefully phrased truthful statements deceived Jeff about the reality of his illness. Jeff, his father, and grandmother assumed when there was no reason for further surgery that it was good news; it was not. There was no reason for further surgery because the tumor had infiltrated the motor cortex of his brain, was too invasive, and could not be resected. Now, despite the radiation, the loss of strength in his hand and leg meant that the tumor was increasing in size. Jeff and his relatives were slowly beginning to realize they had been deceived and were beginning to distrust his health care providers.

What should the nurse in the radiation clinic do? Jeff was asking pertinent questions, and at 13 years, he was capable of making reasoned decisions. He was experiencing the side effects of the radiation and high dosage of steroids, and he wanted to know what benefit they were offering him. Still, his mother, the custodial parent who rarely visited the clinic, did not want him to know the whole truth. The neurosurgeon supported the right of the mother to decide in her child's best interests and was unwilling to tell Jeff or his father any more about his prognosis and treatment without her consent. But the physician was not listening to Jeff's persistent questions. The surgeon did not realize how unsuccessful the carefully chosen phrases had become at hiding Jeff's true prognosis, nor did he realize the depth of Jeff's fears.

- Should the nurse make a decision and tell Jeff the truth on her own?
- Does she have the authority to make such a decision?
- Should she attempt to arrange a conference between herself, the physician, and Jeff's divorced parents to discuss the situation?
- Or, should the nurse merely answer Jeff in the same half-truths that the neurosurgeon had used, keeping him guessing and wondering about his true condition?

Informed Consent: How Can a Nurse Determine if a Patient Has Been Adequately Informed?

Mr. Grimes, a 32-year-old man, was admitted to a tertiary medical center for evaluation of frequent infections and severe bruising. Early on the evening of his admission, a medical student, two interns, a resident, a nurse, and an attending physician entered his room during rounds. One of the interns presented Mr. Grimes' case to the group and concluded by stating the patient had acute lymphocytic leukemia. The intern then turned to the patient and told him that he had leukemia. The intern stated the names of the chemotherapy agents anticipated, listed possible side effects, and asked the patient to sign a general consent for treatment. When asked if he had any questions, Mr. Grimes just stared at the entourage. After the patient signed the form, most of the group left to continue rounds on another unit. Was this an example of informed consent?

Consent is another issue that has both legal and ethical implications. When a patient gives consent, she or he agrees to the treatment or procedure. Legally, treating or touching without consent is battery, even if the treatment is appropriate and has no negative effects. Consent is usually implied rather than written for "routine" procedures, like dressing changes or most medication administration. It is also implied when a person goes to an emergency department acutely ill and unresponsive. However, for most complex procedures, written informed consent should be obtained.

Jameton tried to determine a pattern to how health care providers decided if informed consent was required prior to the performance of a procedure.[10] He could not identify one. In one setting, it appeared that procedures done by physicians, residents, and medical students required consent, while procedures done by nurses did not.

> Consent is often implied rather than written for routine procedures, such as taking a blood pressure or giving a bath. However, written informed consent should be obtained before complex procedures that might have serious side effects or consequences for the patient.

In another setting, giving things to patients (blood, routine medications) did not require consent, while taking things from patients (biopsies, thoracentesis, DNR) did. Riskiness and risk-benefit ratio did not appear to have a place in determining which interventions required informed consent in his analysis.

Comeau notes that from a legal perspective, informed consent "is usually necessary for treatments that are invasive or have potentially serious side effects, risks, or complications."[14] She states that health care facilities usually have policies identifying which procedures require informed consent in that setting. Common procedures that require specific informed consent include surgery, procedures requiring anesthesia, procedures (such as chemotherapy) that may involve more than a slight risk of harm, radiological therapy, and experimental therapies or medications.

Informed consent has three components. The decision to permit the treatment or procedure must be made voluntarily by a competent adult who understands her or his condition and the possible treatments. Patients must be able to make rational decisions concerning medical care and demonstrate competency as discussed earlier in this chapter in order to give informed consent.

> Components of informed consent:
> - Competent patient
> - Adequate information to make a decision
> - Voluntary participation

The patient's decision must be an autonomous choice, not coerced by health care providers or family members. An exception is made for children whose parents should consent for procedures for them.

Adolescents are legally and ethically a special case, since they exist in an interlude between childhood and adulthood. Since many adolescents are capable of rational, autonomous decisions, various ethicists and legal scholars suggest that adolescents older than age 14 should be treated differently than common law prescribes. Common law considers adolescents incompetent to make decisions until they reach the age of 18, unless they have been emancipated. States vary considerably in their definitions of emancipation, and thus the conditions for which adolescents may legally be treated without their parents' consent vary from state to state.

Additionally, adolescents often view the hazards and benefits of treatment differently than adults. Health care providers and parents may need to decide whether to impose their decision on the adolescent, a risky course of action, or negotiate with the adolescent to plan a course of treatment to which the adolescent will consent. For example, a 17-year-old adolescent was discovered to have Hodgkin's disease during the spring of her senior year in high school. Both her parents and her health care providers wanted her to begin chemotherapy immediately. She was insistent that the treatment could wait for several weeks until after her senior prom. When they tried to force her to begin chemotherapy, she ran away from home.

For this adolescent and her parents, as with any patient, in order to obtain informed consent and comply with existing laws, the following information has to be provided:

- The nature and purpose of the proposed treatment or procedure
- The expected outcome and likelihood of success
- The material risks involved
- The alternatives to treatment
- The effect of no treatment or procedure, including the prognosis and the material risks if no treatment is selected

When determining how detailed the information provided to the patient ought to be, most states utilize either the reasonable practitioner or reasonable patient standard. Under these standards, the practitioner does not need to provide the patient with a laundry list of every possible treatment and complication. Rather the practitioner should use her or his judgment to convey to the patient the information any other "reasonable practitioner" would under the same circumstances, or whatever information a "reasonable patient" would be expected to desire to know.

The completion of an informed consent form may offer the health care provider and institution some legal protection, but there are additional reasons for requiring informed consent for treatment. Requiring informed consent may emphasize the power of choice and the autonomy of the patient. The focus on informed consent for treatment arose as medicine switched from an emphasis on paternalism (making choices for patients) to autonomy (assisting the patient to make choices for herself or himself). Informed consent requires truth telling by the practitioner and the family. This prevents the deception and confusion about goals of care previously associated with the paternalistic use of deceit at the end of life. Truth telling also demonstrates respect for the patient as a person and her or his ability to make autonomous decisions. In a more practical vein, patients who are given enough information to make informed decisions, sign consent forms,

> The reasonable practitioner standard means a practitioner must provide the information another practitioner would in a similar circumstance. The standard also means a practitioner must provide the information a reasonable patient would be expected to consider significant and desire to know under the circumstances.

and participate in the development of their treatment plans may become more committed to complying with their treatment plans.

Opponents of informed consent usually question the value of patient autonomy in medical settings. They do not deny the importance of autonomy in general, but according to Jameton, feel that autonomy is impossible in the medical setting.[10] In a hold-over from paternalism, opponents of informed consent may take the position that medical decisions should be made only by those with accurate, complete medical knowledge, usually physicians. They may believe that acutely ill patients are much too emotionally distraught and vulnerable to engage in the rational decision-making necessary for informed consent. A paternalistic approach is also favored by physicians, who avoid describing the possible side effects of treatments and medications to their patients because they fear their patients will be more likely to develop the complications.

Some practitioners may believe that obtaining consent has degenerated into a formal procedure, a chore rather than a process, from which the patient can recall little useful information. For example, consider the situation with Mr. Grimes. The intern was conveying the necessary information and completing the informed consent form without considering if the situation was conducive to Mr. Grimes hearing or understanding the information required for consent.

Other opponents of informed consent in medical settings state that consent is merely an illusion. They believe the practitioner may sway the patient to the practitioner's perspective by the information chosen for presentation or the tone of the presentation. This represents a subtle form of coercion to obtain the patient's consent for treatment. However, it masks a serious issue surrounding informed consent. How much of his opinion should the practitioner reveal to the patient about appropriate treatment? Should the practitioner rely on a catalog of treatment possibilities and side effects?

Most ethicists would argue a physician initially ought to describe the benefits and risks of each treatment to the patient, clearly distinguishing between conservative, progressive, and experimental approaches. The practitioner has a moral obligation to present therapies that are effective. This obligation includes offering therapies that are not provided by the practitioner, or are not available in the patient's geographic area. Despite gag rules, the physician also has an obligation to describe treatments that might benefit the patient but that are not paid for by the patient's insurance. If the physician will be providing the intervention, she or he should identify to the patient her or his experience with the procedure. After this information, the patient should be allowed to ask questions. If the patient asks what the physician would recommend, the physician should state a professional recommendation and the rationale. Still, the decision about exactly what information to present, and more importantly how the information is presented and shaded, remains a personal and subjective one by the individual health care provider. Thoughtful practitioners consider how their presentations of information may influence their patients.

In general, it is the responsibility of the person who is going to perform the procedure or prescribe the treatment to obtain informed consent. In most institutions, this means the physician, nurse practitioner, or physician's assistant. However, an independent nurse provider or therapist in the home is also required to obtain informed consent before beginning any procedure. Legally, a nurse may witness the patient's signature of the consent form, translate what the physician has said, or actually bring the form to the patient. However, the nurse is not supposed to provide the initial education for consent to the patient unless the consent is for a procedure that the nurse will be delivering independently.

In the larger perspective, whose responsibility is informed consent? It is undoubtedly the problem of all those involved in the consent process: the patient, the physician, the nurse, other health care providers, and the family. The patient must recognize that it is her or his duty to understand and take responsibility for the decision. This means that the patient must actively pursue information about the treatment plan and then participate and cooperate wholeheartedly in the plan.

The physician must recognize that the decision belongs to the patient. This does not mean the physician can relinquish the decision to the patient. Rather the physician must be willing to allot sufficient time to the patient for explanations, questions, and explorations of alternatives. The physician must also realize that when the patient questions various options, she or he is not necessarily questioning the competency of the physician. The physician may wish to allocate some of the translation of medical terms and supplemental education to another health care provider, possibly the nurse.

The nurse should assure that the patient has received sufficient information to understand the proposed treatment, comprehend that information, and consent to treatment.

The nurse might ask the patient the following questions:

- What did the physician tell you about the treatment?
- Do you have any questions about your prognosis or the recovery you can expect to make if you have the treatment?
- What problems do you anticipate during the treatment?
- Do you understand the alternatives to the treatment and know their consequences?

Let's return to the situation with the leukemia patient. Since it is the physician who has the legal responsibility to obtain informed consent, it was the intern who had obtained the consent. Yet, it is usually the nurse who prepares the patient for the procedure or administers the treatment. It would be the night nurse the next night who would be administering the initial dose of chemotherapy while Mr. Grimes was sleeping. Thus, the nurse would be unable to discuss the therapy with Mr. Grimes.

When a nurse is preparing a patient for a treatment or procedure, she or he should have no reason to doubt the validity of the consent. Therefore, following evening rounds with the physicians, the evening nurse remained in the room with Mr. Grimes. The patient turned to her with tears in his eyes and said,

> Before preparing a patient for a treatment or a procedure, the nurse should ascertain that the patient has sufficient information to understand the proposed treatment, comprehends the information, and consents willingly to the treatment.

"All I heard was leukemia—that's cancer. Am I going to die?" The nurse spent a considerable amount of time that evening with Mr. Grimes explaining in simpler terms precisely what the intern had told him and allowing him to ask questions about the proposed treatment, its effects, and its side effects.

The evening nurse assured that Mr. Grimes' consent was an informed one. Nurses have encountered legal difficulties when they have "interfered with the physician-patient relationship" by providing information on nontraditional therapies not mentioned to the patient by the physician. However, defining terms for patients, clarifying physicians' statements, and offering clear explanations of procedures' risks and benefits are essential components of the nurse's role in informed consent.

If the nurse is not able to provide the additional information necessary to assure an informed consent, then the nurse should recommend delaying the procedure until the patient can be adequately informed. On occasion, the nurse may discover that the patient has signed a written consent form for a procedure that she or he did not mean to authorize. In this situation, the person who obtained the consent should be contacted and the procedure, if necessary, delayed while consent is renegotiated.

For example, a student nurse was preparing Mrs. Smith for an amputation of part of her right leg. The patient had signed a consent form for a possible below-the-knee amputation, and preoperative preparation called for a povidone-iodine scrub from toes to mid-calf. When the student began to scrub the patient's leg at mid-calf, the patient immediately stopped the student, insisting that she had never consented to so high an amputation. Mrs. Smith insisted she had agreed to an amputation of several toes on her right foot with the possibility of a portion of her right foot but never to a below-the-knee amputation. Just then, the operating room (OR) called, requesting the patient be premedicated for surgery. After consulting with the charge nurse and her instructor, the student held the premedication while the charge nurse phoned the surgeon and the OR.

An angry surgeon arrived on the unit soon afterward. The student, her instructor, and the charge nurse accompanied him to the patient's room. Despite repeated attempts by the surgeon to influence her decision, the patient refused to change her mind. The hospital's risk manager was eventually contacted. She concurred it was the patient's legal right to refuse the more extensive surgery and added that the patient could rescind her written consent by an oral refusal of the surgery. A new consent form for surgery was signed, authorizing partial amputation of her right foot, and the patient was prepared for surgery. The student nurse had protected her patient's autonomy by notifying the physician and delaying the preoperative medication, so the patient could remain alert and competent while renegotiating her consent with the physician.

Consent for Experimental Treatment: What Should the Patient Know?

A nurse in an oncology clinic was preparing to administer a new chemotherapeutic agent to Mr. Eta, a patient with cancer of the brain. The patient was from a Middle Eastern country, spoke some English, and had a marked short-term memory deficit. The drug was in the earliest stages of clinical trials in humans, so very little was known about its effects or effectiveness. Since the drug was new and the situation potentially problematic, the nurse had carefully reviewed the informed consent form in the patient's chart to be certain that it was complete before bringing the medication to him.

When the nurse reached Mr. Eta, he asked the name of the drug, which the nurse told him. He next asked why he was receiving the medication and what its side effects might be. The nurse started to explain that it was for his brain cancer, when the patient announced angrily that he did not have cancer. Mr. Eta's brother began to calm him in Arabic and motioned to the nurse to administer the drug and leave the room. Should the nurse administer the drug?

Since the development of the Nuremberg Code in 1947, following the experimentation by Nazi German physicians on Jewish prisoners of war, there has been a growing realization that human subjects in medical research studies require protection. Requiring each research subject to give an informed consent to participate in each study is one attempt to protect subjects. Since the unethical studies at Tuskegee and Willowbrook were revealed, concerns have begun to accumulate that even in the United States we do not provide adequate information or obtain informed consent before delivering experimental treatments.

In 1998, families and ethicists expressed concern that some psychiatric patients were shuttled into studies where their medications were withdrawn and psychosis induced. This was done without the patients' or their families' knowledge of the probable consequences.[15] What heightened the anger of activists about these psychiatric drug studies was that some of the physicians involved in the studies appeared to be obtaining financial benefits from drug companies by enrolling large numbers of patients. Who was supposed to be protecting the interests of these patients?

In 1966, the National Institutes of Health began to require that peers of the researcher, sitting on an Institution Review Board, approve all proposed research using human subjects. The purpose of these boards is to assure that each subject's participation in every study is voluntary and free of coercion, demonstrated by informed

> Patients participating in medical research studies should be protected from unnecessary or harmful research by their voluntary informed consent and the review of the risks and benefits of the proposed research study by an Institution Review Board before human subjects may participate.

consent, and that there is an acceptable balance of risk versus harm for each of the subjects. The review of research proposals by the Institution Review Board is designed to protect the interests of the research subjects.

According to Kravitz, there are several principles that are necessary to assure that consent has been acceptably obtained from subjects in medical research:[16]

- The person must have volunteered and must have all the information needed to make an informed decision.
- The subject must realize that she or he can withdraw from the study at any time.
- All unnecessary risks must have been eliminated from the study.
- The research should only be conducted by fully qualified individuals.
- Subjects should be aware of any financial settlement they will receive if they are injured.
- The benefits either to the individual or to society must outweigh the possible risks to the subjects in the study.

This last point has been the source of considerable controversy: the benefits of the research either to the individual or to society outweigh the possible risks to the subjects in the study. Arguing that the benefits to society may outweigh the risks to an individual is stating that a person may be treated as a means to an end. This is in direct opposition to some schools of philosophy, such as deontology, which state that each person be respected and treated as an end in her or himself. More importantly, in the Tuskegee experiment, which is now recognized as unethical, the prisoners' syphilis was ignored so that the long-term effects of the disease could be observed. One of the arguments for allowing the men's syphilis to go untreated was to benefit future patients. Researchers in some of the recent psychiatric drug studies argued that withdrawing medications, causing an exacerbation of psychosis, and then treating the psychosis with the experimental antipsychotic drug was necessary to establish the effectiveness of the new drug and benefit future patients.

In Tuskegee, the men were neither informed they had syphilis, nor that as part of a research study their syphilis was not being treated. In the psychiatric drug studies, the patients did give consent to participate in a study of psychotropic medications. However, patients and families charged that violations of informed consent occurred. One patient was given a notebook of consent forms to be signed all at once without any explanation. Participants in other studies signed consent forms saying that their "condition might improve, worsen, or remain unchanged," while researchers were aware that psychosis would reoccur in many of the patients. One patient was alleged to have committed suicide due to the psychosis that reoccurred during the withdrawal of his previously prescribed psychotropic drug.[14] Another patient entered a drug study because she had no other way to pay for her psychotropic medications, and the experimental drugs were free. Critics have charged that consent for these studies did not serve as the primary protection for the patients because consent was possibly coerced and not fully informed.

The Citizens for Responsible Care in Psychiatry and Research have circulated questions that a potential subject should consider before consenting to psychiatric research.[17] However, most of the questions are pertinent to other types of medical research as well. The questions include:

- Is there an independent doctor, not connected to the research team, assigned to monitor your well-being and to assure that patient safeguards are followed?
- Is there a nonmedical patient advocate assigned to you? What authority does the person have?
- Is a medication washout or withdrawal period required? For how long?
- Will the research involve any painful or uncomfortable procedures?
- Who is available during off-hours for you to contact if you wish to withdraw from the protocol?

- What follow-up care is available to patients who complete the research or who withdraw from the research?

When a nurse is preparing to administer experimental treatments to a patient, she or he should be convinced that the patient has considered the ramifications of the treatment and believes that the benefits outweigh the risks. The nurse might want to pose questions similar to those that should be considered before any informed consent. These questions include:

- Can the patient explain the experimental treatment?
- Does the patient understand the problems she or he might encounter during the treatment?
- Does the patient believe that the benefits of this treatment outweigh the risks?
- Was the patient coerced, or was she or he able to make up her or his own mind about the treatment?

When the nurse who had been preparing to administer the experimental medication to Mr. Eta detected his anger, she quietly excused herself from the room. From his questions about the medications and his adamant denial that he had cancer, the nurse was concerned that his consent might not have been informed. Therefore, the nurse contacted the physician who had obtained the informed consent and the nurse who had administered the initial dose of medication. She also re-examined the consent form, as she had previously observed, clearly spelled out that little was known about the experimental medication.

After speaking with both the physician and the other nurse, the clinic nurse learned that because of Mr. Eta's limited English and his short-term memory deficit, he reacted as if the information about his illness was new each time he heard it. The physician had discussed the medication with him in detail several times and the other nurse once, with his brother as translator. Each time, after reacting with initial anger and surprise, he consulted with his brother in Arabic and eventually deferred to his older brother's decision that the medication was his best option. Each time, he stated in his limited English, "My brother has my father's approval to decide for me; I will listen to him." Mr. Eta's brain tumor was inoperable, and standard treatment was not providing him any relief. Early human studies demonstrated very little toxicity for this medication and a chance for improvement. The physician and nurse suggested that if the clinic nurse said she was bringing him medication for his headache rather than for cancer, he would accept it without difficulty. When the nurse returned to the room, Mr. Eta again asked her the name of the medication and what it was for. When she answered it was for his headache, he was willing to take the medication. Should she administer it?

Noncompliance: How Should the Nurse Respond to the Noncompliant or Nonadherent Patient?

A parish nurse saw several people for monitoring of hypertension and medication counseling one morning. Only one of the people, Mr. Denver, had his blood pressure (BP) below 140/85 and had taken his medications as prescribed. The only reason he had been compliant was he knew the nurse would be checking his BP. He could neither state the name of his antihypertensive medication nor its side effects.

The other people all had different reasons for not managing their BP as directed. A 50-year-old perimenopausal woman, whose BP was 140/90, had agreed to phone her physician if her BP remained that high for three measurements. Now after 4 months of continued high readings, she did not want to phone for fear she would be started on antihypertensive medication. Mr. Thames, an 87-year-old, only took his diuretic when he was planning to stay at home in the morning. Since he rarely stayed home, he rarely took his diuretic. A 34-year-old had just started on an ACE inhibitor and could not remember to take the medication on a consistent basis. An 80-year-old with a dangerously high BP had run out of samples of a new diuretic that her physician wanted her to try. She had no one to take her to the pharmacy, so the prescription had gone unfilled. The last patient had taken her medications as prescribed, but had fallen earlier in the week, was anxious, and her BP was 180/70.

Compliance in health care has been defined as "the extent to which the patient's behavior (in terms of taking medications, following diets, or executing daily lifestyle changes) coincides with medical or health care advice."[18] It has also been more truthfully described as the patient doing what the health care provider wants her or him to do. Noncompliance usually implies that the person appears not to be following the directions of the health care provider, either some or all of the time. Since some providers believe that the term noncompliant has developed a negative connotation, they prefer the term non-adherent.

Compliance or adherence to a medical regimen is a complex process. It usually requires that the patient has met all of the elements of informed consent. The patient should understand the disease process, agree that treatment is necessary, and have made a commitment to carrying out the treatment plan.

Managing hypertension highlights some of the problems with compliance. Although the hypertensive person may have an intellectual understanding of the disease process, she or he usually does not feel ill. The hypertensive person must accept the word of the health care provider that she or he has hypertension and thus is at an increased risk for stroke or heart

> Noncompliance or nonadherence implies that the patient is failing to follow some or all of the health care providers' recommendations for health care.

attack. This places the person in a very dependent role, submissive to the medical authority, who measures the blood pressure and determines how the person is progressing, regardless of how the patient feels. This can establish the patient role as one of passive submission to medical treatment at least in the view of the health care provider.

In truth, according to Playle and Keeley, most patients evaluate treatments "in the light of beliefs about treatments, the nature of health, measures that improve health, and the effects of the treatments on their life-style."[19] They often modify a treatment regimen to adapt to their lifestyle. For example, Mr. Thames would not take his diuretic on the mornings he was planning to leave the house.

The person may give an informed consent to the plan of treatment but subsequently find that the planned course of action results in physical discomfort, is inconvenient and expensive, or interferes with her or his lifestyle. Without a commitment to the health care plan, it often is forgotten and falls by the wayside. The nurse's role when a person has made a rational decision to follow a plan but is unable to follow it for practical reasons is relatively simple and without ethical overtones. It is the nurse's responsibility to assist the person to develop a plan that she or he can live with. It means the nurse needs to listen to the person and hear what the person is saying about problems with the treatment plan. Then it means adjustment of the plan, memory aids, changes in scheduling of medications, assistance with procuring medications, and discussion of ways to limit side effects. Crucial to the discussion is the realization that the person is usually evaluating her or his care and is searching for a way to integrate the treatment regimen in a lifestyle definition.

What should the nurse do to persuade the patient to comply with therapy? Consider the situation of Mr. Denver: he only took his antihypertensive medication because he liked the nurse and wanted to please her with a BP reading within normal limits. He had no understanding of his medication regimen. Was it paternalistic for the nurse to encourage this behavior by praising him and telling him how well he was doing? Can the consequences justify the paternalistic action? The results had been impressive. Mr. Denver was taking his medication almost every day, and his BP had dropped from 182/92 to 140/82.

It is still more problematic when the patient makes a rational decision not to follow the treatment plan. Suppose that Mr. Thames announced he had stopped taking his diuretic, as well as his other antihypertensive medications. He had decided the medications were causing him unpleasant side effects, dizziness and frequent urination, and were far too expensive. His BP had risen to 198/92, but he said he felt great, except for a little arthritis. There are several questions a nurse might want to consider when working with a noncompliant patient.

- How far should the nurse go to convince the patient to follow a course of action the nurse believes is right for the patient?
- Should the nurse threaten the patient with complications, scold, try to persuade, or encourage with praise?
- Should a nurse ever slip from support for patient autonomy to paternalism?
- Should the potential consequences of the patient failing to take his medication have a role in the nurse's decision?

Clearly, the nurse needs to determine that Mr. Thames made an informed decision when he chose to terminate his medications. The nurse would need to be certain that he could identify the likely consequences of stopping the medications. The consequences to Mr. Thames could be devastating if he had a stroke. However, there could also be possible consequences to others. Should the nurse consider who else might be affected? If Mr. Thames had a stroke, he would probably be unable to continue to provide care to his disabled wife, so she would most likely be affected.

Society as a whole might be affected by Mr. Thames' decision to discontinue his medication. The expense of any hospitalization and possible long-term care placement following a stroke would be borne by the taxpayers. Therefore, should the state have a right to require that he continue his antihypertensive medications? Most states have laws requiring some measure of injury prevention. For example, many states require motorcyclists wear helmets. The re-establishment of many of the helmet laws was based on the excess cost to the states of the care following head injuries to people who rode without helmets. States also may require some patients to take medications before engaging in hazardous activities. For example, most states require people with epilepsy to be seizure-free for a specific amount of time before they are allowed to resume driving.

However, while states have consistently regulated who may drive and other safety factors on the road, they are not normally in the business of requiring people to take medications. The exemption is that states may require some groups of people to follow a medication regimen to protect the public health and welfare. For example, incompetent psychiatric patients who are a danger to themselves or society or people with a communicable disease such as tuberculosis may be required to follow a medication regimen. But for most people, despite the states' interests in keeping people well, it is the individual's decision whether or not to comply with therapy.

If the decision not to comply with antihypertensive therapy is one Mr. Thames ought to be able to make autonomously, how far should the nurse go to encourage him to continue or modify his treatment plan? Since stopping his medication would increase the likelihood of stroke and heart attack, the parish nurse might consider invoking the principle of beneficence. If she or he invoked the principle of beneficence, the nurse would attempt to act paternalistically, to convince or manipulate Mr. Thames to continue his medication, overruling his autonomy in an attempt to prevent potential harm to him.

There have been circumstances where nurses have attempted to act beneficently to prevent harm to large groups of patients and limited these patients' autonomy. Until 15 years ago, it was common practice to restrain frail residents in nursing homes to prevent them from falling.

> How should a nurse balance paternalism and beneficence with autonomy when attempting to gain a patient's compliance with medical therapy?

Long-term care nurses stated that their primary motive in restraining these residents was beneficence, acting to prevent frail elders from the harm they might incur if they tried to walk or get out of bed unassisted and accidentally fell.

However, the consequences of the nurses' actions were different than they had envisioned. When residents are restrained, they are unable to exercise and are more likely to become weak, incontinent, and constipated. Ironically, they are also more likely to fall and injure themselves more severely if they do fall. So, there is reason to doubt that the nurses' actions when restraining elderly residents were in fact beneficent. There is also reason to believe that in acting to prevent one potential harm, a fall, nurses were causing an actual moral harm, the deprivation of the residents' autonomy. One study demonstrated that residents who had been restrained for prolonged periods of time became so demoralized they remained as if they were still restrained after the restraints had been removed.

Thus, the nurse ought to be exceedingly careful when considering overriding any person's autonomy to prevent a potential harm to that person. Perhaps as health care providers we should realize it is our duty to point out the risks, but it is not our responsibility to decide for our competent patients which risks are worth taking.

> Nurses ought to be exceedingly cautious about overriding a patient's autonomy in an attempt to benefit the patient.

Are there circumstances when it is not possible to let the patient determine which risks are worth taking? Benjamin and Curtis suggest that health care providers may be justified in making a decision for a patient, also called acting paternalistically, if and only if the patient is:[20]

- Incompetent or incapacitated and thus unable to make a rational decision
- Likely to be significantly harmed
- Would probably approve of the decision if or when her or his capacity to make a rational decision returns

In such situations only, they would recommend the patient be required to follow the health care provider's plan of care. Mr. Thames' situation does not appear to meet these conditions.

Limited Paternalism or Negotiated Consent

Mrs. O'Neil, an 83-year-old, lived in her home with her 51-year-old gambling, alcoholic, occasionally employed son. A home health aide, who had been assisting Mrs. O'Neil with her hygiene, became concerned that the home was becoming unsafe for her client. Mrs. O'Neil had burned herself on the stove several times in the past week. Her medication bottles had remained empty and unfilled on the kitchen table for the previous 2 weeks. In addition, Mrs. O'Neil was becoming depressed. She would only rarely get out of her lounge chair to clean up or to eat, and she was losing weight.

When the nurse and social worker evaluated the home, they learned that Mrs. O'Neil's son had taken money from her pocketbook, and she was unable to buy food or obtain prescription renewals. Her blood pressure was 220/110, and she became short of breath after walking only a few feet. Also, one of the burns on her arms had become infected. Although the son was verbally abusive to his mother while the nurse and social worker were in the home, Mrs. O'Neil denied that he had ever physically abused her.

Mrs. O'Neil refused to move away from her home. She stated that she wanted to remain there because the cost was affordable, and her memories were there. Her daughter had asked her to live with her, but the daughter had two teenagers and a troubled marriage. Mrs. O'Neil did not want to move in with her daughter. She also stated she needed to stay in her house, so her son could live there for free until she died and he inherited it. After all, she said, "I made him what he is today, I need to take care of him."

This circumstance is different from that of Mr. Thames because Mrs. O'Neil's predicament is currently unsafe and immediately harmful to her rather than only potentially damaging. Still, Mrs. O'Neil is able to express a rational, informed reason for wanting to stay in the dangerous situation. When the situation becomes immediately harmful to the person, should the principle of beneficence take precedence over autonomy? After all, the duty to remove harm is the primary obligation of beneficence. Is the duty to remove her from harm sufficient reason to override Mrs. O'Neil's autonomy and protect her against her desire?

Home health care providers consistently say that determining when a person's safety should take precedence over her or his autonomy is one of the most difficult dilemmas they encounter. In certain circumstances, legal concerns take precedence. For example, suspicion of abuse mandates reporting the situation to the appropriate authority for action. Yet, there are other circumstances when the situation is dangerous but neither neglectful nor abusive, and the decision of whether to protect the competent patient against her or his will seems to rest with the health care provider.

How might the provider make such a decision? Caplan suggests that if any group of people have established a set of authentic values, which ought to be respected when articulated, it is the elderly.[21] He believes that someone who has experienced a full life and acquired the wisdom that only experience can bring should be able to use that wisdom to determine the course of her or his life during its final years. In short, Caplan believes that autonomy should trump beneficence and safety when those values conflict in an elderly client.

Collopy cautions against too narrow a definition of safety or autonomy.[22] He suggests that the elder, who rejects protection and services to keep safe, may be searching for a different type of safety. She or he may be trying to protect herself or himself from dislocation, to establish areas of control, or to maintain a connection with the past by fulfilling a role she or he believes is important. This does not match well with health care providers, who may focus on the potential harms of "injury, poor nutrition, missed medications, and poor personal care."[22]

Thus, most health care providers have a difficult time relinquishing their concept of safety and allowing elders to choose their own course of action. A nurse involved with an elder such as Mrs. O'Neil would want to establish that the elder was indeed competent, that she or he had considered all possibilities and had a realistic view of the alternatives before making any decisions. If the elder was competent and consistent, the nurse and social worker might try to negotiate some compromise between risk limitation and autonomy that would be minimally acceptable to all those concerned.

Moody, a gerontologist, advocates obtaining such a negotiated consent when the health care provider(s) is concerned that an elder's autonomous decision might be very dangerous to her or him. "Negotiated consent is more appropriate for situations when the ideal outcome is not attainable, but making the best of a bad situation is the most that can reasonably be expected."[23] It requires active participation and negotiation by an elder or the proxy, who must be aware of her or his legal and ethical rights. The process involves an active bargaining to attain an agreement that is at least minimally acceptable to all those involved. Since the original, autonomous decision of the elder is being negotiated, Moody recommends that the agreement be widely disseminated, so there will be a critique of the compromise to protect the interests of the elder.

> Older adults and health care providers may have differing views of what is really important. While health care providers may focus on safety-related issues, the older adult may be more concerned about autonomy, role fulfillment, and continuity of values and lifestyle.

Mrs. O'Neil agreed to hospitalization for management of her hypertension and heart failure. During that time, a referral to protective services was made because of her son's verbal abuse and his theft of her medication and food money. Mrs. O'Neil refused to repeat the charge that her son had taken her money and adamantly denied any verbal or physical abuse. She insisted on returning home after her hospitalization but was willing to establish new banking habits, limit the money available in her home, and have supervision of her medication purchases. She also was willing to receive increased home health services, meals on wheels, and a home visit from protective services to evaluate her home. The nurse might consider the following questions in this and similar circumstances:

> Components of negotiated consent:
> • Active participation by a competent elder or agent
> • Bargaining and negotiation to obtain an agreement
> • Wide dissemination of compromise

- Was this a negotiated consent?
- Did the plan strike an acceptable balance between autonomy and risk limitation for the patient?
- Was the patient's autonomy respected and a safer environment arranged?

Confidentiality: Should Only the Patient and Selected Health Care Providers Have the Right to Information About That Patient?

A hospice nurse was making a home visit to Mrs. Wilson, a 62-year-old woman with breast cancer who lived alone. Since the nurse's previous visit, Mrs. Wilson's condition had deteriorated considerably, and the nurse recognized her patient probably had only a day or two left to live. The nurse helped Mrs. Wilson to plan her care, manage her symptoms, and discussed the progression of the disease.

Mrs. Wilson's daughter lived 200 miles away. The daughter had previously asked the hospice nurse to keep her informed about her mother's health and had expressed her anger with the hospice nurses for not informing her of her mother's deteriorating condition. The nurse asked Mrs. Wilson if she could contact the daughter and tell her that her mother's health was declining quickly and death was approaching. Mrs. Wilson was adamant in her refusal.

"My daughter's life is difficult enough. I haven't told her how much worse I am doing. I have no intention of having her come flying up here and making her life more complicated by imposing my dying on her. She gets so upset about everything." What should the hospice nurse do?

Keeping patient information confidential means that the nurse does not reveal personal or health-related information concerning the patient without either the patient's consent or sufficient cause. Since 1972, the American Nurses Association has included the following statement as the second plank in its Code for Nurses: "The nurse safeguards the client's right to privacy by judiciously protecting information of a confidential nature."[24] Most nurses view respecting patients' confidential information as an essential part of building a trusting nurse-patient relationship. If the patient did not believe the nurse would maintain the confidential nature of the information, why would she or he want to reveal sensitive or personal information to the nurse? Without accurate information about the patient's behaviors and practices, it can be very difficult for health care providers to plan and deliver appropriate care.

However, there are certain circumstances when the nurse is obligated to break confidentiality concerning her or his patient. A specific legal "duty to warn" was established 25 years ago in California with the Tarasoff decisions.[25] Since these decisions, mental health professionals have had a "duty to warn" the potential victim when they predict one of their

> Confidentiality of patient information is recognized as an essential first step in the establishment of a trusting nurse-patient relationship.

clients will become violent. The state appellate court in these cases determined that the duty to protect and warn a vulnerable person of potential injury was more important than protecting the client's confidentiality. Since Tarasoff, mental health professionals have worried that their patients will not trust them if they know that their violent fantasies may be disclosed to police or other individuals. But studies have demonstrated that when therapists describe at the onset of therapy that there are confidences they cannot keep, and if they tell the patient they cannot keep the confidence after it is disclosed, most clients will continue to trust and confide in their therapists. Therefore, many therapists begin their relationship with clients, as well as each therapy session, by describing the limits of confidentiality.

In general, confidentiality may be broken when there is a suspicion that the patient may have been injured by someone, or has injured or plans to injure someone else (as in Tarasoff). Legally, the nurse must report suspected cases of abuse or neglect, and in most states gunshot wounds must also be reported to the appropriate authority. Contagious diseases must be reported to the health department, and in some states, health care providers have a duty to warn the sexual partners of people with human immunodeficiency virus (HIV) of their partner's condition. Additionally, health care information is released within the health care system to the patient's insurance company for reimbursement to consultants and to numerous health care providers once the patient has signed a general release of information. Finally, information about the patient's medical status is relayed to her or his health care proxy or guardian. As previously noted, the nurse should inform the patient of those circumstances in which confidentiality cannot be maintained.

The problems associated with breaching confidentiality and requiring reporting of medical care are most apparent in the care of adolescents. In most states, parents, as guardians, must be informed of the medical care their offspring receive. This may cause difficulties when an adolescent is seeking care for problems of a sensitive nature, such as a sexually transmitted disease. When parents must be informed about and consent to adolescent health care treatment, the adolescent usually delays seeking treatment until the condition has progressed and treatment may be more complicated. Therefore, the American Medical Association states that confidential care to adolescents is critical to improving their health.[13] Yet, even if the health care provider and adolescent agree to maintain the confidentiality of the treatment, the insurer usually does not. Since the adolescent's parents are usually the insured, they often discover the treatment when an itemized bill arrives from the insurance carrier.

Concerns about leakage of information to and from insurers has been especially intense since the Health Insurance and Portability Act of 1996 required that each American be assigned at birth a unique health identifier. Information about each person would be maintained in a national data bank with links to all health care plans and providers. With every health encounter from a person's life available to all insurers and health care providers, as well as anyone else who might gain access to the data bank, the potential for misuse is immeasurable. For example, the daughter of a staff member at a Catholic long-term care facility obtained a prescription for birth control pills. The treasurer of the institution received knowledge of the prescription as part of the information supplied by the insurance company. The employee and his daughter were called to the treasurer's office to justify the use of the birth control pills. Should such information have been provided to the treasurer of the long-term care facility?

Congress has been preparing legislation to protect patient privacy. Unfortunately, some of the proposed laws actually assure the patient of less privacy than many state laws currently require. One proposed law would require institutions, health care plans, and providers to reveal their confidentiality practices to patients, but would not require patients' consent for release of their health care records. Thus, the records could be released to a wide variety of health care concerns without the patient being notified. If patients realize all their health information is being tracked and circulated to other insurers and providers, many of their complaints and concerns may go unvoiced and untreated.

The patient should be able to trust that only the people involved directly in her or his care will know the details of the illness, its management, and the prognosis. More importantly, the patient should know that no one would reveal the intimate face of her or his illness with its uncertainties and suffering. That means that only the health care providers involved in the patient's care should see the record and know the particulars of the patient's care. Health care records should never be released without the patient's consent. There should never be discussion of patients' conditions in public places, such as elevators, hallways (even surgeons with patients' families), cafeterias, and waiting rooms. When the patient is a public figure, the media should only be provided with information approved by the patient or her or his proxy. The patient needs to know that neither his friends, nor the general public, nor insurance carriers and other health care providers will have access either by accident or intention to information about her or his condition without consent.

Should confidentiality also mean that the patient's family is not provided with information about the patient's illness? When members of the patient's family are among the caregivers, it seems they need to be provided information about the patient's condition. Since in some states a family member is assumed to be the appropriate proxy decision-maker, if the patient does not have an advance directive, then family members should be kept current on the patient's condition. There are a number of questions a nurse might want to consider:

- What should family members who are not involved in delivering care or do not have proxy decision-making authority expect to be told about the patient's illness, prognosis, and care?
- What are the boundaries between keeping the family informed and protecting the patient's confidentiality?
- Are there times when the nurse ought to consider the needs of the family to know what is happening to the patient, as well as the stated desire of the patient to keep the information confidential?

Mrs. Wilson's hospice nurse picked up the phone and said to Mrs. Wilson, "I understand you don't want me to call your daughter, and I won't if you insist or try to stop me. However, I need to tell you something even if I am being too forward. You are very ill and will die soon. Your daughter has asked to be told how you are doing and I believe she wants to be with you when you die. If I were your daughter, I would resent not being notified that my mother was dying. I would want to have a chance to be with you. I would not want you to die alone. If I don't call now, I am taking away that chance for the two of you forever. There will be no other chance to do this a different way. I'll call now unless you stop me."

> Patients should be able to trust that their health care information will not be released to members of the public, other health care providers, or insurers without their consent.

Should the hospice nurse have called Mrs. Wilson's daughter? Is protecting the confidentiality of Mrs. Wilson's condition the most important moral good in this case? Or, was it reasonable for the nurse to phone the daughter and notify her that her mother would be dying soon?

Mrs. Wilson did not make any effort to stop the hospice nurse, and the nurse phoned the daughter. The daughter arrived several hours later, obviously distraught, and informed the hospice nurse she "needed a scotch." After the scotch, the daughter managed to relax a little, and she and the hospice nurse prepared her mother for death. Mrs. Wilson died before morning with her daughter present. If the hospice nurse had not called the daughter, Mrs. Wilson would probably have died alone.

Did the hospice nurse breach her patient's confidentiality? Did she act paternalistically? Was her action ethically justifiable?

REFERENCES

1. Chell B. Competency: what it is, what it isn't, and why it matters. In: Monagle JF, Thomasma DC. eds. *Health Care Ethics: Critical Issues for the 21st Century*. Gaithersburg, Md: Aspen Publications; 1998:116-127.

2. United States Department of Health and Human Services. Omnibus Budget Reconciliation Act of 1990, Sections 4206, 4751, Public Law 101-508 (Patient Self Determination Act).

3. Emanuel L, Emanuel E. The medical directive: a new comprehensive care document. *JAMA*. 1989;261:3288-3293.

4. Pellagrino ED. Ethics. *JAMA*. 1992;268:354-355.

5. American Nurses Association. *Compendium of ANA Position Statements*. Washington DC: American Nurses Association; 1996.

6. Hardwig J. What about the family? *Hastings Center Report*. 1990;10:5-10.

7. Hebert PC, Hoffmaster B, Glass KC, Singer PA. Bioethics for clinicians: 7. truth telling. *Can Med Assoc J.* 1997;156:225-228.

8. Oken D. What to tell cancer patients: a study of medical attitudes. *JAMA.* 1961;175:1120-1128.

9. Seo M, Tamura K, Shijo H, Morioka E, Ikegame C, Hirasako K. Telling the diagnosis to cancer patients in Japan: attitude and perception of patients, physicians, and nurses. *Palliat Med.* 2000;14:105-111.

10. Jameton A. *Nursing Practice: the Ethical Issues.* Englewood Cliffs, NJ: Prentice Hall;1984:184-199.

11. Harrison C, Kenny NP, Sidarous M, Rowell M. Bioethics for clinicians: 9. involving children in medical ethics. *Can Med Assoc J.* 1997;156:825-829.

12. Bandman E, Bandman B. *Nursing Ethics Throughout the Lifespan.* 2nd ed. Norwalk, Conn: Appleton & Lange; 1990:166-167.

13. American Medical Association Council on Scientific Affairs. Confidential health services for adolescents. *JAMA.* 1993;269:1420-1424.

14. Comeau CJ. The nurse's role in informed consent. *Journal of Nursing Law.* 1994;1:5-14.

15. Marwick C. Bioethics commission examines informed consent from subjects who are decisionally incapable. *JAMA.* 1997;278:618-619.

16. Kravitz M. Informed consent: must ethical responsibility conflict with professional conduct? *Nursing Management: Critical Care Management Edition.* 1985;15:34A-34H.

17. Kong D. Debatable forms of consent. *The Boston Globe.* 1998;Nov16:A1, A10, A11.

18. Haynes RB. Introduction. In: Haynes RB, Sackett DL, Taylor DW, eds. *Compliance in Health Care.* Baltimore, Md: Johns Hopkins University Press; 1978:2.

19. Playle JF, Keeley P. Noncompliance and professional power. *J Adv Nurs.* 1998;27:304-311.

20. Benjamin M, Curtis J. *Ethics in Nursing.* 3rd ed. New York, NY: Oxford University Press; 1992: 54-68.

21. Caplan AL. Let wisdom find a way. *Generations.* 1985;Winter:10-14.

22. Collopy BJ. Safety and independence: rethinking some basic concepts in long term care. In: McCollough LB, Wilson NL, eds. *Long Term Care Decisions: Ethical and Conceptual Dimensions.* Baltimore, Md: Johns Hopkins University Press; 1995:137-142.

23. Moody HR. From informed consent to negotiated consent. *Gerontologist.* 1988;28(suppl):64-70.

24. American Nurses Association. *Code for Nurses.* Kansas City, Mo: American Nurses Association; 1997.

25. Chaimowitz G, Glancy GD, Graham D, Blackburn J. The duty to warn and protect: impact on practice. *Can J Psychiatry.* 2000;45:899.

MULTIPLE-CHOICE QUESTIONS

1. Which of the following is true about the determination of patient competence?
    A. Competence is an ethical term without legal implications
    B. If a person is incompetent in one area of life, the patient is incompetent in all areas
    C. Patients are assumed to be competent until it is demonstrated otherwise
    D. If a patient disagrees with the health care plan, she or he is most likely incompetent
    E. All of the above

2. The Patient Self-Determination Act (PSDA) requires that:
    A. All patients present their health care directives on admission to health care institutions
    B. All health care institutions provide written information to their patients about their rights to make advance directives
    C. Health care institutions identify patients without advance directives and provide them with aggressive, intensive treatment
    D. All of the above
    E. None of the above

3. Which of the following does Hardwig believe about patient and family decision-making?
    A. The patient should always be the primary decision-maker about her or his care
    B. The family should be involved in promoting and protecting its needs when patient care is planned
    C. The seriously ill patient should be encouraged to consider her or his needs unhampered by the needs and concerns of the family
    D. All of the above
    E. None of the above

4. Which of the following is a component of informed consent?
    A. The consent must be voluntary
    B. The patient must be competent
    C. The patient must understand her or his condition and its possible treatment
    D. All of the above
    E. None of the above

5. Which of the following is true for a patient who is consenting to treatment with an experimental protocol? The patient:
    A. Is not allowed to know all of the possible side effects of the protocol to prevent the effects from being exaggerated
    B. Cannot withdraw from the study until it is concluded
    C. Must have volunteered for the study and been provided with adequate information to give an informed consent
    D. Is unlikely to receive any benefits from the study since studies are done only for the benefit of society at large
    E. All of the above

6. Benjamin and Curtis suggest that health care providers might be justified in acting paternalistically in which of the following circumstances? When the patient:
   A. Is competent and able to make a rational decision
   B. Might be harmed by her or his choice
   C. Would probably approve of the decision at a later date
   D. All of the above
   E. None of the above

7. Which of the following is true concerning negotiated consent? It:
   A. Is appropriate when all that can be hoped is making the best of a bad situation
   B. Involves overriding the autonomy of a compromised adult
   C. Provides for decision-making by health care providers for incapacitated elders
   D. Should be done quietly and with minimal publicity to protect the privacy of the patient
   E. All of above

CHAPTER 4 ANSWERS

1. C
2. B
3. B
4. D
5. C
6. C
7. A

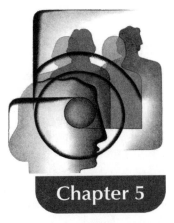

How Should Health Care Resources be Allocated?

Kathleen Ouimet Perrin, RN, CCRN, PhD(c)

Jon Allen, a 39-year-old father of two young children, had scheduled a routine physical. When the laboratory results of his complete blood cell (CBC) test were obtained, he was hospitalized immediately by his primary care provider. His white blood count (WBC) was 1000, his platelets were 17,000, and his hemoglobin and hematocrit were 3 and 8. Following a bone marrow aspiration, his possible diagnoses included myelodysplastic disease and aplastic anemia. Two specialists in aplastic anemia were unable to decide which diagnosis was accurate. However, since the anemia was so severe, a bone marrow transplant was the recommended procedure for both conditions. Jon's insurance company agreed to pay for a bone marrow transplant for aplastic anemia but not for myelodysplastic disease.

As health care consumes increasingly more of the gross domestic product (GDP), people have begun to wonder if there ought to be a limit to how much money is allocated to it. Economists, ethicists, politicians, insurers, and health care providers have begun to ask such questions as:

- Is health care rationing ever justifiable?
- If rationing is acceptable, what procedures should be rationed? Which people should have their health care choices limited?
- Are there limits to the amount of health care an individual has a right to receive?
- How should decisions about rationing be made?
- Who should make decisions about access to and allocation of health care?
- How should expensive or scarce resources be allocated?

IS HEALTH CARE RATIONING EVER JUSTIFIABLE?

Historically, health care rationing has focused on which patients should have access to a limited supply of staff or equipment. In times of scarcity of medical supplies or personnel, rationing of health care has long been accepted. During World War II, penicillin, in short supply, was allocated first to the soldiers expected to survive. Triage is an approved method of prioritizing emergency care to those who need and will probably benefit from the care. People who have only minor injuries and those expected to die from their injuries are required to wait for medical care. What is unusual about the current health care situation is that experts are suggesting that spending on health care should be curbed and medical care limited during a period of relative abundance. Why is this happening?

Since 1950, the amount of the United States' gross national product allocated to health care has tripled. The United States spends more of its GDP on health care than any other country in the world. Despite attempts to reign in health care costs, they continue to rise while Americans grumble ever more loudly about inadequacies in the health care system. Many experts argue that the term *health care*

> In the past, rationing of health care supplies and services has been accepted during times of scarcity. Currently, the talk of health care rationing is occurring during a time of relative abundance.

system is a misnomer because there is no coherent system of health care in this country. Rather, there is an entangled web of financing from private insurers through employers patched with city, county, state, and federal government programs. Attempts to produce a more coherent system to this point have failed.

In the 1980s and 1990s, insurers along with state and federal governments developed a consensus that they could not afford the spiraling costs of health care. This resulted in changes in the way health care is reimbursed, with retrospective reimbursement giving way to prospective payment for health care. Hospital stays were shortened and changes were made in the skill mix of hospital units. Hospital administrations were streamlined. Health care agencies such as the Agency for Health Care Policy and Research (AHCPR) began to identify the most appropriate and cost-effective treatments for various medical conditions. Nurse practitioners and physician assistants were employed by many health maintenance organizations (HMOs). In nonprofit HMOs, an emphasis was

Attempts to reduce the cost of health care:
- Changes in the health care delivery system
  - use of prospective payment
  - emphasis on wellness education and health promotion
  - AHCPR recommendations for effective treatment
- Changes in the hospital
  - decreases in the length of stay
  - changes in the skill mix on hospital units
  - reductions in the numbers of administrators
- Changes in health care providers
  - increases in advanced registered nurse practitioners (ARNP) and physician assistants
  - increased preparation of primary care physicians
  - reductions in the numbers of specialists

placed on wellness education and disease prevention. All of these measures resulted in some savings in health care expenditures.

Although the rate of increase of health care costs has slowed with the changes described above, the United States still spends approximately 15% of its GDP on health care. Unfortunately, there is no indication that our health outcomes are better than countries that spend significantly less, and in some instances our outcomes are not as good. For example, we rank 22nd in the world in infant mortality. In addition, economists and politicians declare that we are short-changing many other important areas of American life in an effort to fund medical care. Politicians have stated we should spend more money on teachers' salaries, roads, bridges, and public transportation. Businessmen have noted that the cost of health insurance drives up the cost of their products and makes them less able to compete with companies from other parts of the world. Critics of limitations to health care spending note we also spend billions of dollars on such "goods" as cigarettes, cosmetics, and Super Bowl commercials, but no one recommends we cap those discretionary expenses. The debate about how much of the GDP should be allocated for health care is not likely to be resolved soon.

WHAT PROCEDURES SHOULD BE RATIONED? WHICH PEOPLE SHOULD HAVE THEIR HEALTH CARE CHOICES LIMITED?

The current level of debate centers on whether health care can justly be rationed and what would constitute a fair distribution of the health care resources we currently have available. Although some ethicists and politicians argue that rationing is not an ethically appropriate alternative, many argue that planned, explicit rationing might be more acceptable than the haphazard, implicit system of rationing that presently exists. Lamm, the former Governor of Colorado, has noted that we ration by the following:[1]

1. **Geography**. Patients in remote rural areas receive less care; care in certain geographic regions, such as New England, tends to be more up-to-date and appropriate than in others.

2. **Economic factors**. The wealthy and employed are usually cared better for.

3. **Attractiveness to the media**. If a patient is denied an experimental procedure, an appeal to the media or a politician may help secure financial assistance or free care.

4. **Scientific interest**. If a disease is currently endowed with research funds, there may be better possibilities for treatment.

5. **Full-time employment**. Usually people with full-time employment have access to medical insurance.

What criteria do experts suggest would be more acceptable for health care rationing? Lamm and Callahan have been advocates of age as a criterion for health care rationing. Callahan states that with the rapid increase in the population over the age of 85, there will be a steady increase in the amount of chronic disease.[2] Thus, the gap between health care needs and limited

---

Arguments for age-based health care rationing:
- End of natural life span
  - at 80 years of life
  - accomplished life goals
  - fulfilled responsibilities
- Change goals of health care
  - no further curative treatment
  - comfort care only

---

medical resources will widen. Both Callahan and Lamm suggest that when an individual has reached the end of her or his life span, she or he should not be provided with life-sustaining interventions, rather only with comfort care. Callahan suggests that this occurs somewhere around the age of 80, when a person should have accomplished life goals and fulfilled responsibilities.[2]

However, there are several problems with this argument. First, it is not always clear when a person has reached the end of her or his natural life span or fulfilled responsibilities. One 82-year-old woman with severe treatable pneumonia requested antibiotics and mechanical ventilation so she could return home to provide care for her daughter with multiple sclerosis. The woman survived and cared for her daughter for another 8 years. Next, there is not always a clear distinction between interventions that are life sustaining and pain relieving. One obvious example is treatment of the chest pain associated with angina or myocardial infarction.

A final problem is that most of the cost associated with care of older adults during the last year of their lives is not associated with high-technology care. Rather, it is the cost of providing simple comfort measures at the end of life that encompasses most of the medical expense.[3] Only 20% of those 85 and older who were admitted to hospitals in one analysis of Medicare data were admitted to intensive care units. Aggressive cardiovascular procedures and chemotherapy were unusual. Instead, the majority of the procedures for the oldest adults admitted to hospitals were to relieve hip pain and stabilize or pin hip and femur fractures.[3] Some research studies have suggested that limiting expensive technologies for the oldest adults would only result in a 3.5% to 6% savings in the Medicare budget. In order to save significant amounts of health care dollars by rationing care to older Americans, simple pain-relieving interventions like hip and femur fracture repairs as well as penicillin and oxygen administration would have to be limited. Even the ethicists and politicians who recommend limiting care to older adults do not usually recommend limiting interventions that relieve pain and discomfort.

ARE THERE LIMITS TO THE AMOUNT OF HEALTH CARE AN INDIVIDUAL HAS A RIGHT TO RECEIVE?

Some health care providers and ethicists recommend limiting access to procedures that are unlikely to be successful or will be futile. They argue that it makes little sense to provide interventions that have only a minimal chance of restoring health to the patient. Although one might imagine this means limiting highly technical, expensive interventions, this is not always the case. In Mr. Allen's situation, there were two possible treatments. The conservative treatment for severe aplastic anemia involved blood transfusions and immunosuppressants. This offered him about a 5% chance of long-term survival and meant he would be less likely to accept a bone marrow transplant. The more aggressive bone marrow transplant offered him an 85% chance for a 3-month survival and a 50% chance of survival for more than 1 year.

In most instances, we expect health care providers to be stewards of the medical resources available to them and use resources wisely when they offer some hope of benefit. We expect health care providers to identify treatments that will not provide benefit to their patients and either dissuade

> Physicians are expected to be the medical experts and deny patients treatments that will be of no benefit to them or that could harm them or their community (eg, antibiotics for viral infections).

their patients from requesting those treatments or refuse to provide their patients with those treatments. Consider the implications of patients who ask for antibiotics for cold and flu symptoms. Primary care providers are expected to explain to their patients that antibiotics will not help a viral infection, and prescribing antibiotics inappropriately will only increase the incidence of bacterial resistance to antibiotics. In short, we normally expect the health care provider to be the best judge of what is a medically appropriate or inappropriate treatment.

Certainly, the stakes rise when the intervention might offer a small possibility of sustaining or prolonging life. Moreover, saying that an intervention offers minimal hope and is futile is a very difficult thing to do. Who is to decide when an intervention is futile? When it leads to a less than 5% chance of improvement or survival, less than 1%, or when no one will survive? Ethicists and medical experts are having a difficult time defining futility.[4] Futile interventions have been defined as those which do not lead to a restoration of a heartbeat, result in immediate survival but no change in the likelihood of death within a few weeks or months, or result in survival at an unacceptable quality of life.

> There is no current consensus of a definition of futility.

One group of medical experts trying to develop a policy for futile interventions concluded, "We can't define futility, but we know it when we see it."[5]

To compound the problem, there are a few people who will survive in even the most dire circumstances following dramatic, normally futile interventions. The information gained from their care may contribute to medical knowledge and improve medical care in the future. When should the health care provider have the ability to overrule the patient's or family's desire for treatment and declare a procedure futile? Obviously, if the procedure would appear to be contraindicated or is based on a patient or family's misunderstanding and request for inappropriate treatment, or offers no hope of benefit, the procedure should not be performed. But, who should make the decision when an expensive procedure offers a 5% chance of a cure? Should futility be the guide, or should there be some national or statewide rationing plan?

HOW SHOULD DECISIONS ABOUT RATIONING BE MADE?

Ethicists have proposed several ways in which health care could be justly distributed. Some of the ways Jameton suggested health care benefits might be distributed were described in Chapter 2. These included:[6]

1. To each equally
2. To each according to merit
3. To each according to past or future social contribution
4. To each according to what can be acquired in a free market
5. To each according to need

Those who advocate health care be allocated to each person equally suggest that each person should have a specific amount to allot to health care throughout their lifetime. Thus, Jon Allen might use his lifetime allotment of health care money to pay for the bone

> To each equally fails to consider that health care needs are not equally distributed.

marrow transplant, even if it were considered futile. This system fails to consider that health care needs are not evenly distributed throughout the population. So, while one child might exhaust the allotment on cleft lip repair and Jon might use his for a bone marrow transplant, a third person might spend her or his money on a tummy tuck or a rhinoplasty. Does this type of allotment seem just or fair? How would the government or health insurer identify what amount of money a person would need to purchase a lifetime of acceptable health care?

Others argue that people should receive health care by merit. They explain that an alcoholic with a damaged liver due to alcohol abuse should not be allowed a liver transplant. But it is not always clear what a person merits. How much risk does a skier assume for a broken leg or an overweight, middle-aged man for a myocardial infarction? Mr. Allen had worked as an industrial hygienist. He had visited numerous polluting industrial plants and had worked to help them meet federal and state standards. It was postulated

> To each according to merit fails to consider how much risk each person can assume and still merit treatment.

that the long-term effects of exposure to industrial pollutants plus his ethnic heritage might have contributed to his development of bone marrow depression. Did he merit treatment? Or was his behavior similar enough to that of the alcohol abuser that he should not be treated? He too had continued to expose himself to toxins despite his knowledge of the potential long-term effects.

When kidney dialysis was in its early stages, many centers used the criterion of past or future contribution to decide who should receive dialysis. It is extremely difficult to weigh past and future contributions justly. What contributions did Mr. Allen make in cleaning up industrial pollution? What will he most likely contribute to society and to his 4-year-old daughter and 8-year-old son if he survives? How might that be balanced with the requirements of a 50-year-old man with a successful business and two college-aged children to support, who needed treatment with a thrombolytic, coronary artery bypass surgery and rehabilitation after a myocardial infarction?

> To each according to contribution fails to consider how difficult it can be to balance the societal contributions of various individuals.

The system we currently have in the United States uses the fourth criterion listed—to each according to what she or he can acquire in a free market. Although few will argue that it is the most appropriate way to allocate health care, it is the primary method of rationing health care in the United States today. People receive the health care that they are

> To each according to what can be acquired in the free market is unfair to the poor, especially to women and children.

able to pay for or failing their ability to pay, the care they can demand. This system is failing a significant percentage of Americans; approximately 15% are uninsured and as many as 25% have been described as underinsured. Many in this underinsured group are women and small children. By any other rationing strategy, this group would most likely be among the first group to receive at least preventative health care.

Jameton believes that to each according to her or his need is the most appropriate way to allocate health care because health care is a benefit only as long as it is needed, and it should be distributed in accordance with the benefit it can provide.[6] However, there are two major criticisms of this argument. First, a rapid and steady increase in the number of older adults having chronic conditions is expected as the baby boomers enter old age. Thus, the legitimate health care needs of this population are anticipated to increase substantially within the next decade. Secondly, Americans have been criticized for being unable to distinguish between a health care need and a desire. For example, is menopause a natural process or should a woman receive hormone replacement to limit the symptoms and prevent some of the potential side ef-

> To each according to need fails to consider the increasing legitimate health care needs of the aging baby boomers. In addition, it highlights Americans' difficulty in distinguishing health care needs from desires.

fects like osteoporosis and bone fractures? If it is a natural process and preventing the side effects is simply a woman's choice, why should insurance pay for hormone replacement? If the patient cannot determine what is a health care need and what is a luxury, who should be making that decision?

WHO SHOULD MAKE DECISIONS ABOUT ACCESS TO AND ALLOCATION OF HEALTH CARE?

In most recent instances, efforts to alter the American health care system, such as Clinton's health care reform proposal, have failed. However, in 1989, after the death of a 7-year-old boy waiting for a bone marrow transplant, Oregon attempted to develop a system to provide access to health insurance to all its citizens.[7] In order to pay for such widespread coverage, it was necessary to develop a means of rationing health care to the people receiving Medicaid in the state. Initially, this was done by developing a list of prioritized services by citizens at public meetings as well as by panels of experts. Supporters believed that this explicit priority setting was important because it required public accountability for health care decisions. When the state established its budget for any year, it set a level for the medical services that would be provided to Medicaid recipients. All services available at that funding level or below would be offered to Medicaid recipients and services above the level would not be allowed. For example, in 1997, Oregon funded the first 505 treatments on the priority list. This meant that some potentially beneficial treatments were not available to patients receiving Medicaid. Thus, Oregon attempted to define a basic health care package for all of its residents by limiting the types of care provided to some of its citizens.

Oregon needed federal approval and waivers to begin this rationing system. In order to meet federal guidelines, initially older adults and people with disabilities were not included in the group whose care would be rationed. Critics of the plan were concerned because most of the people affected were women and young children.[8] Since the institution of the plan in 1994, a number of significant changes have occurred. The low-income elderly and disabled have been included in the insured. Mental health and chemical dependency services were added to the health care package, and services were moved up or down on the list. Since 85% of the Medicaid recipients are now in managed care programs, it is becoming more difficult to determine how to follow the priority list of funded services. Still, Oregon has attempted to develop an explicit, ethical way to ration health care while increasing access to health care for the indigent citizens of the state. Does increasing the number of people with access to health care make explicit rationing of the amount of care available to individual people justifiable?

While ethicists and politicians have proceeded slowly and cautiously in limiting access and rationing health care, for-profit health care insurance companies and HMOs have rushed to take the lead. For-profit institutions have limited health care expenditures by both implicit and explicit rationing on a case-by-case basis rather than on a state or national level. Where nonprofit HMOs saved money primarily through preventative care, staff physicians, and nurse practitioners, for-profit HMOs used methods such as capitation, risk sharing, gate-keeping, and gag rules to implicitly ration health care. Many states are outlawing these prac-

> Some for-profit insurers are implicitly rationing care through such methods as capitation, risk-sharing, gate keeping, and gag rules.

tices because they prevent the patient from being adequately informed about her or his condition and thus giving informed consent for treatment.

Capitation, risk-sharing, and gatekeeping were originally developed to constrain health care costs, and they essentially do so by rationing health care on the individual patient level. Capitation means that a health care provider is given a specific sum of money to provide all of a patient's health care needs over a period of time, usually a year. If the patient requires less care, the provider makes money, but if the patient requires more care, the provider loses money. Risk sharing is money that is held out of the provider's capitated funds and placed in a pool with other providers' withheld funds to provide for the care of high-risk patients and high-cost procedures. A provider who overspends the risk share allotment will

> Capitation and risk sharing may result in loss of money for health care providers who prescribe certain expensive diagnostic procedures, referrals, or treatments for their patients.

see the amount increased in the next time period. The shorter the time periods and the smaller the risk pool, the more the health care provider will feel the financial impact of any high-cost referral or procedure. If the provider repeatedly overspends a risk allotment, the provider may be dropped from the insurance program.[9] Gatekeeping means that the patient must see the primary care provider before being referred to a specialist or the plan will not cover the cost of the specialist's care. Each of these payment methods encourages the primary care provider to undertreat rather than overtreat any patient. Finally, gag rules, now illegal in most states, prevent the health care provider from telling the patient of his or her financial arrangement with the insurance carrier. Gag rules may also prevent the provider from describing potentially beneficial treatments to a patient that the insurer would not fund. These measures have resulted in significant cost savings to insurers while placing patients at risk for inadequate health care.

Health care providers may experience a conflict of interest between providing the most appropriate care for their patients and providing care that will not result in financial or employment loss for them. It can be very difficult to distinguish when a health care provider is being influenced by such monetary considerations. For example, Mr. Allen was a member of an HMO that required gatekeeping and practiced capitation and risk sharing by both primary care providers and specialists. His primary care provider immediately referred him to a hematologist associated with the health care plan. The hematologist could not determine whether Mr. Allen had severe aplastic anemia or myelodysplastic disease. Despite the fact that transfusions would make Mr. Allen less likely to accept a bone marrow transplant and immunosuppressants rarely work in severe aplastic anemia, the hematologist recommended that course of treatment for Mr. Allen.

When approached about a bone marrow transplant, the hematologist stated Mr. Allen should only have a transplant at a national center across the country that was not covered by Mr. Allen's health care plan. In addition, the hematologist initially refused to refer Mr. Allen to the regional transplant center, where a nationally known expert in aplastic anemia performed bone marrow transplants. This transplant program was covered by Mr. Allen's health care plan. This case presents unanswered questions: Why would the hematologist recommend a markedly less costly procedure that was unlikely to benefit Mr. Allen and would probably harm him? Why would the hematologist initially refuse to refer him to the expensive but covered bone marrow transplant program? Was he being influenced to avoid these referrals because of capitation and risk sharing or was he unaware of the appropriate treatment options that the insurer would cover?

Although bone marrow transplant is an expensive procedure, there have been instances in which it appeared that primary care providers were avoiding even simple essential tests (eg, mono spot and cardiac enzymes) to lessen the cost of diagnosis and care. This type of health care rationing is implicit and often undiscovered. Does this type of rationing happen frequently, and is it likely to result in untoward consequences to the patient? It is difficult to say since many of the lapses are slight and do not significantly harm patients. Also, most health care providers will not openly admit when they have been influenced to ration care for their personal monetary gain.

To describe how difficult it can be to identify the extent of the problem, here are examples of patients admitted to a 14-bed ICU in a community hospital by three different physicians in the same week. The first patient was admitted with a BP of 70 systolic, her serum sodium was 104, and her other electrolytes were also severely out of the normal range. She had a bronze coloring, and her symptoms were a textbook example of Addison's disease. Her physician, who had not performed laboratory studies, had told her that she was not physically ill and should not return to the office. The second patient had been seen in her physician's office for strep throat; the physician had sent her to the outpatient lab of the hospital for blood work. The phlebotomist in the lab, concerned about the woman, brought her to the emergency department (ED). The woman was admitted to the ICU with septic shock, a BP of 60 systolic, a rash from her throat to her knees, inability to swallow because her throat was so swollen, and a temperature of 105° F. The last patient, a 52-year-old male, developed vise-like chest pressure at 5 AM. When he called his physician (his health plan required physician approval before it would reimburse for an ED visit), he was given a 3 PM appointment for an office visit. Despite repeated calls to the office during the day, he was told to keep his 3 PM appointment. When he arrived, nauseated and still having chest discomfort and shortness of breath, the physicians took an additional hour and a half to read his EKG before transferring him to the ED. When he arrived in the ED, it was clear he was having an untreated myocardial infarction (MI). Each of these patients was a textbook example of the disease afflicting them. Was the lack of treatment due to health care provider incompetence? Was it due to intrinsic rationing related to a payment system that rewards physicians for limiting diagnostic assessments and health care delivery?

Rationing by health care insurers is not necessarily intrinsic and hidden. It may also be extrinsic and defined in the health care insurance policy. Even though Mr. Allen was eventually referred to the aplastic anemia specialist at the regional transplant center, his insurer would not agree to finance the bone marrow transplant until it was established that he suffered from aplastic anemia and not myelodysplastic disease. Mr. Allen's HMO stated that a bone marrow transplant for myelodysplastic disease was an experimental treatment and its position on experimental treatment was clear in Mr. Allen's insurance policy.

Many business experts compare buying health care insurance to buying a car. They state that people select the level of protection they desire and can afford. Just as people choose a car with or without antilock brakes or dual air-bags, they choose a health insurance policy with or without certain levels of protection or coverage of certain procedures.[8] Although a few women might think to check if their insurance covered bone marrow transplants for breast cancer, few people would consider determining the level of coverage

> Buying health care insurance has been likened to buying a car. A family might purchase a Mercedes or a Ford, depending on their personal tastes, needs, and budget.

for conditions as rare as aplastic anemia and myelodysplastic disease. Is selecting a health care plan really comparable to buying a car? For most Americans, their place of employment does not offer them a limited number of cars from which they can choose and then assist them with payment for the car. Also, most Americans can more realistically anticipate their requirements for a car than they can foresee their needs for health care.

Additionally, health care activists are worried because, in most instances, HMOs and insurance companies are protected from liability for the medical care or diagnostic studies for which they deny payment. Usually, they cannot be sued for anything more than the actual cost of the procedure denied. For example, a health insurance company or HMO might refuse to pay for a pap smear every year for a woman because its plan covered it only every 3 years after three negative test results. If the woman developed cervical cancer, it went undetected for 2 years and was found only at a late stage, the woman could only sue the insurer for the cost of the denied diagnostic procedure. Instead, the health care provider who did not perform the pap smear could be sued for the additional cost of the woman's care and any pain and suffering the woman incurred. Thus, the health care provider accepts the liability for not providing the care, while the insurer has minimal liability and the potential to make a consider-

> Most health care insurers assume minimal liability for the health care they deny because they are only held responsible for the cost of the care denied and not for the consequences of the denied care.

able profit by limiting the amount of care provided. Should for-profit insurance companies be allowed to implicitly and explicitly ration health care and enhance their profits while incurring minimal liability for their decisions?

HOW SHOULD EXPENSIVE OR SCARCE RESOURCES BE ALLOCATED?

Organ Donation

If insurance companies cannot always be trusted to determine appropriate coverage, and ethicists and politicians have not agreed on criteria for rationing, then how should expensive or scarce resources like organ transplants be allocated? When hemodialysis was initially available in the United States, few dialysis machines were available and the procedure was privately insured and costly. Committees were formed to determine who should receive treatment, and they established lists rather like Jameton's criteria for just distribution of health care resources described earlier.

Most of the people who received dialysis in the early years were white, middle-aged, middle-class men. When the federal government became responsible for payment for dialysis in the early 1970s, minorities, women, and older adults began to receive dialysis in greater numbers. A similar imbalance exists now in the people selected for organ transplants. Many health care ethicists and activists have raised the question: How might we justly distribute the organs available for transplant to assure the fairest distribution and the best outcomes?

There are two separate avenues of approach to the problem: increasing the supply of organs and assuring just distribution of the available organs. Currently in the United States, organs may be donated from one living, usually related individual to another, but they may not be sold. Family members may also donate organs on an individual's death. The individual may have "opted in" to the donor system by signing an organ donor card, which only about 20% of the American population has done. Even when the person has not signed a donor card,

> Patients may "opt in" to the organ donor system by signing an organ donor card indicating their willingness to donate their organs after death.

the hospital must comply with required request legislation. This means if a patient meets the criteria to be an organ donor, the regional organ donor bank must be notified and the family must be asked if they are willing to donate the patient's organs.

Within the current system, nurses have a significant role in enhancing donations. Nurses are often the health care providers most intimately involved with the bereaved family. The amount of trust that is established between the family and the health care team during the period just preceding the patient's death is a major factor in which families decide to donate organs. In some institutions, nurses, because they have come to be trusted by the family, are among the people who request the family consider donating the patient's organs. When

> In the United States, if a patient is a potential organ donor, required request mandates that the family be approached and asked if they are willing to donate the patient's organs.

and how the family is approached also affects whether they will donate. Families are more likely to donate organs if they are not asked to donate at the same time that they are informed their family member has died. They are also more likely to donate if they are approached in a quiet, private place where they can consider their options. These simple interventions can increase the percentage of families who decide to donate by as much as 20%.[10]

Normally, between 30% and 50% of the families approached and asked to donate organs decide not to donate. Some of the reasons are lack of time and private space as described previously, but many people are unsure whether the patient would have wanted to donate her or his organs. In the absence of a donor card or the patient discussing donation with her or his family, many families believe that they cannot be sure that the patient would have wanted to donate. Therefore, they do not consent to donation. Thus, many experts believe that "opting in," requiring people to indicate their desire to donate by obtaining a donor card, and required request, requiring health care institutions to request family members to donate a dead patient's organs, are not working as well as intended.

Presumed Consent

Several European countries are using a system called *presumed consent* or "opting out" instead. In this system, the presumption is that a person would wish to donate her or his organs. This presumption is based on several provisions.[11] The first provision is that human organs are scarce commodities. They are of vital use to living persons but of no value at all to people once they are dead. The next provision is that each person would want to receive an organ if she or he needed one. Since each person would desire an organ, she or he would desire that there be an adequate supply of organs and that all potential donors be willing to donate an organ. Therefore, each person ought to believe that all people should be willing to donate organs after death. The final provision is that people would not want to be "free riders." A "free rider" is defined as a person who is willing to receive but not donate an organ.

> Presumed consent assumes that patients would have wanted to donate their organs unless they have notified a registry with an objection to donation.

With presumed consent, if a person does not desire to donate, there is a choice to "opt out" and remove herself or himself from becoming an organ donor by notifying a national registry. Or, the family has the option to "opt out" for the patient at the time of death. In one Austrian county, presumed consent resulted in a 55% increase in organ donations over 5 years.[11] Presumed consent has encountered obstacles in several countries. There are fears that organs might be donated illegally to wealthy foreigners. There are unfounded worries about HIV, and concerns that organs might be taken before a family has had an opportunity to object. In Brazil, citizens were so fearful that organs would be removed before a patient was clinically dead that presumed consent laws were overturned.[12]

In an attempt to increase the number of organs available for transplantation, should it always be assumed that people would want to donate their organs unless they had previously indicated their objection?

Should the United States change to a presumed consent system in an attempt to increase donations and alleviate the suffering of the more than 50,000 people currently awaiting transplants?

Directed Donations

A few people advocate *directed donation* as a means of increasing donors. With directed donation, a family may indicate the person to whom they desire their family member's organs to be given. This happens when the recipient is a member of the same community as the donor or the media has highlighted the recipient's need for an organ. Advocates of directed donation say that it is rather like directed adoption. The donor's family and the birth mother both have an interest in being sure that their gifts are well cared for. Thus, family members of cadaver donors ought to be able to direct their donation.

Those who do not support the concept of directed donation state it does not increase the number of donors, rather it shifts the organs to specific individuals, making the selection process less fair. In directed donation, the recipient may jump ahead of others who are also awaiting organs and may actually need the organs more. Some fear that directed donation is merely a first step toward providing payment to the family of the deceased

> Directed donation allows a family to specify to whom one or all of their family member's organs should be donated.

just as some parents offer money to the birth mother in directed adoption. This would essentially result in the ability of people to buy cadaver organs. Opponents of directed donation fear that if such events occurred routinely, people would be less willing to donate organs out of concern for the unfairness in the system. A final point is that if directed donation became widespread, the person who could attract the most media attention would be the person most likely to acquire a new organ. Ability to attract media attention appears nowhere on any ethicist's list of just ways to allocate scarce health care resources. Should directed donation be continued as a means of increasing cadaver organ donations?

Ways to increase donations by living donors are also being explored. Some people have advocated reconsidering the prohibition against paid, living donors. The reasoning behind this idea is that a person's body is her or his own and she or he ought to be able to allot it or parts of it as she or he chooses. In countries without prohibition against paid donation, there has been exploitation of the poor, who need money for a specific purpose, by rich people needing organs. For example, one woman in India donated a kidney for money for her daughter's dowry. In the past, most living donors were related to the recipient. There has been a loosening of that restriction recently and donations have been occurring between employer and employee, brother of fiancée and future groom, as well as between close friends. In at least one of these donations, it was suspected that money was exchanged. Another donation resulted in a lawsuit when the future groom declined to marry his fiancée after the successful transplant.

Are there limitations to what should be acceptable in the quest to find more living donors? Should donors be paid for their organs or should we expect donation to be a voluntary, altruistic process?

We presently allow unrelated people to donate renewable sources like blood and bone marrow to strangers; should we allow the donation of solid organs, like kidneys that cannot regenerate themselves, for profit or to acquaintances?

Mr. Allen was lucky. He had a family member who was a complete match and was willing to donate bone marrow. He did not need to wait to determine if there was a match in the national registry. Nor did he need to locate a donor of his ethnic origin by attracting media attention. Because he had a living related donor and severe aplastic anemia, he jumped to the top of the waiting list and received a bone marrow transplant as soon as a bed became available in the transplant unit. Most people would argue that preferential treatment of people with severe disease and available living donors is just. Does such preferential treatment increase the pressure for donations from living related donors? How should the potential donor be protected from being coerced into making a donation?

In an attempt to prevent living related donors from being coerced into making a donation, some physicians and transplant coordinators sometimes equivocate with the patient and family. Transplant physicians and coordinators meet with the prospective donor prior to the transplant. If the donor admits to being coerced into donating or is clearly uncomfortable about the donation, the physician may offer to prevaricate and say that further compatibility testing has indicated that the candidate would not be an acceptable donor. Transplant coordinators and physicians who employ such a technique believe offering the donor candidate an opportunity to back out without the patient's and family's awareness is the only way they can be assured the donor's consent was not coerced. Is it justifiable to offer to lie to the family and patient to assure the donor's consent was not coerced and provide the potential donor an opportunity to decline to donate?

Just Distribution of Available Organs

In addition to attempts to increase the supply of organs, efforts are also being made to assure that organs are justly distributed. When first examining the issue, most people would argue that the person with the greatest need, who is the best match for an organ, should be the recipient of that organ. However, there are problems with such a simple approach. The first concern is whether providing organs only to those with the greatest need is the best way to allocate all organs. When organs are transplanted into the sickest patients, those with the greatest need, the organs' and the recipients' chances of survival are less than when they are transplanted into less gravely ill patients. Some ethicists argue from a utilitarian perspective that being good stewards of the limited organs available means that the organs should be transplanted into those people who are most likely to benefit from the organs. Thus, they contend organs should be transplanted into people who are most likely to survive for an extended period of time and assume the responsibility of caring for the transplanted organs.

> Just allocation of health care resources such as organs has been interpreted to mean either:
> - The patient who has the greatest need should always get the organ
> - The patient who is most likely to benefit from and care for the organ should receive the organ

How should an organ be justly allocated when there are several acceptable matches? Should it always be the person who is most gravely ill and has the most serious need for the organ? Should it be the person who needs an organ and will most likely survive for a long time after transplantation? Or should there be a balance between need and survival? Who has the right to make that decision?

The question of who should make the decision has become an increasingly complicated one in the United States. In the past, organs were allocated through regional organ donor banks first, and then if an appropriate candidate was not found, a national search was conducted. Recent legislation has established a national rather than regional waiting list for organs, with the person who has the greatest need and is the best match for the organ on the national list receiving highest priority. Health and Human Services officials have argued that a national list is the only fair way to allocate organs. However, opponents argue that such a system will "waste" organs since only the sickest recipients will be chosen. Opponents also worry because national waiting lists are being championed by large transplant centers that could establish longer waiting lists and earn more money by performing more transplants if they had access to a national supply of organs. If local

> One current controversy concerns whether donated organs should be allocated on the national or local level.

transplant centers were forced to close because organs were donated nationally not locally, critics fear fewer people would donate since they could no longer appreciate the effects of their donation. How can organs be most fairly distributed? Should distribution be at a local or national level?

Allocation of Another Scarce Resource: Nursing Staff

There are other medical resources in short supply. Nurses available to provide patient care are becoming scarce commodities. There is currently a national shortage of nurses with severe shortages of registered nurses in such specialties as emergency department and intensive care units. Staff nurses may be faced with the question of just distribution of their services on a daily basis. With reductions in the professional nurse staff and increases in unlicensed assistant personnel, individual nurses must constantly evaluate how to justly distribute their time among several needy patients.

Nurses in supervisory positions must determine how to adequately staff units. This entails deciding on an acceptable mix of professional staff, technicians, and assistant personnel. When deciding on the most appropriate staff mix, the nursing administrators are frequently reminded that staff salaries constitute the most expensive category in the budget of a health care institution or organization. Who should determine which patients deserve nursing care and if financially viable staffing patterns are fair and safe for patients?

Sometimes nursing department directors are faced with an even more serious question: How can severe staffing shortages be justly resolved? A 375-bed community hospital had an intensive care unit with 16 beds. The usual occupancy rate was 10 patients, and it was habitually staffed by five experienced ICU nurses. For several months the ICU had been at full occupancy. More nurses than anticipated were required to care for the patients. Although nurses from a step-down unit were partially cross-trained to float to the ICU, all of the patients in the ICU at the time required skills that the step-down nurses did not have. Even though the department director was attempting to hire additional ICU nurses, there had been no qualified nurses responding to advertisements for ICU staff positions, and even traveling nurses had been difficult to obtain. Many of the ICU nurses had been working 60 hours or more each week to make up for the staff shortage. As the overtime continued, the staff nurses were tired and several became ill with the flu.

One evening, there were five nurses scheduled to care for 14 unstable patients, when three nurses called in sick. The charge nurse and department director called all the potential staff and could find no one willing to work that evening. The hospital had a policy that allowed the director to mandate overtime in staffing crises. However, one of the nurses had already been working for 14 hours, another had no one available to pick up her children after school, and a third was clearly becoming ill.

In such a situation, one might ask the following questions:

- How can the nurse administrator arrange for adequate staffing to provide safe patient care?
- Would it be fair if the department director mandated nurses from the previous shift to stay and care for patients?
- What are the consequences if the nurses made errors because of exhaustion, worries about children, or illness?
- Did the director have the right to utilize nurses from the step-down unit even though they were not fully cross-trained?
- Who would have the duty to supervise the step-down unit nurses?

The ICU patients had a clear moral and ethical right to safe, competent nursing care, and the ICU director had a duty to arrange for that care. How can these moral imperatives be fairly and adequately fulfilled in this staffing shortage? The director had not worked as a staff nurse in years and was not sure that she would be safe delivering patient care. Other services (such as respiratory therapy) might be used to manage the ventilators of some patients so that float nurses could fill the gap. Several surgeries had already been postponed, so delaying surgery of patients who would normally be transferred to ICU was not an option. Should some of the patients be transferred to other facilities? Should additional pay or benefits be offered to persuade some of the nurses to work extra hours? How could the department director arrange for nursing care to be delivered safely and competently to these 14 patients?

The department director in this situation determined that her goal was to provide adequate staffing for safe patient care while being as fair to the exhausted nursing staff as she possibly could. She had never mandated a nurse with child care responsibilities or illness, to work overtime, and she stated that she would not do so now. With the outbreak of the flu, most other health care facilities in the area were similarly short-staffed, so transferring patients was not an option. Instead, the department director elected to pay an additional incentive for overtime that persuaded some staff to stay later and other staff to come in early. She stayed, providing some of the care herself with the assistance of the charge nurse, and she asked for help from other departments, especially the step-down unit and respiratory therapy. Finally, she redoubled her efforts to hire qualified ICU staff to prevent such a circumstance from occurring again. Was this a just way to overcome the staffing shortage? Are there other more appropriate methods she should have utilized?

Nurses are actively involved in the delivery and distribution of health care. The American public also trusts them more than other health care providers. It is therefore important for nurses to work on both individual and professional association levels to assure that nursing and health care resources are justly distributed. Ways that nurses might choose to work to assure just distribution of health care resources will be discussed in two subsequent sections. How should the nurse proceed when she or he encounters illegal, unjust, or unethical practices?

REFERENCES

1. Lamm RD. Rationing of health care: the inevitable meets the unthinkable. *Nurse Pract.* 1986; 11:581-583.
2. Callahan D. *Setting Limits: Medical Goods in an Aging Society.* New York, NY: Simon and Schuster; 1987.
3. Levinsky G. Can we afford medical care for Alice C? *Lancet.* 1998;352:1849.
4. Brody BA, Halevy A. Is futility a futile concept? *J Med Philos.* 1995;20:126-128.
5. Department of Medicine and Center for Medical Ethics and Health, College of Medicine, Houston, TX. Multi-institutional collaborative policy on medical futility. *JAMA.* 1996;276:571-574.
6. Jameton A. *Nursing Practice: the Ethical Issues.* Englewood Cliffs, NJ: Prentice Hall; 1984:130-134.
7. Ham C. Retracing the Oregon trail: the experience of rationing and the Oregon health plan. *BMJ.* 1998;316:1965.
8. Daniels N. Is the Oregon rationing plan fair? *JAMA.* 1991;265:2232-2235.
9. Woolhandler S, Himmelstein DU. Extreme risk, the new corporate proposition for physicians. *N Engl J Med.* 1995;333:1706-1707.
10. Randhawa G. Coping with grieving relatives and making a request for organs. *Medical Teacher.* 1998;20:247.
11. Kennedy I. The case for presumed consent in organ donation. *Lancet.* 1998;351:1650.
12. Csillag C. Brazil abolishes presumed consent in organ donation. *Lancet.* 1998;352:1367.

MULTIPLE-CHOICE QUESTIONS

1. Which of the following measures to control health care costs were attempted during the 1980s and early 1990s?
    A. Identification of most appropriate and cost-effective treatment for various types of medical conditions
    B. Increasing the number of physicians trained in various specialties
    C. Primary care nursing with all RN staffs providing holistic care
    D. Reliance on retrospective reimbursement for payment of health care costs
    E. None of the above

2. Limiting expensive, life-saving technologies for the frail elderly would most likely result in what percentage of savings in the Medicare budget?
    A. 5%
    B. 10%
    C. 20%
    D. 30%
    E. 40%

3. Which of the following practices have been used by for-profit HMOs to implicitly ration health care and control costs?
    A. Capitation
    B. Gag rules
    C. Gatekeeping
    D. Risk sharing
    E. All of the above

4. What is the ethical justification for presumed consent for organ donation (also known as "opting out")?
    A. Organs are a scarce commodity that are of value only to living persons
    B. Most people would wish to be "free riders," that is they would like to receive but not donate an organ
    C. Only those people with organ failure awaiting transplant would desire all potential donors to be willing to donate
    D. All of the above
    E. None of the above

5. Why do business experts compare buying health insurance to buying a car?
    A. Employers usually provide both health insurance and company cars
    B. Health care needs are as easy to anticipate as requirements for a car
    C. People can choose the level of protection and safety they desire in both health care insurance and automobiles
    D. All of the above
    E. None of the above

6. Some politicians criticize the health care system for implicit rationing of health care services. Ways in which services have been implicitly rationed include by:

A. Geographic area: people in rural areas often receive less care
B. Economic factors: wealthy people are able to receive better services
C. Attractiveness to the media: publicizing cases may result in approval or payment for health care
D. Full-time employment: people employed full-time are more likely to have health insurance
E. All of the above

CHAPTER 5 ANSWERS

1. A
2. A
3. E
4. A
5. C
6. E

Encountering Unjust, Incompetent, or Illegal Behavior

Kathleen Ouimet Perrin, RN, CCRN, PhD(c)

On July 4 at 10 PM, Mr. Raymond was admitted to a large university medical center. The nurse noted he was short of breath, had a respiratory rate of 36, a heart rate of 180, and a blood pressure of 94/60. After the nurse admitted Mr. Raymond, she phoned the medical resident to notify him of Mr. Raymond's condition. As the nurse returned to his bedside, Mr. Raymond's respiratory rate increased to 48, then he stopped breathing and became unresponsive. The nurse called for the cardiac arrest team.

The room was immediately flooded with interns, residents, and nurses. One physician grabbed an endotracheal tube and a laryngoscope and proceeded to the head of the patient's bed. The nurse assistant director of the unit turned to the physician and said,

"Hello, I'm Jean Day, the assistant ICU director. I don't believe I know you."

"I'm Doctor John Marks," the physician replied.

"What specialty are you doing your residency in and how long have you been here?" Jean Day queried.

"I'm an OB-GYN intern," responded the physician.

What should the nurse do in this situation?

Do patients in our hospitals and other health care institutions need protection from health care provider errors? They probably do. Over the past 30 years, the health care error rate has been high but steady. Mistakes occur to as many as 45% of patients during their hospital admissions; and in 18% of patients, the errors result in serious complications ranging from temporary disabilities to death.[1] The longer the patient stays in the hospital, the more likely she or he is to be affected by a health care provider error. Only about one-third of the

> Of the 31 million patients admitted to hospitals annually, over 5 million will suffer an unexpected occurrence that will seriously harm them and 500,000 of them will die.

errors are reported in the medical record. Some are described in internal unexpected occurrence reports (also called incident reports), and some are not reported at all. Thus, studies that attempt to determine the extent of health care provider error by chart review are doomed to underestimate the extent of mistakes.

Unfortunately, many health care providers fail to inform anyone when they have committed an error. Without knowledge of the initial error, the subsequent health care can be inadequate and inappropriate, or health care errors can be compounded. One study found that most patients who had one initial error committed eventually had three additional errors committed as the situation worsened.[1] What can the nurse do to limit health care errors?

INFORMED DISCUSSION AND PEER PRESSURE

Nurses will encounter situations where they realize that other health care providers are not competent to provide care. What should the nurse do when she or he encounters such a situation? In the simplest situation, a nurse might identify a usually proficient peer who is unable to perform a particular procedure. The peer might have difficulty gaining intravenous (IV) access and make repeated attempts to start an IV on a patient. After several attempts, when it is apparent the patient is experiencing unnecessary discomfort, the nurse ought to suggest to her or his peer that an expert in IV insertion be called to attempt the procedure.

This is a simple case, since the patient has experienced only minor delays in therapy and some mild unnecessary discomfort. The nurse also does not have any concerns about the overall competence of her or his peer, only the peer's ability to perform this procedure at this time. Additionally, if the nurse is tactful in suggesting an expert, there is mini-

> When a nurse suspects a colleague is unable to perform a procedure, the nurse should:
> - Determine if the colleague has the capacity to perform the task
> - Discuss the situation privately with the colleague
> - Offer alternatives (assistance, alternate provider, and instruction) to the colleague

mal disruption in the relationship between the two professionals. In such a simple case, when the patient is not in danger of serious harm, the nurse might observe the behavior to be certain that the professional is not capable of competently performing the procedure. If the provider cannot intervene competently, the nurse ought to initiate a discussion and suggest an alternative way to complete the procedure.

The next approach uses informed discussion but also peer pressure to encourage the health care provider to deliver care competently. Nurses commonly use such an approach when they provide sterile gloves to a surgeon hurrying to change an abdominal wound dressing, or offer to complete the dressing change themselves after the surgeon has examined the wound. Some nurses argue that merely supplying the gloves to the surgeon perpetuates the nurse-doctor game. These nurses believe that a simple statement that sterile gloves are needed to change the dressing should accompany the presentation of the gloves.

Nurses can be caught in a difficult situation when they recognize a specific intervention would aid their patient, but the intervention requires a physician's order or physician compliance. This can be especially difficult if the physician does not believe the intervention is needed or has no desire to order the intervention. There are no ethical problems when a nurse directly describes her or his concerns to the physician and requests an intervention. However, some physicians become irritated, believing the nurse has overstepped her or his boundaries by suggesting medical interventions, and will refuse to respond to the nurse's suggestion. Thus begins

> The nurse-doctor game, where the nurse attempts to indirectly influence a physician to prescribe an intervention the nurse believes is in the patient's best interests, should be avoided.

the nurse-physician game, where nurses attempt to indirectly influence physicians to obtain interventions that they believe are in their patients' best interests.

Imagine a surgeon examining an abdominal wound that had been left open to heal by secondary intention when the patient developed peritonitis following a perforated bowel. After the surgeon examined the wound, he verbally directed the nurse to pack the wound with half-strength povidone-iodine solution, a practice he had followed for years. The nurse was aware that povidone-iodine, even in minute quantities, has been demonstrated to slow granulation and is harmful to a healing wound. How should the nurse respond?

The most direct, honest response would be for the nurse to explain the studies that she or he had read to the physician outside of the patient's hearing and request that they attempt packing the dressing with only saline-moistened gauze for a few days. However, as one nurse commented, this is not an easy option and may not be realistic for a new nurse. As a less appropriate choice, the nurse might also offer to provide the articles to the physician for her or his perusal, while continuing to pack the wound with half-strength povidone-iodine until the surgeon has read the articles. If the nurse believed any packing of the wound with povidone-iodine would cause substantial damage to the wound tissue, and the surgeon would not listen to the nurse's reasoning, she or he might notify the physician that she or he would not pack the wound with povidone-iodine. This approach is similar to conscientious refusal.

Indirect and deceitful actions, which perpetuate the nurse-doctor game, would be for the nurse to pretend she or he had misheard the surgeon and pack the dressing with a saline-soaked gauze. Or, the nurse may imply that the surgeon's partners usually employ another method of packing, would the surgeon like to choose that method? The most deceitful approach would be for the nurse to pack the wound with a saline-soaked dressing without informing the surgeon. Some nurses do practice such deceit when they consider the physician's order to be inappropriate or harmful to a patient. Is it ever justifiable to deceive a physician or patient to protect their best interests? In such a circumstance, the physician would probably continue to believe that her or his choice of intervention had been successful or at least not harmful and would therefore continue to prescribe a potentially harmful treatment. What if the nurse believed the procedure would cause the patient significant harm?

IS IT EVER JUSTIFIABLE TO REFUSE TO COMPLY WITH A PHYSICIAN'S ORDER OR TO PREVENT A PROCEDURE?

Conscientious Refusal

In Chapter 2, situations when a nurse might refuse to comply with a physician's directive because the nurse disagreed with the physician's or health care team's ethical reasoning were described. Conscientious refusal, the refusal to assist or proceed with an intervention, might also be utilized when a nurse believes that the planned intervention will result in significant medical harm to the patient. In this situation, the nurse refuses to participate in the intervention; but she or he does not actively prevent the procedure. However, there might also be situations in which the nurse believed that it was necessary to prevent a procedure.

Preventing a Procedure

There are situations that call for a rapid response, when it is not possible to offer the health care provider repeated explanations or several attempts to perform a procedure before identifying another professional who would be more capable of delivering the needed care. When Jean Day realized that a beginning OB-GYN intern was planning to attempt to intubate Mr. Raymond, a cardiac arrest patient, she gently took the laryngoscope and endotracheal tube from his hands, turned to the pulmonary resident standing in the doorway, and said, as she handed him the intubation equipment, "I'm sure Dr. Andrews would be glad to demonstrate the appropriate way to intubate a patient for you. He is one of the most proficient physicians I know, and I'm confident you could learn a lot from observing his technique."

Dr. Andrews quickly and competently intubated Mr. Raymond while the OB-GYN intern observed the procedure. If Jean Day had not intervened, it was unclear whether Dr. Andrews would have allowed the intern to attempt the intubation.

Benjamin and Curtis have argued that in urgent situations, nurses should comply with physicians' directives unless there is clear and convincing evidence that the directives will cause harm to the patient.[2] They base this conclusion on the principle that the physician is usually the expert in medical care. Therefore, they believe the physician's opinion ought to be followed, especially in situations that require immediate response. They argue that in less urgent situations, the nurse should approach the physician in private and explain why she or he disagreed with the chosen action, perhaps presenting an alternative choice, as the nurse might have done with the povidone-iodine-soaked dressing.

Nurse Jean Day did not have time to fully evaluate the skills of the intern. However, she could surmise, based on the time of the year and his current specialty, that his medical knowledge and skills were limited and the patient's health in jeopardy if his plan was followed. Even though this was an urgent situation, the nurse chose to prevent the intern from intubating and provided another, safer course of action. Was such a limited evaluation sufficient to determine that the intern was not yet an expert in medical care or should the nurse have complied with the intern's desire to intubate the patient? Does the urgency and severity of the situation mean that the nurse has more of an obligation to intervene and protect the patient or more of an obligation to yield to the physician's medical expertise as Benjamin and Curtis have suggested?

Preventing a procedure can be hazardous to the nurse's position in the institution, similar to the way in which conscientious refusal can be perilous. In the previous situation, Jean Day was a well-known and respected nurse with an administrative position. Her clinical skills and judgment were excellent, as were her interpersonal skills.

> The nurse might refuse to comply with a physician's directive she or he believed would be harmful to the patient.

She prevented an intern from attempting a procedure that he ought not to have been trying and was polite in the process. The ramifications to her were insignificant. In fact, the pulmonary resident thanked her for her intervention when the intern had departed.

However, there are times when a staff nurse might believe that a powerful physician or nurse colleague is preparing to perform a procedure that the staff nurse believes the person is incapable of performing. For example, one New Year's Eve in a large medical center, all of the interns, residents, and fellows began drinking at 11 PM. By midnight, when a postcoronary artery bypass patient developed an extremely rapid atrial dysrhythmia, the physicians, including the chief fellow, were drunk. The chief fellow wanted to defibrillate the patient, an inappropriate intervention, when all that was required was IV medication to control the dysrhythmia. The nurse found herself in the position of attempting to block the performance of the procedure without incurring the anger of the chief fellow. How should the nurse proceed?

Enlisting the Support of Other Health Care Providers

The nurse might want to enlist the support of other nurses, administrators, and physicians to prevent the proposed action. Sometimes, the overwhelming number of people who oppose an action will persuade the person not to attempt it. The ICU staff nurse was able to enlist the other nurse in the ICU and one of the medical residents to remove the defibrillator from the fellow's hands. The nurses and the medical resident next informed the fellow that they were administering the appropriate medication immediately.

In each of these situations, where nurses prevented physicians from performing procedures, the nurses had reason to believe that the physicians lacked the capacity to make an appropriate medical judgment. In the first circumstance the intern was inexperienced, and in the second the chief fellow had been drinking and was impaired. A nurse might also have reason to doubt a physician's capacity if he had made a series of errors in judgment in the past. Thus, nurses who intend to prevent a procedure should consider the physician's ability and medical judgment at the time of the procedure, in addition to the procedure's potential for patient harm. If there is adequate time, discussing the refusal with the physician and reporting the incompetent behavior along institution channels should coincide with the refusal to perform the procedure. However, in crisis situations, because of time constraints, the explanation and reporting often occur after the incident or the attempt to prevent the procedure.

> Nurses should consider preventing a procedure when:
> - The nurse has reason to believe the health care provider performing the procedure lacks the capacity to make an appropriate medical judgment or perform the procedure
> - The situation is urgent
> - The nurse is unable to discuss alternatives with the health care provider
> - The procedure is likely to result in significant harm to the patient

Reporting Along Appropriate Channels Within the Institution

Reporting along appropriate channels can be more productive than many nurses believe. The reporting may be of either health care errors or incompetent behavior. Without tracking health care errors through unexpected occurrence reports, it is difficult to identify problems within the institutional system that lead to errors. Adverse drug reactions have been reduced through the use of sophisticated computer programs that identify drug interactions. These computers were developed following an analysis of health care medication errors.

If health care errors are not reported, then they cannot be rectified; and as previously noted, the harm to the patient can be compounded. For example, one day a student nurse was finishing a report to a per diem evening nurse when the tube feeding supplement and enteral feeding pump arrived for the start of a patient's nasogastric tube feedings. The patient, a 16-year-old, had his jaw wired the previous day, following a motor vehicle accident. He also had a fracture of his left femur that was in a cast, and a mild concussion, which left him lethargic and disoriented. The evening nurse started the feeding at 50 mL per hour while the student completed her charting. After finishing her charting, the student nurse entered the patient's room to discover that the enteral feeding pump had been incorrectly threaded and the patient had received 900 mL of tube feeding in 15 minutes. The student discontinued the feeding and immediately notified the evening nurse of the error.

> Reporting unexpected occurrences along appropriate channels allows tracking of health care errors and permits the institution to recognize and rectify problems within the patient care delivery system.

The per diem evening nurse was distressed. She stated she would clamp the nasogastric tube and allow the patient to digest the tube feeding over the entire shift. However, she had no intention of informing the physician of the error or completing an unexpected occurrence report. The student nurse left the unit and arrived at her post-clinical conference distraught, believing that something else ought to be done. What should she do?

If the student allowed the evening nurse to take no further action, she would be contributing to any subsequent iatrogenic illnesses that the patient might develop. By allowing the nurse to avoid reporting the incident to the physician, the student also would be preventing other health care providers from remedying the error. This patient had taken nothing by mouth (NPO) before the tube feeding began. The amount of tube feeding that had run in was substantial, a larger than normal amount of a bolus tube feeding for a 16-year-old of his size and weight. Worse, this patient was only supposed to be beginning tube feedings at 50 mL per hour. In addition, the patient's jaw was wired and he was lethargic. If he began to vomit, he might be unable to protect his airway and aspirate. Thus, the potential for harm to the patient was substantial if corrective action was not taken. The student considered the consequences and realized that the potential for harm to the patient was more serious than any problems the per diem nurse or she might encounter by reporting the error.

The student and her instructor returned to the clinical unit. They informed the evening nurse of their deliberations and asked her if she would prefer to notify the physician and complete the unexpected occurrence report herself or if she would prefer

> Failure to report an error can result in the error being compounded.

they did it. The per diem nurse insisted an unexpected occurrence report would not need to be filled out, that she would personally assure the patient was all right and would not aspirate. What should the instructor and student do?

Without unexpected occurrence reports, it is more difficult to track defects in equipment and to observe patterns in employee behavior. The student nurse and instructor decided to initiate the unexpected occurrence report and began the procedure by notifying the physician and unit director. The physician requested the patient's nasogastric tube be reconnected to low continuous suction to lessen the possibilities of vomiting and aspiration. In the following year, risk management noted a pattern of recurrent problems with nurses incorrectly threading this brand of enteral nutrition pump and recommended purchasing a different brand.

Unfortunately, the per diem nurse had a history of errors. The reason she had been so insistent about not reporting this error was that she had been informed that further errors would result in her being placed on probation. Because this error could have resulted in serious complications for the patient, but more importantly because she had attempted to cover up the error despite the potential harm to the patient, she was placed on temporary suspension.

Reporting along appropriate channels can be an effective method of dealing with incompetent health care providers. Some nurses become impatient because the incompetent provider usually continues to practice while the process is occurring and nurses worry that additional patients' health is being jeopardized. Still, when nurses join with physician colleagues to report incompetent providers' behaviors, it can result in the following actions: suspension of the per diem nurse, removal of a surgeon from the trauma team of an institution, an oncologist being asked to leave a group practice, a nurse manager being asked to resign his position, and revoking a surgeon's hospital privileges. While preventing a procedure protects current patients, reporting incompetent practitioners to the appropriate authority protects future patients.

Nurses may also need to act beneficently and protect patients from errors that can occur from unsafe working conditions. The nurse's first response to unsafe working conditions, such as unacceptable staffing levels, should be to report the condition along the appropriate institutional channels. When a nurse is forced to deliver substandard care because of poor staffing, she or he is still legally and morally responsible for the care that she or he delivers. Thus, it is in the nurse's, as well as the patient's, best interests to obtain adequate staffing. Documenting complaints of staffing shortage along the appropriate channels is important, as is assuring that unexpected occurrence reports are filed for all errors that occur because of understaffing.

Prevarication

Are there any situations when a nurse ought not to complete an unexpected occurrence report or report an error? Should a nurse or physician ever lie to an insurer about a patient's condition? Some nurses argue that in an unjust system, lying or failing to disclose health care errors is acceptable. These nurses state that most health care providers make small errors but few report the errors, believing they are insignificant. For example, Jamie Green, a nurse, hung an IV of D_5NS instead of D_5 ½ NS, and the patient received 200 mL of IV fluid. There were no problems with the patient's electrolyte or fluid balance. Should Ms. Green complete an unexpected occurrence report?

Many staff nurses would decline to write the report because they would fear that several small, accumulated errors that did not harm their patients might significantly hurt their careers. Since their error rate would look higher than the rates of other nurses, they fear they might be denied a promotion, placed on probation, or suspended as was the per diem nurse. They might also suggest that filling out unexpected occurrence reports is time consuming and subtracts further from the time available for nursing care. The nurses might announce that phoning the physician over insignificant errors, which is required by the unexpected occurrence report, often annoys physicians. The nurses might insist that the error was in part due to understaffing and the institution was to blame. Finally, they might declare that many errors are in part due to other departments within the institution like pharmacy or supply services. Jamie Green's error happened because a stocking room worker had placed D_5NS in the bin reserved for D_5 ½ NS. Ms. Green had taken the IV from the appropriate bin but while hurrying had not noted she was carrying the incorrect solution. The error was clearly hers, because she should to have rechecked the IV solution. However, it is not solely her mistake.

Suppose Ms. Green is a single mother who is supporting her two sons with her income alone. This error would be her third insignificant one in 6 months and would result in her being placed on probation. Should she report the error? Would it make a difference if the nursing administration had a policy of working with nurses to identify patterns of errors and correct them rather than a policy that stated that after three errors a nurse was on probation and after the fourth she or he was suspended? How many errors should a nurse be allowed to make? How much education and assistance should a nurse who has committed several errors be allowed to receive

> Nurses might choose not to fill out unexpected occurrence reports because:
> - The minor errors might not have any effect on the patient
> - By reporting minor errors, they might appear less competent
> - Filling out reports is time consuming
> - Physicians do not appreciate being informed of minor errors
> - The error might be due to institutional problems

before she or he is placed on probation or suspended? What approaches are in the best interests of the patient? Should the nurse's best interests also be a consideration?

Proponents of telling the truth and reporting all errors maintain that only when all errors are reported is it possible to identify problems and propose new approaches. Once errors in stocking are uncovered, the bins might be checked more carefully before carts are transported to the floor and stocking efficiency improved. Some institutions have discovered that the majority of their errors were due to the illegibility of physicians' handwriting and ward clerks attempting to transcribe illegible orders. They developed systems in which physicians entered their orders directly into the hospital computer. Other institutions now use a pharmacy computer to check all medication orders for patients to detect any drug interactions or contraindications. If errors are not reported, problems may not be identified and new approaches may not be attempted.

Proponents of telling the truth also wonder who ought to decide when an error is insignificant and does not require an unexpected occurrence report. Certainly, the per diem nurse did not believe her error with the tube feeding was significant, yet all the other members of

> Proponents of reporting all errors argue that only when all errors are reported can the institution accurately identify problems and rectify them.

the health care team did. Proponents of truth telling believe that health care providers ought to report all errors to the institution, the physician, and even to the patient. However, until the system becomes more truthful, many health care providers will continue to ask the question: Why should health care providers tell the truth and admit mistakes in a system that punishes truth telling and rewards keeping quiet?

Nurses who are thinking about reporting an error might want to consider the following questions:
- Are current or future patients likely to be harmed if she or he fails to disclose the truth?
- Will failing to disclose this error lead to additional errors for this patient or other patients?
- Could a recurrent problem be rectified if she or he reports this error?

- What are her or his personal interests in the situation and is she or he making an egoist decision if she or he fails to report the error?
- Does she or he believe that it is important to be known as a person who is truthful?

Jon Allen was a patient with severe bone marrow depression. His physician was wavering between a diagnosis of aplastic anemia and myelodysplastic disease. Several hematologists suggested Jon's physician should not attempt to determine his actual diagnosis but should inform the insurance company and state that Jon had aplastic anemia. The insurance company would only cover a bone marrow transplant for aplastic anemia, and the hematologists believed that denying bone marrow transplant for myelodysplastic disease was unjust. They argued that since the treatment for both diseases was the same, the insurance company would have no way to determine whether Mr. Allen was being treated for aplastic anemia or myelodysplastic disease and it would need to fund the care. Such a lie would allow an immediate bone marrow transplant for a severely ill patient. Furthermore, the other physicians believed if the hematologist persisted in obtaining an accurate diagnosis and it was determined Jon had myelodysplastic disease, Jon would be forced to wait until the appeal to his insurer was completed. With Jon's platelet count at 7000, he could bleed spontaneously at any time and could die during the appeal process.

Jon's physician believed that a policy of lying was shortsighted. He believed that although bone marrow transplant was indicated for the treatment of both conditions, there were variations in the procedure that were more appropriate for one or the other of the diseases. He was also concerned for future patients and believed if he argued for a bone marrow transplant for myelodysplastic disease for Jon, he would be better able to provide transplants for those patients in the future. Both for the benefit of providing the best possible treatment for Jon as well as for the benefit of his future patients, Jon's hematologist requested an opinion from several other specialists across the country. While awaiting their response, the hematologist began preparation of an appeal of the insurer's denial of the transplant in the event Jon did have myelodysplastic disease. No appeal was ever necessary. The other specialists concurred that Jon most likely suffered from aplastic anemia. Should the hematologist have lied to expedite Jon's treatment?

Nurses may also encounter situations in which they are asked to mislead insurers. In order to obtain home-health services, a client must be designated as homebound. Clients who are very ill often confront home-health nurses and need home-health care, yet benefit immensely from going to church services on Sunday or playing cards with friends. The nurse might believe the homebound rule is unjust since several studies suggest that regular socialization enhances the quality of life for homebound patients as much as medications. Still, leaving their homes for such activities makes the clients ineligible for home-health care. If the

> Some health care providers argue that it is acceptable to lie or mislead insurers to obtain necessary services for patients from an unjust health care system.

home-health nurse knows that her or his client is leaving the home for brief periods, should the nurse inform the insurer? Should the nurse warn the client she or he suspects the client is not homebound and she or he will need to report the client to the insurer if trips outside the home continue? Or should the home health nurse look the other way, continuing to provide services to clients she or he suspects are not completely homebound because the system is unjust?

The last option is becoming increasingly more hazardous to the home-care agency since the federal government radically changed the way that Medicare pays for home-health services and the ways in which home-health agencies are being evaluated. Home-health agencies that the federal government determines engage in fraud are being severely punished. However, what constitutes fraud can be controversial. Allowing a client to receive home-health services when the client is not homebound is considered fraud and can cost a home-health agency as much as $30,000 per occurrence.[3]

What should a nurse do when she or he believes a client would benefit from socialization outside the home? Act beneficently toward the client and jeopardize her or his agency? Force the patient to make an autonomous choice between two competing goods—home-health care and socialization? Or, should the nurse work for changes in the homebound requirement for home-health care, essentially appealing the process that denies care to the client as the hematologist was willing to do if Jon Allen had been diagnosed with myelodysplastic disease?

Whistle-Blowing

A large southern medical center had an eight-bed step-down unit for patients requiring mechanical ventilation. The patients in the unit were too complex to be cared for on a routine medical surgical unit but were medically stable. This unit was usually staffed with two RNs, but at least once or twice a week was staffed with one RN and an aide. A respiratory therapist was available for assistance but was also covering an adjacent unit. The RNs assigned to the step-down unit were convinced that the unit was purposefully and dangerously understaffed. There were several instances when the only RN in the unit was unable to respond to patients who had become disconnected from their ventilators for several minutes because she or he was responding to another patient's urgent needs. The nurses were afraid that eventually a patient would die because no one was available to evaluate a ventilator alarm. The nurses reported their concerns to the nursing and hospital administration. They also completed unexpected occurrence reports on the occasions when patients were disconnected from mechanical ventilation.

After each of their reports of short staffing, the nursing and hospital administration agreed to provide at least two RNs to staff the unit at all times. Still, the short staffing continued. The nurses, weary of unfulfilled promises, decided that they could not improve staffing through hospital channels and brought their concerns and documentation of the short staffing to the local newspaper. A reporter interviewed several of the nurses, collected confirmation of their complaints, and informed them a story would be printed the following day. That night the nurses were unable to sleep. They drove about the city, agonizing about the consequences of their whistle-blowing to themselves and to the medical center.

As soon as the newspaper was available, the nurses searched the headlines, believing their allegations would be on the front page. The story consisted of a paragraph buried on the 14th page of the paper. When they contacted the reporter later, he informed them the editors did not believe their allegations were of major news interest. The nurses wondered if the medical center had intervened to protect its interests but were unable to validate their concerns. Although the nurses were worried about retaliation, there were no obvious repercussions. Over the following year, they all left the step-down unit, most leaving the medical center and community completely. The short staffing on the unit continued.

Whistle-blowing, notifying an outside agency or organization, may be considered when available avenues for reporting unsafe, illegal, or incompetent behavior within the institution have been exhausted. Before considering whistle-blowing, nurses must be convinced that there exists a clear, grave danger to their patients or themselves. Whistle-blowing should not be used for trivial, insubstantial issues. Rather, it should be reserved for situations in which there is reason to believe that substantial harm could occur to current and future patients. Nurses should have personal involvement and objective documentation of the dangers they are considering reporting. Reports based on hearsay and rumors are inaccurate, misleading, and disruptive.

Whistle-blowers may also be concerned about danger to themselves if the unsafe situation continues. The nurses in the step-down unit were held liable for the nursing errors that resulted from short staffing. They were afraid that they might be placed on probation, suspended, lose their licensees, or be sued because of errors related to the unsafe short-staffing practices. The nurses in the step-down unit had accumulated several folders of reports of incidents that documented nursing and respiratory therapy errors due to short staffing. Several of the errors had resulted in harm to patients. The nurses were apprehensive that if the pattern continued, a patient death would result.

Before considering external appeal to an outside agency, the nurse should be convinced that all internal channels for rectification have been exhausted. When nurses believe they are practicing in an unsafe environment, the internal channels for correction of the problem can appear to be excruciatingly slow.

> Nurses might consider whistle-blowing if:
> - A grave danger to their current patient or themselves exists
> - All other avenues of recourse have been exhausted
> - The person or agency is engaging in unsafe, unethical, or illegal behavior

However, they can also be very effective. Most authorities recommend reporting internally first because internal reporting is most likely to correct the problem and least likely to destabilize the situation. With internal reporting, there is less disruption in the health care team. Health care teams and institutions function most effectively when there is a sense of loyalty among the members. Whistle-blowing can disturb the sense of trust and loyalty among team members and have a negative impact on patient care. Few of us are perfect in all of our interventions. Who would want to work in an environment where she or he was constantly worried that any of her or his actions might be reported to an outside authority without her or his knowledge? The nurses in the step-down unit no longer trusted either the nursing or hospital administration. By failing to correct the staffing problem after agreeing to do so, the administration had belied the nurses' trust.

Only when there has been clear evidence that the internal process has failed should nurses consider whistle-blowing. The nurses in the step-down unit had already reported along appropriate channels. In fact, both hospital and nursing administration had agreed to improve staffing; it was only when the short-staffing continued several months after their agreement that the nurses considered whistle-blowing.

When considering whistle-blowing, nurses should identify the expected consequences of their action. Do they anticipate that an incompetent practitioner will be removed from staff? Do they hope that unacceptable policies or inadequate staffing patterns will be reviewed and revised? Without a clear goal, it is difficult to determine if the whistle-blowing has accomplished its purpose. The whistle-blowing nurses in the step-down unit wanted to have two RNs assigned and present in the step-down unit each shift.

Nurses considering whistle-blowing should also review their motivation for advocating an appeal to an outside authority, especially the media. They should be certain that they do not have impure motives, such as a grudge, against an individual or institution, or a desire for media attention. For example, a particular nurse might accuse a physician of incompetence because she or he resented the physician. Perhaps the nurse had been repeatedly embarrassed in front of peers and patients by derogatory remarks made by the physician. Retaliation is not an acceptable rationale for whistle-blowing. Nor is personal gain from media celebrity an acceptable reason to consider whistle-blowing. Some people, enticed by the notoriety from media exposure, might be motivated to inflate errors and whistle-blow. There was no reason to suspect the motives of the nurses in the step-down unit.

Finally, nurses considering whistle-blowing should consider the personal risk such an action might entail. Although whistle-blowing is protected under the law, laws cannot protect a nurse from subtle social ostracism by her or his peers and co-workers. If the nurse has implicated a well-known individual or institution in wrongdoing, supporters and friends of the individual or institution may blame the nurse for any problems that develop. When community members or peers use subtle discrimination, life can be made difficult for whistle-blowers. The nurse may eventually desire to leave the institution and community, just as the step-down unit nurses did, without ever being overtly punished for whistle-blowing.

> Nurses need to consider the repercussions of their actions on their personal and professional relationships before proceeding to blow the whistle.

Since whistle-blowing may be fraught with hazards for all those involved, a nurse might want to consider the following questions before proceeding:

- Do I have a legitimate concern? If the situation is uncorrected, will it result in grave danger to present and future health care providers, patients, or the community?
- Why am I involved in this situation? Do I need to be?
- Have I reported my concerns along the appropriate channels within the institution?
- Have I exhausted my avenues for redress within the institution?
- What do I envision will be the result of my action? Is it a worthwhile goal?
- Am I likely to accomplish my purpose?
- What are my motivations for reporting this activity to an outside authority?
- Are there any reasons why someone might distrust the purity of my motives?
- What are the likely personal consequences if I engage in whistle-blowing?

The step-down nurses did indeed have a legitimate concern about short-staffing, which they believed was already resulting in nursing errors and patient harm. They were directly involved in the situation and believed that if they were to continue to be employed in the unit, they needed to improve the conditions for patient care. They had already exhausted all avenues within the institution without any change in the unsafe staffing patterns. They wanted to increase staffing to a minimum of two RNs per shift and believed this was a reasonable, realistic, safe goal. The nurses' motivation for reporting the staffing problem was frustration at the institution for not correcting the problem and notification of the public of the unsafe situation.

Three years after the whistle-blowing, one of the nurses still felt victimized by the entire process. She stated that the nurses had been immensely concerned about safety issues and had worked for months to improve the situation through hospital channels. During that time, they had continued to provide nursing care to patients with multiple needs in very disturbing circumstances. They had agonized about the decision to notify the newspaper. They feared that current as well as future patients of the institution would worry about their safety during their hospitalizations. The nurses blew the whistle because they believed that once knowledge of the unsafe practices became widespread, the hospital would be forced to increase staffing.

After all their hard work, both in caring for patients as well as amassing data and notifying the media, being told that their concerns were not significant or newsworthy by the newspaper reporter was like being slapped in the face. They believed that the newspaper would be the first to print a story if a patient had died because of short-staffing. But no one was interested in the nurses' struggles to provide care to patients against huge odds.

When asked if she would consider whistle-blowing in the same situation again, the nurse believed she would not. She doubted the action had benefited anyone. The staffing had remained the same, at least for the year she remained employed at the institution, and patients were still subjected to unsafe conditions. She had heard rumors of a patient death due to short-staffing the following year, but since no one she knew still worked on the unit, she was unable to verify the story. The nurses had suffered through the process of notifying the media, and they were reluctant to trust media or hospital and nursing administrations. All of the whistle-blowing nurses had relocated to communities away from the medical center. A few of the women had left nursing.

The decision to blow the whistle should never be made lightly. Whistle-blowing ought to be reserved for circumstances when the nurse has encountered gross negligence or incompetence, has exhausted all internal channels for remediation, recognizes that there may be social ostracism for her or his action, and believes that good can be accomplished by publicizing the problem.

Collective Action or Striking

Nurses in a northeastern, urban medical center approached their state's nurses association because they were considering the formation of a bargaining unit. The nurses at the institution were concerned about several issues: their salaries, their work schedule, and shift rotation. Their salaries were somewhat below others in the metropolitan area. The nurses had every third weekend off rather than every other weekend and were required to work a 7-day stretch before the weekend. They were also required to rotate for 6 weeks at a time to evening or night shifts. As soon as the hospital administration realized that the nurses were in earnest, they offered the nursing staff a substantial raise and decreased the duration of shift rotation to 4 weeks at a time. Talk of formation of a bargaining unit and collective bargaining ceased at that institution.

Within months of the nurses' discussion of collective bargaining at the medical center, the hospital workers' union did call a strike. After filing the necessary notice, all licensed practical nurses (LPNs), aides, unit clerks, and admission clerks at selected institutions in the metropolitan area went on strike. On the first day of the strike, picketing hospital workers blocked an ambulance from transporting a very sick patient to the hospital. There were rumors, none substantiated, that the oxygen supply to the institution was going to be sabotaged. On the third day of the strike, the picketers misidentified one RN as a LPN scab who was crossing the picket line. The picketers threw stones at her, sending her to the emergency department for treatment.

Inside the medical center, many elective procedures were postponed. Patients were discharged if possible or transferred to facilities outside the metropolitan area. Administrators and physicians assisted with patient care, and nursing staff worked overtime. The strike was short-lived, and at this facility no patients appeared to suffer. In fact, a few nurses commented it was nice to have the hospital administrators rediscover what it was like to deliver patient care.

After 4 days, the striking workers and administration agreed on a settlement, and the strikers returned to work. These former strikers now had to work with the people whom they had jeered (or stoned) as they entered the building as if nothing had happened. They were soon providing care to the same person whose ambulance they had attempted to prevent from entering the hospital grounds.

When the American Nurses Association (ANA) initially established its economic security program, it purposefully prohibited collective action, thus relinquishing the right to strike. The ANA believed that by behaving responsibly and voluntarily giving up the right to strike, nurses would be demonstrating their good faith to hospital administrators.[4] Therefore, the ANA anticipated that state nurses associations would be able to bargain collectively with hospital administrators and establish minimum employment standards for nurses. Twenty years later, it was clear that the policy was not working. Nurses were underpaid in comparison to other workers and were dissatisfied with their benefits. Worse, conditions in American hospitals and quality of care were deteriorating, and nurses were reconsidering their decision to enter the profession. The ANA finally rescinded the no-strike policy in 1968.

Since then, the Code for Nurses, with interpretive statements, has supported the nurses' right to collective action by stating that "Nurses should support the profession's efforts to establish and maintain conditions of employment that are conducive to high quality nursing care." In the interpretive statements, nurses' right to participate in collective bargaining consistent with appropriate labor law is established. This statement implies the ANA supports nurses' right to strike since that has been established under current labor laws.[5]

For nurses employed in most institutions, the legal right to strike was established when the National Labor Relations Act of 1974 extended the right of collective bargaining and action to non supervisory personnel in all health care facilities. The act also mandated special dispute-settling procedures and longer notice of any intent to change the bargaining agreement than for other industries. Finally, it mandated a 10-day notice of intent to picket or strike, so that provisions could be made for patient care.

Although critics feared that the act would open a floodgate of nursing strikes, it did not. When nurses initially obtained the right to strike, issues including ones similar to the issues of the nurses in the situation described above were the most common ones: long hours, understaffing, poor working conditions, and low pay. Now, nurses are more likely to strike for what they perceive as deficiencies in the health care system. For example, in 1994, nurses in Michigan protested a restructuring plan at their institution that they feared would have a negative impact on quality of patient care. In Canada, nurses have focused on securing ways to protest operational deficiencies within institutions. Strikes by nurses are not common. During the mid 1990s, there were between 6 and 12 strikes at health care institutions in the United States each year, ranging from 1 to 187 days, not all of which involved nurses.[6]

Although nurses have established their legal right to strike, some experts contend that they do not have an ethical right to strike. These individuals believe, as the ANA did in the early years of its Economic Security Program, that collective bargaining alone should be sufficient to assure reasonable economic protection for nurses. They cite examples, such as the situation described previously when the threat of nurses engaging in collective bargaining was sufficient for the medical center to offer the nurses a more attractive package. These critics believe that no circumstance would warrant nurses striking and leaving patients without adequate nursing care.

Supporters of collective action, picketing, and striking for nurses state that it is not collective bargaining that moves the institution to negotiate with nurses, it is the implied threat of collective action. They emphasize that during the early years of the ANA's Economic Security Program, when the ANA advocated collective bargaining but renounced the use of collective action, institutions did not bargain in good faith with nurses. They believe that actual strikes may not be needed, but the threat of a strike is what forces institutions to bargain in good faith.

Critics argue that one cannot threaten to strike if one is not prepared to carry through with the actual strike. They believe that no current or future condition in a health care institution would warrant putting patients' safety in jeopardy. During strikes, even in the best of situations, they contend staff are stretched thin and overworked. Nurses who staff institutions during a strike have described the situation like an "aneurysm waiting to blow." "It was just threatening all the time like a time bomb. We just tried not to think about it."[7] Nurses who continue to provide patient care during strikes worry about the exhausting pace of work in short-staffed units day after day with no end in sight. They fear that as short staffing continues and they become more and more exhausted that they

> Reasons nurses should not strike:
> - Current patient safety may be jeopardized
> - Nonstriking staff may be overburdened
> - Substitute staff may not be competent
> - Media may portray nurses unfavorably
> - Strikers may cause damage to the facility
> - Strikes may damage relationships between co-workers

could make a serious and irreparable error. When substitute nurses are provided, perhaps nurses from differing units or administrative positions, staff nurses may be unable to depend on the substitutes to deliver care competently in their temporary positions. Thus, the staff nurses may need to constantly verify the assessments or interventions of nurses who were not qualified to deliver care. Critics of strikes believe that placing current patients in such potentially harmful predicaments cannot be justified by a concern for the welfare of future patients or the quality of nursing care.

Proponents of strikes and collective action argue that the 10-day period of notice should be sufficient to develop plans for care of the institution's patients. In that time, elective procedures may be delayed, and patients may be discharged or transferred to other institutions, as in the situation described previously. Once it becomes clear how many patients will remain in the institution, the bargaining unit should meet with the institution to determine how many of its nurses would be needed to cross picket lines to deliver care safely to the remaining patients. Thus, proponents of strikes believe that it is possible to protect the safety of present patients during a strike, while promoting the interests of nurses as well as future patients by striking for higher quality nursing care. Opponents of strikes argue that even the most carefully planned action may have unintended consequences. Nurses at one institution had filed their plan to strike and the hospital had decreased the number of patients in the institution just as flu season began. The number of ill patients increased rapidly while the number of available, nonstriking nurses dropped because of the flu. Short staffing in the institution was pronounced. Not only were patients in jeopardy, which the nurses had not intended, but the hospital notified the media and succeeded in portraying the nurses as heartless and greedy, avoiding their responsibility to care for the public during a flu epidemic.

During the duration of a strike, the strikers as well as the nurses who continue to work usually suffer hardships. The nurses who continue to work encounter staff shortages at the least, and if they are crossing a picket line, they may experience guilt, anger, or discrimination, as the RN who crossed the health care workers' picket line did when she was stoned. The nurses who picket or strike will suffer lost wages. They may be portrayed by the institution as heartless and uncaring or whiners and complainers. They must be prepared to counter such an image in the media and among their nonstriking peers.

Striking nurses may have to fight to continue what they believe is a fair strike. Nurses at one hospital found they "had to take control of their own strike." A local labor union was offering to help by shutting down the hospital, overturning a bus of scab nurses, and torching a car.[8] In the hospital workers' union strike example, an ambulance was initially prevented from entering the medical center, and there were rumors of sabotaging the oxygen system. Although no one was harmed and the oxygen had not been tampered with, it caused considerable expense to the hospital and inconvenience for nonstriking health care providers. Oxygen canisters had to be imported and used throughout the hospital until it could be ascertained that there had been no damage to the oxygen supply.

Following a strike, it can take some time before emotions have calmed completely and strikers and nonstriking workers can work together cooperatively again. The nurse who had the stones thrown at her during the strike had seen a ward clerk from her unit standing among the picketers who were throwing stones.

> Reasons nurses should strike:
> - Ten-day strike notice should ensure patient safety
> - One way to improve patient care and assure the safety of future patients
> - Improvement in nurses' working conditions
> - Empowerment of striking nurses

Though the nurse believed she had a good relationship with the ward clerk previously, the clerk never told the stone throwers the nurse was a RN, not a LPN scab. When the ward clerk returned to work, she was embarrassed to be in the RN's presence for several days. Finally, she explained that she was afraid of what the other picketers would have done to her if she had risen to the RN's defense. The ward clerk expected that the RN, who had been physically bruised and emotionally troubled by the stoning, would understand and forgive her immediately.

The ward clerk's and RN's relationship, like many others damaged by the strike, could not be repaired so easily or quickly. If the strike has been a difficult one, relationships between the bargaining unit and the administration of the institution may also take a while to improve. If there has been name calling by the administration, if strikers have revealed problems within the institution to the community, or if strikers have resorted to dirty tricks like threatening to sabotage the oxygen supply, it may take some time for the two sides to trust each other again. If the strike has been unusually bitter, it may also have an impact on future negotiations.

Nurses ought to consider carefully before committing to any collective action, particularly a strike. Questions that a nurse might want to answer before joining a strike include:

- Is there a sufficient cause for this strike?
- Is the quality of patient care or reimbursement for nursing services so poor that a strike would be the most effective way to improve them?
- Have all provisions of the collective bargaining agreement been maintained?
- Have all alternatives to a strike been attempted and found ineffective?
- Have all provisions of the law been met and is this a legally defensible strike?
- Have provisions been made to maintain safe patient care during the strike?
- Are there any damages that might occur as the result of a strike?
- How will this strike affect my family and me?
- Can I afford financially, physically, emotionally, and ethically to strike?

Nurses who have lived through a strike are often reshaped by their experience. Some female nurses have stated that during the strike, they developed from girls into women. They became empowered and would never again accept substandard compensation for nurses or inadequate nursing care for patients.[8] Nurses who worked during a strike have commented on the camaraderie that developed as all health care providers attempted to make due in difficult circumstances. They have spoken of their disappointment that strikers could endanger vulnerable patients for personal gain. For most nurses, the question becomes how dangerous or unacceptable a condition must exist for nurses to strike? Nurses must weigh the potential harm to current patients, the disruption of trust within the institution, and the potential for personal damages against the possibility for an improvement in unsatisfactory or dangerous working conditions and patient care.

The nurses in the initial situation were very fortunate they were never required to organize, never mind threaten collective action. The mere hint of a union caused the medical center to improve the nurses' working conditions. Perhaps that is what most nurses hope for—that the institution they are employed by will be coerced by the threat of unionization or collective action to recognize their patients' needs and worth, and respond by creating an acceptable employment and patient care environment.

REFERENCES

1. Gross ML. *The Medical Racket: How Doctors, HMOs, and Hospitals are Failing the American Patient.* New York, NY: Avon Books; 1998:60.
2. Benjamin M, Curtis J. *Ethics in Nursing.* 3rd ed. New York, NY: Oxford Press; 1998:98-102.
3. Carroll AJ. Home health care: the winter of our discontent. *Bay State Nurse News.* 1999;7:1,7.
4. Grando VT. The ANA's economic security program: the first twenty years. *Nurs Res.* 1997; 46:111-115.
5. American Nurses Association. *Code for Nurses.* Kansas City, MO: American Nurses Association; 1997.
6. Ketter J. Nurses and strikes: a perspective from the United States. *Nursing Ethics.* 1997;4:322-329.
7. Hibbard JM, Norris J. Striving for safety: experiences of nurses in a hospital under siege. *J Adv Nurs.* 1992;17:487-495.
8. Chipman D. Strike. *Revolution: The Journal of Nursing Empowerment.* 1993;Winter:24-25,80-84.

MULTIPLE-CHOICE QUESTIONS

1. What percentage of patients has health care errors during hospital admission resulted in serious complications?
    A.   3%
    B.   12%
    C.   18%
    D.   24%
    E.   30%

2. What is an appropriate first step when a nurse is concerned that a colleague is not competent to perform a particular procedure?
    A.   Conscientious refusal to assist the colleague with the procedure
    B.   Informed discussion with the colleague about how to perform the procedure
    C.   Initiation of an unexpected occurrence form
    D.   Prevention of the procedure
    E.   Reporting the incompetence along institutional channels

3. In which of the following situations might whistle-blowing be appropriate:
    A.   If the nurse hears repeated rumors of illegal or incompetent behavior
    B.   Prior to attempting to rectify the situation through internal channels at the institution
    C.   When there exists a clear, grave danger to patients
    D.   All of the above
    E.   None of the above

4. Why did the American Nurses Association rescind its no strike policy in 1968?
    A.   Conditions and quality of care in American hospitals were deteriorating
    B.   Nurses were leaving the profession
    C.   Nurses were underpaid in comparison with other health care workers
    D.   All of the above
    E.   None of the above

CHAPTER 6 ANSWERS

1. C
2. B
3. C
4. D

Ethical Issues at the End of Life

Kathleen Ouimet Perrin, RN, CCRN, PhD(c)

WHEN IS A PERSON DYING?

Mrs. Eva Boucher was an 89-year-old widow who had resided for 2 years in a long-term care facility. During those years, she had had recurrent strokes. Her left side had become progressively weaker, and she could barely move her arm. She had a pronounced left-sided facial droop and required careful feeding and observation so that she did not pocket or aspirate her food. She rarely spoke and was often incontinent of urine. Her deterioration from an active, talkative 87-year-old was pronounced, and her family mourned the vivacious woman she had been.

Mrs. Boucher's daughter was concerned because her mother was eating less each week and had lost 10 pounds, a significant amount for a 4-foot 9-inch woman. One afternoon, the daughter had finished feeding her mother lunch and was considering whether she ought to request her mother be started on tube feedings, or allow her mother to eat what she desired and perhaps slowly fade away. Mrs. Boucher was napping peacefully while her daughter sat beside her, fingering rosary beads. The daughter was remembering years earlier when she had also sat peacefully in the sun saying the rosary as her grandmother lay dying. Without warning, Mrs. Boucher's loud, clear voice interrupted her thoughts.

"What do you think you're doing? I'm NOT dying yet."

It can be difficult to determine when a person is dying. Chronic illnesses such as multiple strokes, degenerative neurologic conditions, cancer, coronary artery disease, heart failure, or chronic lung disease can result in slow deterioration of health over a long period of time. Patients often develop acute illnesses, such as pneumonia, which worsen their underlying heart failure or pulmonary disease. Some patients recover from the acute illness with minimal medical interventions, such as antibiotics; some recover following aggressive treatment, such as ventilators, and some patients die with or without medical intervention. A patient with multiple chronic illnesses may have several episodes of acute illness during the long period of slow deterioration of health that precedes eventual death.

When had Mrs. Boucher started to die? Was it when she suffered her first stroke and her left side became weaker so that she was no longer able to dress herself? When after several small cere-bral infarcts, she developed multi-infarct dementia? When she could no longer eat and swal-low well and need-ed to be fed and

> The miracles of modern medicine make it difficult to identi-fy and determine when a person is actually dying. Often, a long period of deterioration punctuated by episodes of acute illness, any one of which might lead to death, precedes the actual death.

observed for aspiration? When she started eating less? When she stopped speaking? When her heart failure worsened? When she fell while transferring to the commode, broke her collarbone, and refused to stand or walk any more? Each of these incidents was a step in her steady decline toward her eventual death. However, it is not clear at what point in the several-year period one could say she was obviously dying.

GOALS OF CARE AT THE END OF LIFE

When patients are deteriorating and may be dying, whether in long-term care, home care, or hospital settings, it is important to identify the goal of care and determine what interventions are appropriate to meet that goal. As Mrs. Boucher became incapacitated, the nurses in the long-term care facility asked her daughter to identify the goal of her mother's care and decide which interventions should be instituted should Mrs. Boucher become acutely ill. The health care providers and Mrs. Boucher's daughter concurred that the goal should promote comfort and quality at the end of life, rather than prolong Mrs. Boucher's life. The interventions were then considered at three levels:

1. What should occur if the patient died (cardiac arrested)? Should an attempt be made to resuscitate her?

2. What should happen if the patient developed an acute illness, such as pneumonia? How aggressively should she be treated, and should she be transferred to an acute care facility?

3. If the patient should stop eating, should she be force fed, supplied artificial nutri-tion, or receive gentle spoon-feeding?

When the nurses explained that few patients in long-term care survive cardiac arrest, the daughter easily determined that CPR for cardiac arrest would be excessive treatment. However, she had difficulty deciding whether she believed her mother should be trans-ferred to an acute care facility should she have an exacerbation of an acute, painful illness. Mrs. Boucher had multiple diverticula, several of which had ruptured in the past, causing her severe pain and requiring surgery. The daughter was unsure what she ought to do if this occurred again. She did not want her mother to have unnecessary surgery, neither did she want her mother to suffer needlessly. The long-term care nurses explained that as Mrs. Boucher became more demented, new settings and unfamiliar people frightened her. Therefore, the daughter decided her mother should only be transferred if the staff in the long-term care facility could not keep her comfortable. Finally, the daughter was worried about her mother's difficulty in eating and weight loss; she wondered if tube feeding would be appropriate.

Artificial Means of Nourishment

When Mrs. Boucher's daughter asked about tube feeding at one of the multidisciplinary meetings focusing on her mother's care, several staff members offered recommendations. The speech therapist noted that Mrs. Boucher's mother was swallowing, not aspirating, as long as she was fed gently and not force fed. The nutritionist suggested that Mrs. Boucher seemed to be taking sufficient calories to maintain her current weight. The nurses noted that an older French Canadian nun came to feed Mrs. Boucher most days, and Mrs. Boucher seemed unusually responsive to this nun. Finally, all noted that it was apparent that Mrs. Boucher really enjoyed the texture and taste of some of her foods, especially coffee. The recommendation of the team was that gentle feeding be continued and tube feeding not

> Gentle spoon feeding may be preferred to tube feeding if it provides the patient with pleasant sensations, social interactions, some nutrition, and is not harming the patient.

be attempted. The team believed that tube feeding would rob her of an important social interaction and a pleasant experience during her day, while offering little potential benefit. Mrs. Boucher's daughter concurred.

Mrs. Boucher's care was very labor intensive but not technology laden. Although she denied she was dying, her life was slowly ebbing away. There was no attempt by either Mrs. Boucher or her daughter to accelerate or to fight the dying process. Rather, the daughter and health care providers observed Mrs. Boucher and kept her comfortable as the dying process continued at its own leisurely pace. As Mrs. Boucher had predicted, she was not dying that sunny afternoon. In truth, her weight stabilized and she lived for another year. As will be shown later in this chapter, Mrs. Boucher did eventually die gently and peacefully.

However, not all people believe that death should occur at its own pace. Some people attempt to control their dying process. Later in this chapter, situations such as assisted suicide and voluntary euthanasia, where patients request assistance in prematurely terminating their lives, will be discussed. In contrast, a large group of patients are not ready to die when their time approaches and they, their families, or their physicians may desire to fight to keep them alive.

Aggressive Care at the End of Life

According to Cassem, as stated during an interview with Stein, more patients and families seem unable to recognize when it is appropriate to terminate aggressive care at the end of life than previously.[1] Cassem believes these people have unrealistically high expectations of medical advances and technology, believing that modern medicine has the ability to cure all ills. One reason this might happen is that people do not have much contact with dying patients any-more. Where once

> Americans gain more of their information about death and dying from television than from contact with dying friends and relatives. Unfortunately, the image portrayed on television is unrealistic.

people died at home, now most people die in the hospital. Where once people would have encountered death in their personal lives, now many people get their impressions of death and dying from television.

Unfortunately, the picture of death and dying that people develop from television is usually distorted. On the evening news, the latest technological advances and the medical "miracles" are reported in detail. Thus, many patients and families believe that a medical miracle will happen for them as well. Television programs often distort the success of medical procedures. For example, when researchers watched fictional medical programs (such as *ER*), 75% of patients who had CPR recovered. On TV programs based on real-life medical dramas, all the patients survived.[2] This contrasts to an actual CPR survival to hospital discharge rate of about 13%.[3] Thus, patients' and families' expectations of modern medicine's ability to cure have been raised to falsely high levels.

There are other reasons why families will ask for unusually aggressive care. Often, when family members are feeling guilty, they will refuse to realize that the patient is dying and request exhaustive amounts of care. For example, a 90-year-old patient whose family had relocated him from Canada despite his assertion that relocation would kill him, had an extensive myocardial infarction (MI). He developed cardiogenic shock, had complete heart block, and was clearly dying. The family insisted that a pacemaker, intra-aortic balloon pump, and cardiopulmonary resuscitation be attempted.

Patients and families may also request aggressive treatment because they do not trust their health care insurers and providers to act in the patients' best interests. The increase in patients' and families' demands for aggressive treatment seems to parallel the distrust in for-profit health care providers. Minority groups, especially African Americans, have demonstrated a deep distrust in the health care system's ability to act in their interests. In several studies, they have shown a preference for aggressive health care treatment. When patients and families do not trust the health care system, they may not believe their health care provider when

> Patients and families may request unrealistically aggressive care because:
> - They have falsely high expectations of the capabilities of modern medicine
> - They do not trust their health care providers or insurers to act in the patient's best interests
> - They have unresolved issues with the dying patient
> - The patient is afraid to die or is not prepared to die

she or he states there are no additional appropriate interventions. Therefore, they will often request that maximal medical support and aggressive interventions be provided.

Some patients request aggressive treatment and refuse to acknowledge they are dying because they desperately want to stay alive. Leslie Evers, a 32-year-old woman with cystic fibrosis, wanted to live no matter the cost. She had been married less than 5 years and had a devoted husband and caring family. Leslie was ventilator dependent and had been transferred to the ICU of a community hospital after developing pneumonia in the long-term care facility where she had been temporarily residing. Leslie was insistent that she was on the heart-lung transplant list of two centers that were nearby and demanded that they be contacted. Both institutions declared she no longer met transplant criteria, and they had informed both Leslie and her family that she was no longer on their transplant lists. Although Leslie requested transfer to either institution, both refused to accept her, saying there was nothing more they could do for her. However, the specialist physicians were willing to provide recommendations for her care to the local doctors.

Leslie was determined to survive. She would not give in to cystic fibrosis as her twin sister had 8 years earlier. Every possible therapy and intervention was tried and her ventilator was set at the maximum settings, but still she became increasingly hypoxic. Any slight sound would startle Leslie, and she would awaken terrified, hypoxic, and diaphoretic. Attempts to suction or turn her resulted in such severe hypoxia that her heart rate dropped to the low 40s. Only when she was in a quiet, darkened room with her husband holding her hand did she seem to get any rest. This, however, was not what Leslie wanted; she wanted to get better and live. Thus, she asked to be turned, suctioned, and percussed despite her hypoxia and terror.

Leslie died quickly but not quietly one morning. While being turned, Leslie became severely hypoxic, her heart slowed down suddenly, then stopped. Despite the terror on her face during the last moments, Leslie had left instructions that absolutely every intervention that might prolong her life should be carried out, so resuscitation was attempted. The resuscitation was unsuccessful. Although they had been complying with Leslie's often professed wishes, the nurses who attempted to resuscitate her wondered if their actions were ethically justifiable.

Death will come for all people. Determining when death is inevitable and when further life-prolonging interventions are useless can be a complex problem. Sometimes, it is clearer to the health care providers than to the patient and family, as it was in Leslie's case. Other times it is more apparent to the patient and family than to the physician. Providing apparently futile, painful care to patients is emotionally and physically exhausting to everyone involved. How can health care providers assist patients and families when they encounter such difficult predicaments?

In such situations, some physicians suggest a trial of maximal, aggressive therapy for a limited amount of time. At the end of the predetermined time, the effectiveness of the therapy is reviewed. If the patient is not improving or is deteriorating, the physicians suggest that the interventions are not accomplishing their purpose, are futile, and should be withdrawn. Health care providers, families, and patients tend to appreciate this approach because they can see that an attempt was made to harness the "miracles of modern science," but the patient was too

> When it is unclear if a patient is dying or might benefit from aggressive medical therapy, a trial of therapy for a pre-established length of time may be helpful to make the distinction.

severely ill to benefit. Such an approach often leaves survivors believing that the health care providers did all they could in a difficult situation. Most nurses would agree that such a plan of care is far superior to providing the type of aggressive care and resuscitation that Leslie Evers requested and appeared to be tortured by as she lay dying.

IS THERE SUCH A THING AS A GOOD DEATH?

Mrs. Boucher continued to deteriorate during the year after she had announced to her daughter that she was not dying. She remained in bed most days and never spoke. At a multidisciplinary meeting, her family was asked what would make this period of her life most meaningful for her. They responded that Catholic mass had always been important to her. In the past, she had attended every Sunday and many weekdays. A decision was made to take her by wheelchair to mass in the long-term care facility's chapel on Sundays.

The following Sunday, Mrs. Boucher smiled as she was dressed in her best clothes and was told she was going to mass. She turned to the nurse's aide and said, "Thank you." When she arrived in the chapel, she glanced around the church, sighed, smiled at the nun who often fed her, closed her eyes, and died.

Fifteen years earlier, Mrs. Boucher's son, Bill, had died at home at the age of 52 after developing cancers of the lung, kidney, and skin. Unable to manage his nursery business, he was forced to sell it, and his wife found a job working evenings. While his wife was at work, one of his five children, extended family, or friends would stay with him to be certain he was comfortable. During the last 5 months of his life, his home was filled with people visiting him and helping with his physical care.

Two days before his death, he became less responsive, seldom waking and barely talking. At least one family member remained near him, perhaps holding his hand but not attempting to engage him in conversation. When the physical signs indicated that his death was near, his close family gathered around him. His mother, sister, brother-in-law, and children sat with him and told him what he meant to them. The next morning, he awoke very agitated. His sister-in-law and a close friend arrived with the Catholic priest. He received communion, assured the priest that he had swallowed it, and became very serene. Then, with his wife beside him in bed, embracing him, and telling him she loved him, he died.

What elements might be considered when identifying if a patient died a good death? Callahan would argue that a death does not offend our sense of justice and timeliness when it has occurred at the end of the natural life span, and when the person has fulfilled her or his life responsibilities.[4] Thus, Mrs. Boucher's death was a more timely death than her son's, who still had a family for which he needed to provide. A good death may have cultural and religious components. Both Mrs. Boucher and her son were devout Catholics of French Canadian descent, and these traditions greatly influenced how they experienced their deaths. Mrs. Boucher was not prepared to die until she returned to mass, while her son was agitated until the priest arrived with communion. Recognizing and respecting the patient's religious and cultural traditions and rituals can greatly assist a patient through the dying process.

A consensus seems to be developing among physicians, nurses, and ethicists that a good death is a peaceful death, one aided by limited technology but relieved by the love and concern of family and friends. Callahan defines it as a "time when friends and family draw near, when leave can be taken, when props and devices of medicine can be put aside save for those meant to palliate and assuage."[4] In a similar vein, Cassem defines a good death as one in which "the person was able to depart with a maximum acknowledgment of the importance and meaningfulness of their having been among us." A good death may also mean that the person has put her or his affairs in order, come together with her or his family, resolved lingering conflicts, and is supported by limited technology. Although care at the end of life is usually not easy, there is the potential for considerable personal growth for the patient, caregivers, family, and professionals. The dying patient should have

> A good death may be defined as one which is timely and peaceful, aided by minimal technology, and relieved by the presence of family, friends, and health care providers.

an opportunity to review her or his life, search for meaning, and determine if there is anything significant that she or he has left undone. Dying may allow the patient the opportunity to resolve any longstanding problems in relationships with families and friends. The care that a person receives from her or his family and community may reaffirm the value of care and community in a materialistic society.

During the 5 months before Bill Boucher's death, his family and friends attended him. Long-lost friends from high school visited and recalled youthful indiscretions. Since he had lost his health insurance when he sold his business, an informal group of health care providers found necessities like commodes, offered him suggestions on how to manage common discomforts like constipation, and aided him with his personal hygiene. Most importantly, family and friends emphasized how much they cherished him. His marriage had been strained at times. So, his wife embracing and comforting him in his final moments pointed to the resolution of some longstanding problems.

Byock believes that of the fundamental needs of people as they die "only the control of physical symptoms is uniquely medical."[5] He believes that in order to care for dying persons and to assist them in dying well, the family, friends, and health care providers need to be able to say to the dying person through their words and actions, "We will keep you warm and we will keep you dry. We will keep you clean. We will help you with your elimination. We will always offer you food and fluid. We will be with you. We will bear witness to your pain and sorrows, your disappointments, and your triumphs; we will listen to your stories of your life and we will remember the story of your passing."

As Byock stated, this description of care at the end of life is not uniquely medical. In fact, it is decidedly nursing-care oriented.[5] Kuhse, a philosopher, has advocated that nurses ought to be the primary care providers and decision-makers for dying patients.[6] Wald, a nurse, has wondered, "How can we make the experience of dying not just tolerable but a time of accomplishment for the patient, the family, and the professional?"[7] According to Cassem, nurses should have a central role in coordination of care at the end of life because they understand the emotional impact of the dying process on the patient and

> Appropriate care at the end of life is heavily nursing oriented.

family.[1] Cassem has said, "If there is hope, they (nurses) will pick it up. If there is a sense of hopelessness, they will pick that up too."[1] Nurses can have a significant impact on the way in which a patient dies, by providing nursing care, teaching families to care, and "being sensitive to the patient's lifestyle and attuning our care to fit that lifestyle."[7] Nurses can help patients in any setting to die peacefully and well.

PALLIATIVE CARE

The World Health Organization (WHO) defines palliative care as "the active total care of patients whose disease is not responsive to curative treatment. Control of pain, of other symptoms, and of psychological, social, and spiritual problems is paramount. The goal of palliative care is the achievement of the best quality of life for patients and their families."[8] In order to assist patients to die well, nurses often are involved in symptom management and relief. The nurse may manage the patient's symptoms or she or he may educate the patient and the patient's family in symptom management.

Pain and Symptom Management at the End of Life

Pain is a common symptom, and its management may create misunderstandings and confusion for patients, families, and health care providers. Emanuel estimates that with aggressive use of pain medications, 95% of patients should be pain-free during their dying process.[9] However, many patients, health care providers, and family members are ignorant of essential information about how to provide adequate pain relief. Patients may be concerned that they will be less responsive if they take adequate pain medication. This may be partially counteracted by central nervous stimulants such as methylphenidate. Other patients and health care providers are concerned that the patient will become addicted to the narcotic used to relieve pain. This is not a realistic concern because research has demonstrated that the threat of addiction from commonly prescribed opiates is very small in the patient experiencing pain. Health professionals have expressed fear of prosecution if they prescribe the amounts of narcotics occasionally required for pain relief in dying patients. However, prosecution of physicians prescribing pain relief for dying patients is very rare. Finally, caregivers may fail to realize the importance of maintaining a baseline level of pain medication and pain relief. When a patient or caregiver waits to administer pain medication until the pain is intense, there is little possibility of adequate and consistent pain relief.

However, perhaps one of the most significant fears of caregivers is that by administering an adequate amount of pain medication, they might be morally accountable for the patient's death. Caregivers fear that the pain medications may depress the patient's respiration and hasten her or his death. Actually, adequate pain medication and relief of

> Patients, families, and caregivers need to be educated about appropriate pain management at the end of life.

pain may slightly prolong a dying patient's life. However, caregivers, whether nurses or family members, need to realize that administering medication within the patient's dose range (which may be above the normal dose range for the medication) with the intent to relieve pain is morally acceptable even if it does hasten the patient's death.

A traditional ethical principle, double effect, is invoked in this instance. When an action has two effects, one good (relieving pain) and one bad (hastening death), it has been considered morally permissible to take the action if certain conditions are met. These conditions include:

- The act itself (giving pain medication to relieve pain) is either good or morally neutral.
- Only the good effect (pain relief) is intended.
- The good effect is not achieved through the bad effect (the patient's pain is not relieved because the patient dies).
- There is no other means of attaining the good effect (other alternatives for pain relief are not possible or are ineffective).
- There is a good reason for assuming the risk of the bad effect (relief of severe pain).

There has been substantial criticism of the principle of double effect, since Jack Kevorkian began invoking it to justify assisting suicides. Kevorkian states his intention is the relief of suffering, thus he should not be responsible for the patient's

> Fear of hastening a patient's death should never prevent a caregiver from providing pain medication to a dying patient.

death. However, he violates both the first and third conditions of the principle of double effect because the good effect (relief of suffering) is brought about only by the bad effect (death). Thus, the principle of double effect cannot be used to justify Kevorkian's actions.

Caregivers of dying patients often require explanations of the acceptability of administering pain medications to patients even if the medication might hasten the patients' deaths. Four days before Mr. Boucher's death, he was experiencing increasingly severe back and chest pain. He could rest comfortably for only half an hour between his doses of pain medication. When his sister called his primary care provider, the provider suggested that she increase Mr. Boucher's baseline dose of morphine and provide him some immediate medication for breakthrough pain. After taking the increased dose of medication, Mr. Boucher appeared to fall asleep. However, when he remained unresponsive for more than 2 days, his sister was concerned that the pain medication had induced his unresponsiveness and that she was responsible for worsening his condition and hastening his death.

A hospice nurse volunteering with Mr. Boucher reassured his sister that the medication dose was medically appropriate and relieving Mr. Boucher's pain was a worthy goal. No other medication choices or alternative therapies had been effective at relieving his pain. The nurse explained to Mr. Boucher's sister that because her intent had been to relieve Mr. Boucher's pain and not to hasten his death, even if he died sooner because of her action, her action would still have been justifiable. The nurse also explained that such a period of withdrawal and unresponsiveness is not uncommon just prior to death and might be unrelated to the pain medication that the sister had administered. Palliative care practitioners stress that administering adequate doses of medication at consistent, appropriate intervals is essential to good pain management at the end of life. Fear of hastening death should not to be a barrier to providing pain relief.

Terminal Dehydration

Other symptoms, which may cause dilemmas for patients and caregivers at the end of life, include fluid volume excess (especially of respiratory secretions), incontinence, breathlessness, difficulty swallowing or eating, and anorexia. Many palliative care nurses believe that terminal dehydration is helpful in relieving or preventing this constellation of symptoms. In terminal dehydration, when a dying patient becomes uninterested in food or has difficulty swallowing, then food and fluid are offered but not forced. The patient is encouraged to consume as little or as much food and fluid as she or he desires, which often means the person consumes very little.

Since in many cultures and religions food is associated with nurturance and care, withholding food and fluid may seem unacceptable and unethical to both families and health care providers. Many people believe that food and fluids should always be provided to patients because they represent simple, ordinary means of care. However, only oral food and fluids should be classified as ordinary means. Force feeding or food delivered by artificial methods, such as intravenous or nasogastric tubes, are medical interventions and should not be considered obligatory to provide to all patients. Like

> In terminal dehydration, oral food and fluids are offered to the dying patient but are never forced.

any other medical intervention, patients should be able to refuse force feeding, IV hydration, or nasogastric tube feedings if they offer minimal benefit and are too burdensome.

At some point in the dying process, additional food and fluid appear to offer little benefit and may be very burdensome to a patient. Studies of aggressive nutritional support, including tube feeding, of patients with cancer have demonstrated no benefits in length of survival. In fact, qualitative studies and practitioner's experiences are beginning to suggest that such aggressive feeding may harm the patient.

According to Zerwekh, providing artificial fluid replacement once the patient's organs have begun to fail may be a contributing factor in the development of peripheral edema; ascites; increased respiratory secretions, which may result in dyspnea; and increased gastrointestinal secretions, which may result in nausea and vomiting.[10] Nurses in one hospice service noted that their patients who did not receive IV fluid replacement did not have difficulty with respiratory secretions and did not require suctioning. This was in stark contrast to the suctioning required by patients who had IV fluids administered.[11] During terminal dehydration, patients do not appear to be experiencing pain. There is some indication that the increase in circulating endorphins resulting from ketosis may provide a natural analgesic effect at the end of life.[12] Thus, providing food and fluids by artificial means, such as IVs or nasogastric tubes, appears to offer more burdens than benefits for the dying patient. Most palliative care nurses therefore argue that patients should be offered only the oral food and fluid they desire at the end of life, even if they desire very little.

Palliative care specialists stress it is more important to manage symptoms such as thirst and hunger of the patient than to adhere to any general formula. Byock includes in his promises to dying patients, "We will always offer you food and water."[5] This accentuates the importance of offering oral feedings but permits the patient to determine whether she or he can tolerate them. When the patient is unable to swallow or does not desire food and fluids but is complaining of thirst or a dry mouth, the nurse may teach caregivers to moisten the mouth and lips or provide ice chips. Since the goal of palliative care is the best quality of life for the dying patient, the health care team should re-evaluate a situation in which the patient does not appear to be more comfortable because of terminal dehydration. In the rare circumstance when a patient is suffering from dehydration-induced delirium, artificial hydration might be considered. Palliative care nurses are often required to assist patients and their families in determining whether they should attempt artificial hydration or whether terminal dehydration and natural progression of the disease is more appropriate.

Approximately 2 weeks before he died, Bill Boucher developed anorexia. The sight of food nauseated him. He was not thirsty and was uninterested in drinking or eating. His wife was concerned that he would suffer from the lack of food and fluids, so she consulted with his volunteer hospice nurse. The nurse explained to Mrs. Boucher that her husband had minimal kidney function. Mr. Boucher had had a nephrectomy for renal cancer early in his disease. Subsequently, during a radiological procedure, half of his remaining kidney had been destroyed. Mr. Boucher was not experiencing thirst and there was a specific reason (his lack of kidney function) to believe that limiting his fluids would result in far less discomfort for him than providing extra fluids. During the last weeks of his life, Mr. Boucher was frequently offered those fluids, such as sherbet, that appealed to him. He took only very small amounts of the fluids, never complained of thirst, and had minimal problems with oral secretions, incontinence, vomiting, or dyspnea.

In addition to managing the physical symptoms of the dying patient, palliative care emphasizes the psychological, social, and spiritual aspects of care. A multidisciplinary team approach may be used to assist the patient and her or his family so that the dying process may be a chance for growth and self-actualization. The team attempts to assist the patient and family to deal with any unfinished business. The patient or family may be asked, "Is there something that could be done to make this time especially significant for the patient?" Following such a question, arrangements were made to bring Mrs. Boucher to the long-term care facility chapel for mass.

The patient might be asked to describe her or his emotional responses. Byock recommends a question he discovered while working at St. Christopher's Hospice. He believes asking the patient, "How do you feel inside yourself?" is extremely effective at allowing the patient to describe her or his emotions.[5] Once the patient's emotional concerns are identified, efforts are made to arrange for members of the palliative care team to assist the patient in resolving any underlying issues. Thus, the hospice staff made arrangements for marriage counseling for Mr. Boucher and his wife.

Perhaps one of the best-known methods for delivery of palliative care is hospice. The modern movement began with Dame Cicely Saunders at St. Christopher's Hospice in England. In the United States, hospice has developed in a variety of forms as a means to provide palliative care to patients. One of the major concerns about hospice care in the United States is that hospice referrals are usually not initiated until a few weeks prior to the patient's death. Therefore, although symptom relief may be arranged for the end of the patient's life, it is often too late to arrange for optimum psychological, social, and spiritual care.

There are also concerns about attempts to restrain the costs of hospice care. When referrals to hospice occur during the last few weeks of life, there are cost savings from hospice care over traditional or hospital care of dying patients. However, when hospice care is provided over a longer period of time, the savings disappear and costs

> Important questions that might be posed to a dying patient:
> - Is there anything that could be done which would make this time particularly significant for you?
> - Do you have any unfinished business that you need to complete?
> - How do you feel inside yourself?

may even be greater if the expenses of family care providers missing work and delivering health care are factored into the equation.[13] Previously, many hospice organizations had guidelines requiring nurses to visit dying patients at least daily. With budgetary constraints, this is no longer possible. Hospice nurses are concerned that effective symptom management of dying patients will no longer be possible, since families will not have nurses consistently available to assess the developing symptoms and offer guidance about their management. How to justly allocate palliative care and expense at the end of life is a concern of many health care providers, legislators, insurers, families, and patients.

> Should patients requiring daily care be referred to hospice in the last few weeks of their lives? Should they receive professional assessment and assistance with symptom management on a regular basis?

WHAT MEDICAL, CURATIVE INTERVENTIONS MIGHT BE RECONSIDERED WHEN A PATIENT IS GRAVELY ILL?

Mr. Jeffers was an 85-year-old man with multiple medical problems. He had a history of myocardial infarctions, gout, chronic leukemia, chronic renal failure, and chronic obstructive pulmonary disease (COPD). Following an emergency cholecystectomy, he developed a paralytic ileus and respiratory failure. He was intubated and placed on a ventilator. After his surgery, Mr. Jeffers was sleepy but could be woken. However, his only responses were to smile at his wife, kiss her, and indicate if he was in pain or nauseated. He would not respond to questions about his preferences for treatment. Mr. Jeffers was receiving maximal medical treatments including hemodialysis, and the goal was to cure him and return him to his home. However, after several weeks of attempting to wean him from the ventilator, it became apparent that Mr. Jeffers would never breathe on his own again. Despite medications to enhance gastric motility, he was unable to tolerate tube feedings for more than a few days at a time without becoming nauseated and vomiting. The nurses and physicians providing Mr. Jeffers' care decided to approach his wife and daughter about re-evaluating the goals of his care and implementing do-not-resuscitate order (DNR).

Cardiopulmonary Resuscitation and Do-Not-Resuscitate Orders

In the United States, more people die in hospitals than at home or in any other setting. CPR is required for all patients who die in a hospital unless there is a physician's order stating that the patient is not to be resuscitated (DNR). CPR, even in the hospital setting, is usually unsuccessful, with only approximately 13% of patients surviving to hospi-

> Cardiopulmonary resuscitation is the only medical intervention that is provided routinely without a medical order, yet it is successful only 13% of the time.

tal discharge. Some groups of patients, such as patients with renal failure, cancer, and multisystem organ failure, rarely survive following a cardiac arrest. Some people would argue that CPR is usually a futile intervention. Maintaining the capacity to perform in hospital resuscitation is very expensive. Vrtis estimated that a hospital CPR program costs a total of $23,552,777.10 or $7002.29 per patient who cardiac arrests.[14] The total cost per survivor was $60,327.46. Resuscitation is most likely a painful or at least an uncomfortable process. The patient's ribs may be broken, endotracheal intubation is performed, and electrical shocks may be delivered. Finally, the study discovered "nearly half of the patients who had a desire for CPR to be withheld did not have a DNR order written during their hospitalization.[15] Nearly one-third of those patients died before discharge." Therefore, if a patient is in the hospital, either the patient or the patient's family ought to be asked if CPR should be performed or withheld should the patient cardiac or respiratory arrest.

Most ethicists recommend that patients and families be involved in deciding about the advisability of resuscitation. Since CPR has a small chance of being successful, it is not clearly futile. Thus, the decision about resuscitation is value-laden, not purely medically determined, and one in which patients and families should participate. Resuscitation is clearly an intrusive, expensive, and possibly painful medical intervention, so patients and families may decline the intervention if they believe it will offer minimal benefits or be too burdensome.

Many Americans prefer that aggressive medical care is delivered and resources are expended until a patient's prognosis becomes apparent and physicians, nurses, patients,

> All hospitalized patients ought to be asked if they desire to be resuscitated if they cardiac or respiratory arrest.

and families are certain that it is appropriate to withdraw interventions. However, often patients and families will consider DNR orders before withdrawal of medical interventions since resuscitation is only instituted when the patient's heart or respiration have already stopped, and what is being considered is an attempt, probably futile, to revive her or him. Unfortunately, many physicians are uncomfortable about initiating discussions about end-of-life care, including DNR orders, with patients and families.

Often, it is the nurses who have been listening to the patients' and families' concerns about prognoses and treatment choices, and who alert the physicians to the patients' and families' willingness to discuss resuscitation. How the patient and family are approached has an impact on their decision. If they are asked, "Do you want everything done?" They will often say yes.

Saying they do not want everything done for a dying family member often makes people feel as if they are abandoning the dying patient. However, the response in the following situation may be very different. "Hospital policy states that unless there is an order saying not to attempt it, when a patient's heart stops, we must try to restart it again. I don't believe we could successfully restart your (family member's) heart and I would prefer not to try to do so. Do you agree?" The response may be very different. Nurses may need to spend a significant amount of time explaining the concept of DNR in understandable terms to patients and families so that they can give informed consent.

Nurses should emphasize to patients and families that consent to a DNR order does not imply consent to withdraw other medical interventions or a decision to switch to a goal of comfort rather than cure. These are separate issues that may be discussed simultaneously or at

> Nurses are often responsible for explaining CPR in terms that the patient and family can understand.

a later time. Consenting to a DNR does not imply the patient will receive less care. Patients with DNR orders in ICUs frequently receive more nursing time and nursing care than those ICU patients who do not have DNR orders.

Mr. Jeffers' wife had developed a great deal of trust in two of the ICU nurses. On the day the health care team chose to speak with her about a DNR order, one of the nurses was assigned to care for her husband. Mrs. Jeffers cried repeatedly when the idea that her husband might die was discussed. However, when the nurse explained that because of his renal failure, chronic leukemia, and age, Mr. Jeffers' chance of being successfully resuscitated was less than 1%, his wife consented to a DNR order. However, she insisted that all other therapies (tube feedings, ventilation, and dialysis) be continued

> Providing CPR should never be described as "doing everything possible."

and asked the nurses she trusted to promise to provide the same respectful nursing care to him that they had before the DNR decision was reached.

Withholding and Withdrawal of Life-Sustaining Technologies

Over the following week, Mr. Jeffers deteriorated considerably. He experienced episodes of pulmonary edema that frightened him and required emergency hemodialysis. He was unable to tolerate his nasogastric tube feedings and he developed a urinary tract infection. His daughter conferred with his nurses and physicians and began to consider how to approach her mother about withdrawing some of his medical therapies and allowing her father to die

Most medical ethicists, physicians, and nurses consider both the withholding and the withdrawal of futile, burdensome, or extraordinary means to be ethically justifiable. When a patient is deteriorating and dying from her or his disease process, and the proposed medical interventions, are unlikely to prevent the patient's inevitable death but could prolong suffering the dying process, the interventions offer minimal benefit and may be withheld or withdrawn. Thus, aggressive medical interventions such as mechanical ventilation, chemotherapy, or hemodialysis may be justly withheld or discontinued in the dying patient. Additionally, if an intervention is too burdensome (painful, costly, excessively unpleasant side effects) for a patient to tolerate, the patient may choose to decline or discontinue the procedure. Foregoing, withdrawing, or withholding medical treatment, which offers minimal benefit or is excessively burdensome, is classified as passive euthanasia.

Passive Euthanasia

To understand why such a position is ethically justifiable, one must acknowledge that modern medicine is not capable of curing all conditions and that it is capable of imposing inordinate suffering on patients in attempts to prolong their lives. The principle of autonomy might therefore be invoked to justify the patient being able to determine when the benefits of a slightly longer life are outweighed by the burdens of physical and emotional suffering. Since the treatment is not capable of curing the patient, it is not the withdrawal of the intervention that directly causes the patient's death, but the relentless progress of the patient's disease. That is why withdrawal and withholding are classified as *passive euthanasia*.

Rachels has been a longstanding critic of the concept of passive euthanasia.[16] He suggests that there is no difference between active euthanasia (actively causing a patient's death) and passive euthanasia (withholding or withdrawing interventions and allowing death to occur). He cites, as an example of active euthanasia, purposefully holding a child's head under the water in a bathtub. He offers as an example of passive euthanasia, seeing a child under the water in a bathtub and not lifting the child's head out of the water. The error in this reasoning is that in his analogy there is a simple, effective intervention (reaching into the tub and lifting the child's head) that would prevent the child's drowning and eventual death.

However, in passive euthanasia and withholding of medical care, there is no clearly effective intervention that would cure the patient, only choices that might prolong her or his situation. A better analogy than Rachels' bathtub example would be a child being swept away in a raging river, too deep for the rescuer to enter. The rescuer has a small branch that she or he might throw to the child. If the rescuer throws the branch, the branch might hold the child up a little longer only to have the child drown in the rapids downstream. However, it is also possible that the branch might never reach the child when it was thrown, or it might hit the child on the head when it was thrown and the child might die sooner after becoming unconscious. This is a more accurate analogy to the process of withholding and withdrawal of medical interventions at the end of life. The suggested medical interventions may slightly prolong the patient's death only to make it ultimately more painful, have no effect, or even cause the patient to die sooner. The analogy also demonstrates why the withholding or withdrawal of intervention is not the direct cause of death; rather, it is the disease process that causes the patient's death.

When a patient is deteriorating and possibly dying, many patients and families prefer a trial of aggressive medical management as described previously. Withholding or withdrawing medical interventions may be discussed before medical therapy is initiated, after a predetermined trial of aggressive therapy, or anytime medical interventions do not appear to be benefiting the patient. A sequence for withholding or withdrawal of medical interventions that might be followed is:

- Initiation of a do-not-resuscitate order
- No further aggressive or heroic treatment to be provided
- No further curative treatment to be provided
- Withdrawal of probably discomfort-producing technology
- Provision of comfort measures only

Although Mr. Jeffers was clearly deteriorating, despite maximal medical therapy he remained unwilling to express his treatment preferences, and his wife was not ready to withdraw any of the existing medical interventions (hemodialysis, tube feeding, or mechanical ventilation). However, she agreed that if he developed any new infections, he would not be treated with antibiotics for them. She also agreed that he should not be straight catheterized, since the process was causing him considerable discomfort, and he was producing very little urine. Thus, she agreed to withhold any additional curative interventions.

Mr. Jeffers' physicians, nurses, and daughter next approached his wife about changing the goal of Mr. Jeffers' care, from prolonging his life to promoting his comfort. He was deteriorating slowly but clearly dying. He no longer tolerated tube feedings at all, had increasing respiratory distress even with mechanical ventilation and dialysis, and was frequently grimacing in pain. One of the nurses whom Mrs. Jeffers trusted implicitly described to Mrs. Jeffers how distressed her husband was when he was short-of-breath and how much discomfort he appeared to be experiencing whenever he was turned or positioned. She gently but firmly explained to Mrs. Jeffers that her husband was deteriorating and it was very unlikely he would live much longer. She suggested Mrs. Jeffers consider what type of care her husband would desire at the end of his life. Mrs. Jeffers then consented to changing the goals of her husband's therapy to providing comfort rather than obtaining a cure. After obtaining a promise that the nurses would continue to care for her husband as before, she agreed to allow the health care providers to withhold dialysis while instituting a morphine drip so that her husband did not experience dyspnea. Mr. Jeffers died peacefully that night.

Patients and their families, like Mrs. Jeffers, need to be reassured that the patient will still be cared for when aggressive medical interventions are stopped. The designation of comfort measures only, like palliative care, should be a cue that aggressive nursing care is required to maintain patient comfort and control patient symptoms. Nurses should reassure patients and families by both their words and their actions that they will continue to provide quality nursing care after life-sustaining interventions are withdrawn.

SHOULD LIFE-SUSTAINING INTERVENTIONS BE WITHDRAWN FROM SUDDEN AND ACUTELY ILL CHILDREN?

All of the dying individuals described thus far have been adults, most of them older, who have been chronically ill. What happens when a sudden, devastating event occurs to a child?

On Thanksgiving, Adam Jones, a 2-year-old, rushed away from the dinner table to play with his older cousins. While running he aspirated corn and became unresponsive. It was several minutes before his family found him lying in the hall, and the paramedics were

> The designation of comfort care only, like the designation of palliative care, identifies the need for intensive nursing care.

called. The paramedics had a lot of difficulty with his intubation. When he arrived at the nearest hospital, his pupils were fixed and dilated; he had no corneal, gag, or cough reflexes; no movement to noxious stimuli; and no spontaneous respiration.

Such a death certainly does not meet Callahan's conception of a good death, which occurs at the end of the natural life span when the person has fulfilled her or his life responsibilities.[4] Health care providers and parents may feel such a premature death is unfair. The child has never had a chance to live her or his life, and there is so much potential that will be wasted. Families may experience considerable amounts of guilt. Adam's mother anguished over why she had allowed her 2-year-old to eat corn, and why she had let him run off to see his cousins. Such a sudden injury does not allow the family to come to terms with the illness before they are being asked to understand that any further care is futile and their child is dead or dying.

Health care providers may also become emotionally involved with the child and family. One of the paramedics who had transported Adam to the hospital visited him and brought him a stuffed bear. The attending physician in charge of Adam's care insisted on unnecessarily repeating all of the tests for brain death four times to be sure that Adam was really dead before he pronounced him dead.

Eventually, despite their grief and anguish over the tragedy of the circumstances, the health care providers and family members realized that Adam had died and further intervention was futile. His organs were donated and ventilation was withdrawn. As in this situation, the emotional turmoil surrounding the sudden unexpected death of a child can cloud ethical issues and make decision-making about withdrawal of life-sustaining interventions more difficult than for adults.

What are the Ethical Considerations When a Patient, Family Member, or Health Care Provider Decides to Prematurely Terminate the Patient's Life?

Assisted Suicide

Allen Bacon was a 32-year-old C5-6 quadriplegic. He lived alone in an apartment and had private health care attendants who cared for him at least 16 hours a day. He was unable to perform any of his activities of daily living. He needed to be fed and could not hold his medications or reach either of his hands to his mouth. Since a fall from his wheelchair 2 months earlier, he had been experiencing severe pain in his left shoulder. One evening, he informed his health care attendant that he could not stand his life or pain any longer and asked her if she would help him ingest an overdose of his pain, anti-anxiety, and antidepressant medications.

Mr. Bacon was requesting that his health care attendant assist him to end his life. When an individual knowingly provides the means for a patient to commit suicide but the patient completes the act of suicide, it is termed assisted suicide. Assisted suicide is legal in Oregon in certain situations and in the Netherlands is not prosecuted if certain conditions are followed. Physicians who admit to assisting patients with suicide have rarely been found guilty by juries in the United States, yet there is a growing movement in this country to legalize assisted suicide.

Advocates of assisted suicide state that suicide allows the terminally ill patient to control the time and situation of her or his death. They believe that an autonomous, competent person ought to be able to declare when her or his life has become burdensome and she or he no longer desires to live. They declare that just as a medical intervention that has become too burdensome may be withdrawn, so may a life that has become too burdensome be ended. They maintain that if the patient is able to control the time of death, she or he may complete all necessary business, and death will be both timely and peaceful.

Supporters of assisted suicide argue that dying by medication overdose is a far more humane method of death then dying naturally. They believe by committing suicide, the dying patient does not experience any discomfort at the end and is not forced to endure a protracted, painful dying experience. Supporters of assisted suicide may declare, "We treat our dogs and cats more humanely at the end of life than our relatives." Some physicians will agree and argue that assisted suicide ought to be available for the 5% of dying patients who are unable to obtain pain relief despite the best pain management.

Defenders of assisted suicide may stress the results during 1998, the first full year following the enactment in October 1997 of a law in Oregon that legalized assisted suicide in certain circumstances. They believe that the law was not abused and, in fact, a number of people benefited from its enactment. Fifteen people ended their own lives that year in the state, while a few additional patients obtained the necessary medications but never committed suicide. However, there was a fourfold increase in the prescription of morphine for pain in dying patients and a dramatic increase in the number of patients referred to hospice in Oregon during the same year. Thus, some supporters of assisted suicide believe that the enactment of legal assisted suicide resulted in dramatic improvements in end-of-life care to all dying patients in the state of Oregon.

> Supporters of assisted suicide argue:
> - It allows the patient to take control of her or his own death
> - It is a more humane way to die
> - It prevents the patient from becoming a burden to others

Finally, promoters of assisted suicide will state that assisted suicide allows the dying person to avoid a protracted period of dependency during which she or he is dependent on others to meet her or his most intimate needs. By committing suicide, the dying patient is not a burden to those who would otherwise be required to care for her or him. When dying patients are questioned about reasons why one might commit suicide, being a burden to others is consistently near the top of the list.

Opponents of assisted suicide may declare that there are limits to autonomy and no one has the right to end a human life, even her or his own life. They seriously question whether the person requesting suicide is capable of making a rational, autonomous choice. They note that the majority of people who request assisted suicide are depressed. Depressed patients are not considered to be competent to make a decision about medical treatment, so opponents of assisted suicide are emphatic that depressed patients should not be allowed to make a decision about assisted suicide. In both Oregon and the Netherlands, depression screening is required as a condition prior to medically assisted suicide.

Critics of assisted suicide suggest that assisted suicide would not necessarily result in a more humane death. They stress that suicide is an irreversible condition, which harms the person irrevocably by depriving her or him of life. For most dying patients, the last months of life can be maintained relatively symptom-free and may be full of meaning. They also note that withholding and withdrawing medical interventions is now practiced in about 70% of deaths in American health care institutions. In these instances, patients appear to experience less uncomfortable, though slow, deaths.

Opponents of assisted suicide fear that the slowness and inconvenience of a natural death may eventually result in the "right" to assisted suicide becoming the responsibility of assisted suicide. Opponents fear that if care of the dying patient is perceived as a burden by the caregivers, the dying patient would believe she or he must commit suicide to relieve the caregivers of the

> Opponents of assisted suicide argue:
> - No one has the right to take a life (whether her or his own or someone else's life)
> - Depressed patients cannot make rational decisions
> - The right to die may become the responsibility to die
> - The integrity of the medical and nursing professions could be threatened
> - It may be the beginning of a slide down a slippery slope

burden. They emphasize that America is a materialistic society, where care of children is often relegated to child care centers, care of the ill to hospitals, and care of the old to long-term care facilities. They wonder what happens to a country that ceases to value the care of its most vulnerable citizens.

Critics of assisted suicide also argue that it should not require the presence of legal assisted suicide, as in Oregon, for us to provide adequate care to dying patients. There should be paid leave from employment for caregivers to dying patients, as in some European countries. Hospice referrals should be readily available to dying patients. Physicians should have absolutely no fear of prosecution for prescription of adequate pain medication at the end of a patient's life.

The American Nurses Association (ANA) has taken a stand in opposition to assisted suicide. The ANA's opposition to assisted suicide is based on several points:[17]

- "The profession of nursing is built upon the Hippocratic tradition 'do no harm' and an ethic of moral opposition to killing another human being."
- "Nursing has a social contract with society that is based on trust, and therefore patients must be able to trust that nurses will not actively take a human life."
- "While there may be individual cases that are compelling, there is a high potential for abuses with assisted suicide, particularly with vulnerable populations, such as the elderly, poor, and disabled. These abuses are even more probable in a time of declining resources."

Finally, as the ANA statement implies, critics of assisted suicide are concerned that it is a first step down a slippery slope leading to active euthanasia. In active euthanasia, another individual knowingly administers an agent with the intent to cause the patient's death. This may be done with the patient's consent (voluntary) or without the patient's consent (involuntary).

To return to Mr. Bacon's situation, when the attendant returned the following day, Mr. Bacon could not be wakened. She immediately phoned 911. Mr. Bacon was transported to the hospital, where he went into respiratory arrest and was intubated. He had overdosed on his prescribed pain medications, antidepressants, and anti-anxiety agents.

Mr. Bacon's case highlights some of the problems that may occur when a patient requests assistance with suicide from a health care provider. First, his effort was not successful. What should the person assisting the suicide do when the suicide attempt is not successful? Completing the act (perhaps by placing a plastic bag over the attempter's head) is homicide and clearly illegal. In the state where Mr. Bacon lived, assisted suicide is not legally permissible. Therefore, if the attendant acknowledged assisting Mr. Bacon in his suicide attempt when she sought medical assistance for him, she could have been prosecuted.

Since he was incapable of ingesting his prescription medications without assistance, someone had to have assisted him. However, the attendant continued to maintain that she had refused to help him, had prepared him for bed, and had left for the day. Because the attendant was privately employed by Mr. Bacon rather than an agency, she had no nursing supervisor to notify of his request for assisted suicide. The attendant stated she had left Mr. Bacon for the evening and made no attempt to notify either Mr. Bacon's family or physician of his depression and suicidal thoughts.

The circumstances surrounding Mr. Bacon's attempted suicide illustrate how secretive and hidden the decision to assist a suicide may be, how conflicted the assistant may feel about such an irrevocable choice, and how poorly the patient may be evaluated before assistance is provided. The attendant who cared for Mr. Bacon insisted she had not assisted with his suicide, yet someone had because there were no medication containers anywhere in his apartment. Additionally, it was unclear how Mr. Bacon could have accumulated the huge doses of his medications that he had ingested without the assistance of the person who normally administered his medications. Mr. Bacon's request was obviously a cry for help, and after extubation he did receive that help. An angry, uncooperative Mr.

Bacon was transferred to the pain management unit of the hospital for medication adjustment, psychiatric evaluation, and treatment of his depression.

Voluntary Active Euthanasia

Some would argue that Mr. Bacon's case straddles the line between assisted suicide and voluntary euthanasia. Mr. Bacon had clearly requested assistance with dying. If he were capable of manipulating the medication prepared or prescribed by another individual into his mouth without assistance, then it was assisted

> In assisted suicide, while another person may provide the means of death, the patient completes the action that results in her or his death. In active euthanasia, another person provides both the means and the action that result in the patient's death.

suicide. However, if the attendant or another person had placed the medication in his mouth for him, then it was voluntary, active euthanasia. In active euthanasia, the health care provider or other person takes an action that purposefully and directly causes the patient's death. Concerning voluntary euthanasia, the patient requests that the action be taken to end her or his life; in involuntary euthanasia, the action to end the patient's life is taken without the patient's consent.

In the Netherlands, physicians who commit voluntary active euthanasia are not prosecuted if certain guidelines are followed:

- The death must be reported to the local prosecutor
- The patient's death request must be voluntary and enduring (carefully considered and requested on more than one occasion)
- The patient must be conscious and experiencing unbearable pain (physical pain, psychic suffering, or the potential disfigurement of the personality)
- All other reasonable solutions must have been considered
- The patient's death cannot inflict unnecessary suffering on others
- Only a doctor can euthanize a patient after obtaining a consultation to validate the decision

Most Dutch citizens and physicians support the continued use of active euthanasia in these selected circumstances. Eighty-one percent of the general population believes euthanasia is appropriate, while 83% of physicians believe it is acceptable in the face of unbearable suffering when no alternatives are available. Approximately 53% of Dutch physicians have performed voluntary euthanasia or assisted suicide, and the subjects are currently taught in medical and nursing curricula.

However, there are grave concerns about the Dutch experience. During more than 20 years that voluntary euthanasia has been permitted, the guidelines for euthanasia have been steadily broadening from unbearable pain to psychic disfigurement. One woman was assisted to die when she became depressed after the deaths of her two children and the breakup of her marriage. Most studies indicate that only about 40% of the cases are reported to the local authorities as required. So, the procedures are not all open to scrutiny by outside authorities, as was the original intent. Despite universal access to medical care in the Netherlands, palliative care programs have been poorly developed; and in the mid 1990s, only two hospice programs were in operation. Does this mean that Dutch citizens are experiencing an obligation to die quickly rather than consume medical resources or be a burden to others?

Perhaps the most significant concern, though, is that the Dutch may be sliding down the slippery slope to involuntary active euthanasia, purposefully ending a patient's life without her or his consent. Approximately 1000 deaths per year have been described in government reports as occurring from "life terminating choices not technically called euthanasia." These deaths have been interpreted by some critics of Dutch policy as deaths due to involuntary active euthanasia.

> Concerns about active euthanasia in the Netherlands include:
> - The consistent broadening of the guidelines for euthanasia
> - The lack of reporting of more than half of the cases of euthanasia
> - The lack of palliative care programs for dying patients
> - The potential slide down the slippery slope

Involuntary Active Euthanasia

Mrs. Brown, a 77-year-old woman, was admitted to a medical unit of an acute care hospital. She had undergone extensive surgery for colon cancer several months earlier and was in considerable pain and dehydrated at the time of admission. Mrs. Brown was barely responsive and was accompanied by a daughter, who announced she would be the medical care decision-maker because she had durable power of attorney for health care purposes. The daughter stated that she understood her mother was dying and she did not want any measures to prolong her mother's life but would like aggressive management of her mother's pain.

Mrs. Brown was started on IV hydration and a morphine infusion with intermittent morphine boluses for severe pain. As her pain was controlled and she was rehydrated, Mrs. Brown's vital signs stabilized and she appeared quite comfortable, but she was still either unable or unwilling to communicate. Mrs. Brown's daughter cornered her mother's nurse and proclaimed, "I told you I only wanted you to control my mother's pain. I don't want her life prolonged." The nurse reassured the daughter that her mother was responding favorably to the pain medication and hydration and nothing else was being done for her. "Then," said the daughter, "I want you to give her enough pain medication to end it now. This has been going on for too long and I need it to be over." When the nurse explained that she could not and would not administer that much medication to Mrs. Brown, the daughter announced, "You have to do what I say. I have her power of attorney for health care."

Administering an overdose of pain medication to a patient whose pain is controlled with the intent to end the patient's life is active euthanasia. In this case, it is involuntary euthanasia since the patient is unable to request the intervention, and the daughter has no legal or moral right to make such a request. Active euthanasia is illegal in this country, and the daughter does not have the right as durable power of attorney for her mother to request the nurse perform an illegal act.

Involuntary active euthanasia is usually a private, hidden act because it is illegal. Thus, it is difficult to gain a clear perspective on the extent to which health care providers engage in it. In a flawed study by Asch, it appeared that 16% of critical care nurses had performed active euthanasia, either voluntary or involuntary.[18] The nurses in Asch's study most often provided large doses of narcotics to patients in pain prior to the patient's death. Because of defects in the study, it was unclear whether the nurses' intent was to relieve their patients' pain or solely to cause the patients' death. A well-controlled study by Emanuel and colleagues[19] suggests approximately 12% of oncologists have engaged in active euthanasia but does not distinguish between voluntary and involuntary euthanasia.

Most health care providers who commit involuntary euthanasia state they are acting out of compassion. They argue that the patient's life was no longer worth living and that the burdens of the life far outweighed the benefits. They cite such reasons as the patient was suffering unbearably or the family and health care team were unable to reach a decision to withdraw futile, life-sustaining treatment so the patient was forced to suffer needlessly. They may also declare that the patient would never have wanted to live in her or his current condition and would have requested interventions be halted if she or he had a voice. Involuntary euthanasia is the judgment by another person, in this case a health care provider, that the patient's life is no longer worth living, followed by an action which ends the patient's life without the patient's consent.

Although the public supports the general concept of active euthanasia by physicians,[20] oncology patients in pain usually do not.[19] Perhaps it is telling that people who are dying, whose quality of life may appear limited to others, do not want to have health care providers empowered to determine if their lives are worth living or not. In fact, only 3% of Americans would want their health care providers to make a decision and commit involuntary euthanasia on their behalf if they were not conscious and could not express their wishes.[20] Thus, there is little support for those health care providers who contend that in committing involuntary euthanasia they are acting in accordance with their patients' wishes.

There are numerous other arguments against the use of active euthanasia. First, most medical and nursing professional organizations state their members have a primary duty not to harm, which prohibits them from intentionally causing a patient's death. Many religious groups profess that human life should be respected and health care providers should never intentionally cause their patients' death. Advocates for the poor and homeless wonder how long it would take before sick, vulnerable, poor people would begin to be euthanized if euthanasia were allowed in this society, where 42 million Americans lack health insurance and cost containment is becoming one of the most important medical values. Hospice nurses question whether palliative care would continue to receive adequate funding and referrals, or whether patients would experience pressures to die quickly and stop being a burden. Caring for a deteriorating or dying person takes time, a scarce commodity in our society.

Mrs. Brown's daughter insisted that she did not have time to stay with her mother and wait for her to die, so she wanted her mother's nurse to administer an overdose of pain medication to end things quickly. When the nurse explained that she would not intentionally give Mrs. Brown an overdose because it violated her moral code and she could not give the overdose without fear of losing her nursing license or being prosecuted, Mrs. Brown's daughter asked to speak with the nurse's supervisor.

The daughter repeated her demands for a lethal injection of morphine for her mother to the nursing supervisor. The supervisor attempted to explain that Mrs. Brown was resting comfortably, in no pain, and was receiving excellent nursing care. She explained that occasionally patients rally just prior to death and that although Mrs. Brown's prognosis had not changed, she was unlikely to die in the next few hours. The supervisor reiterated the staff nurse's explanations that they would neither make an attempt to delay or hasten Mrs. Brown's death. She suggested that Mrs. Brown's daughter might want to spend some of her mother's last hours with her. Although Mrs. Brown was not speaking, she did seem aware of her surroundings. The daughter turned and stomped off, announcing she was going to consult a lawyer. The supervisor responded, "We will take care of your mother while you are gone. We will do all that we can to be sure that she is comfortable." Mrs. Brown died in her sleep that evening before her daughter returned.

Although nurses should not be involved in active euthanasia, they can do a great deal to help a patient die a good death. Nurses can advocate for the appropriate use of technology and the withdrawal of futile and burdensome therapies. Nurses can ensure that their patients receive adequate symptom management, that the families are educated about the dying process, and that patients receive human contact, comfort, and support when they are actively dying. When the patient is actively dying and medical interventions can do no more, then nursing care remains essential.

REFERENCES

1. Stein C. Ending a life. *The Boston Globe Magazine.* 1999;March 14:13,24,30-34.

2. Diem SJ, Lanton JD, Tulsky JA. Cardiopulmonary resuscitation on television: miracles and misinformation. *N Engl J Med.* 1996;334:1578-1581.

3. Schneider P, Nelson DJ, Brown DD. In-hospital cardiopulmonary resuscitation: a thirty-year review. *J Am Board Fam Pract.* 1993;6(2):91-101.

4. Callahan D. *The Troubled Dream of Life: Living with Mortality.* New York, NY: Simon & Schuster; 1993.

5. Byock I. *Dying Well: Peace and Possibilities at the End of Life.* New York, NY: Riverhead Books; 1997.

6. Kuhse H. *Caring, Nurses, Women, and Ethics.* Oxford, England: Blackwell Publishers; 1997.

7. Wald F. Finding a way to give hospice care. In: Corliss I, Germino BB, Pittman M, eds. *Dying, Death, and Bereavement.* Boston, Mass: Jones and Barlett Publishers; 1994.

8. World Health Organization. *Cancer Pain Relief and Palliative Care. Technical Report Series 804.* Geneva: WHO; 1990.

9. Emanuel EJ. The promise of a good death. *Lancet Supplement Cancer.* 1998;351(9114):S112.

10. Zerwekh JV. Should fluid and nutritional support be withheld from terminally ill patients? *American Journal of Hospice Care.* 1987;July/Aug:37-38.

11. Dolan MB. Another hospice nurse says. *Nursing83.* 1983;Jan:51.

12. Meares CJ. Terminal dehydration: review. *American Journal of Hospice and Palliative Care.* 1994;May/June:10-14.

13. Emanuel E. Cost savings at the end of life: what do the data show. *JAMA.* 1996;275(24):1907-1914.

14. Vrtis MC. Cost benefit analysis of cardiopulmonary resuscitation: a comprehensive study, Part II. *Nursing Management.* 1999;23(5):44-51.

15. Support Principal Investigators. A controlled study to improve care for seriously ill hospital ized patients. *JAMA.* 1995;274(20):1591-1598.

16. Rachels J. *The End of Life: Euthanasia and Morality.* New York, NY: Oxford University Press; 1986.

17. American Nurses Association. *Position Statement on Assisted Suicide.* Washington, DC: ANA; 1994.

18. Asch DA. The role of critical care nurses in euthanasia and assisted suicide. *N Engl J Med.* 1996; 334(21):1374-1379.

19. Emanuel E, Fairclough DL, Daniels ER, Clarridge BR. Euthanasia and physician assisted sui cide: attitudes and experiences of oncology patients, oncologists, and the public. *Lancet.* 1996;347:1805-1810.

20. Blendon RJ, Szalay US, Knox RA. Should physicians aid their patients in dying? The public perspective. *JAMA.* 1992;267(19):2658-2662.

Multiple-Choice Questions

1. Which of the following is a reason why some Americans might have difficulty believing that a loved one is dying?
   A. Many Americans distrust technology and its ability to prolong or enhance life
   B. Most Americans have had personal experiences caring for dying relatives
   C. Most Americans learn about death and dying from TV programs where few severely ill patients die
   D. All of the above
   E. None of the above

2. According to Emanuel, what percentage of patients should be pain free during the dying process if aggressive pain management strategies are used?
   A. 80%
   B. 85%
   C. 90%
   D. 95%
   E. 100%

3. Which of the following is a *realistic* concern of health care providers about providing adequate pain medication for dying patients?
   A. Concern the patient will become addicted to the narcotics used to relieve the pain
   B. Concern of persecution for prescription of excessive amounts of medication to dying patients
   C. Concern that they will be responsible for the patient's death if the pain medication shortens the patient's life
   D. All of the above
   E. None of the above

4. Which of the following is a reason why a family member might want to provide a dying relative with IV hydration or nasogastric nutrition?
   A. Food and fluid are associated in many cultures with nurturance and care; not to feed seems not to care
   B. Force feeding and IV fluids have been demonstrated to increase the length of life for patients with cancer
   C. Patients who are fed and hydrated have fewer problems with dyspnea, incontinence, nausea, or vomiting than patients who are not fed
   D. All of the above
   E. None of the above

5. A do-not-resuscitate (DNR) order implies which of the following:
   A. CPR will not be attempted should the person respiratory or cardiac arrest
   B. No further aggressive or heroic treatment will be provided
   C. No further curative treatment will be provided
   D. Only comfort measures will be provided
   E. All of the above

6. John Hamilton is dying from amyotrophic lateral sclerosis (ALS). He was placed on a ventilator when he respiratory arrested and now he is asking to have the ventilator disconnected. He understands that he will most likely die. This is considered:
   A. Assisted suicide
   B. Involuntary active euthanasia
   C. Passive euthanasia
   D. Voluntary active euthanasia
   E. None of the above

7. Which of the following arguments might critics of assisted suicide make?
   A. There are limits to any individual's right to exercise her or his autonomy
   B. Assisted suicide results in a person being deprived of a moral good, her or his life
   C. The right to die may eventually become the responsibility to die so that the patient does not become a burden to her or his family
   D. All of the above
   E. None of the above

CHAPTER 7 ANSWERS

1. C
2. D
3. E
4. A
5. A
6. C
7. D

Conclusion

Kathleen Ouimet Perrin, RN, CCRN, PhD(c)
James McGhee, PhD

When is a nurse a professional nurse? Does a nurse owe her or his patients allegiance? Does a nurse have a responsibility to advocate for her or his patients? Why would a patient require an advocate?

Many nurses believe patients require advocates because they are vulnerable, ill people caught in a medical system with which they are unfamiliar. Negotiating such a system may require a guide, a counselor, a patient right's representative, or a nurse. Medical information and options are expanding at a rapid rate, and patients may be unsure of their options. Insurers may be unwilling for the patient to be notified of all viable treatment alternatives, and some physicians are still bound by gag rules from the insurance companies. Additionally, incompetent health care providers and institutions may deliver unnecessary, inappropriate, or unsafe treatment. Who, besides the vulnerable patient and her or his family, is watching out for the patient?

Over the past 20 years, the nursing profession has accepted the premise that nurses owe their primary allegiance to their patients and not to their patients' physicians, the institutions by which they are employed, or the patient's insurance company. The American Association of Colleges of Nursing (AACN) lists advocating for vulnerable patients and for patients' rights as behaviors that are critical to the performance of a caring, professional nurse.[1] Yet, nurses and ethicists are unable to agree on a consistent definition of advocacy. Proposed definitions include:

- Assisting patients to "authentically exercise their freedom of self-determination. By authentic is meant a way of making decisions that is truly one's own decisions that express all one believes important about oneself and the world; the entire complexity of one's values."[2]

- Informing patients "of what their rights are in a particular situation and then to make sure they have all the necessary information to make an informed decision," and "to support clients in the decisions they make."[3]

- Being "a spokesperson for the patient in those contexts in which it is not possible for the patient to speak for her or himself."[4]
- "Securing or checking on quality health care."[4]
- Creating "an atmosphere in which something intangible (human values, respect, compassion) can be realized... That is plain, not so simple, good nursing practice."[5]

Despite these differing definitions, there does appear to be agreement on what nurses owe to their patients. Whether it is termed patient advocacy or good patient care, nurses have a responsibility to:

- Assure their patients have sufficient information to make authentic, informed choices about treatment
- Assist their patients to obtain the health care they need
- Provide or oversee competent delivery of care when their patients are unable to provide or obtain care for themselves
  - assist with the alleviation of their patients' suffering
  - assure competent nursing care from the individual nurse or delegate
  - protect the patient from incompetent care of other health care providers
  - maintain a safe environment for care
- Maintain patient confidentiality and privacy

When nurses need to secure these basic values for their patients, they are often described as providing good patient care, sometimes credited with being patient advocates, and occasionally branded as troublemakers.

Critics of nurses as patient advocates condemn the confrontational approaches that some nurses use when stating they are functioning as patient advocates. These critics of nurse advocacy for patients argue that negotiation, compromise, and reporting along institutional channels are much more effective than confrontational stands. In fact, patient advocacy need not be confrontational, and any one of the other approaches may lead to appropriate outcomes for patients. One study by Sellin reported that by utilizing staff meetings, planning case conferences, and reporting within institutional channels, nurses were able to function as patient advocates, obtain desirable changes from the institution, and behave in an ethically viable manner.[6] Sellin noted that a supportive unit culture and nursing administration influenced nurses to act as patient advocates.

However, not all administrations are supportive of nurse attempts at patient advocacy. Critics of nurses being held accountable for serving as patient advocates charge that nurses are constrained by institutional bureaucracy and prevented from acting in their patients' best interests. These critics argue that nurses are often unwilling to act because they fear that confrontation with the physician or institution may cost them their credibility, their opportunities for professional advancement, or their employment. These critics also seem to equate patient advocacy with confrontation with physicians or institutional administrations. Nurses' self-interest may be another reason why negotiation, compromise, case conferences, or reporting within institutional channels may be more appropriate methods of patient advocacy than confrontation.

However, there are circumstances when advocacy might require confrontation, such as the example in Chapter 6, when the OB-GYN intern attempted to perform endotracheal intubation. There might also be rare circumstances when care to groups of patients might be so compromised that confrontational approaches, such as striking or whistle-blowing, might be indicated.

It is not only the current patients within the health care institutions who are vulnerable. Health care in the United States is evolving rapidly. Since there is considerable discontent within the American population with the current health care system, now is an opportunity for reform of the system. With nurses' knowledge of the defects of the health care system and the numerous contradictory proposals for changes in legislation for health care, nurses ought to become involved in advocating for legislation that will promote the best interests of their patients.

Let's consider the following questions:

- What rights should a member of an HMO have?
- How should primary care providers for HMO patients be reimbursed?
- Should patients have access to emergency rooms or specialists without referral?
- Should patients be able to sue HMOs for pain and suffering, for care that was denied to them?
- Who should have access to a patient's confidential computerized health care record?
- How should the health care dollar be distributed?
- Should 20% be allocated to benefit for-profit health care plans?
- How should hospitals, rehabilitation centers, home care, and long-term care facilities be reimbursed?
- Should people be able to ask for assistance in committing suicide?

All of the previous questions have a direct bearing on the type and quality of nursing care. Nurses ought to be involved in advocating for legislation that will benefit their current and future patients on both the state and national levels. Perhaps, at the moment, this is the most pressing type of patient advocacy required of nurses because nurses have a chance to shape the policies that will guide health care delivery as this millennium develops.

REFERENCES

1. American Association of Colleges of Nursing. *The Essentials of Baccalaureate Education for Professional Nursing Practice*. Washington, DC: AACN; 1998.
2. Gadow S. Existential advocacy: philosophical foundations of nursing. In: Pence T, Cantrall J, eds. *Ethics in Nursing: An Anthology*. New York, NY: National League for Nursing; 1990:41-51.
3. Kohnke MF. The nurse as advocate. In: Pence T, Cantrall J, eds. *Ethics in Nursing: An Anthology*. New York, NY: National League for Nursing; 1990:56-58.
4. Abrams N. A contrary view of the nurse as patient advocate. In: Pence T, Cantrall J, eds. *Ethics in Nursing: An Anthology*. New York, NY: National League for Nursing; 1990:102-105.
5. Curtin P. The nurse as advocate: a cantankerous critique. In: Pence T, Cantrall J, eds. *Ethics in Nursing: An Anthology*. New York, NY: National League for Nursing; 1990:121-123.
6. Sellin SC. Out on a limb: a qualitative study of patient advocacy in institutional nursing. *Nursing Ethics*. 1995;2(1):19-29.

Index

Keep up with the Latest in Nursing!

Other Exciting Books in the Nursing Concepts *Series Include:*

Title	Author	Book #	Price
❏ Nursing Concepts: Oxygenation	Sheldon	25236	$21.95
❏ Nursing Concepts: Pain	Kazanowski	25228	$21.95
❏ Nursing Concepts: Mobility	Durette	25201	$21.95
❏ Nursing Concepts: Symptom Management in the Acute Care Setting	Laccetti	25198	$21.95

Subtotal $_____
NJ and CA Sales Tax* $_____
Handling Charge $ 4.50
Total $_____

ORDER TODAY!

Name: _____

Address: _____

City: _____ State: _____ Zip Code: _____

Phone: _____ Fax: _____

Charge my: ❏ [AMEX] ❏ [MasterCard] ❏ [VISA] Account#: _____

Exp. date: _____ Signature: _____

Prices are subject to change. Shipping charges may apply. Shipping and handling charges are non-refundable.
*Purchases in NJ and CA are subject to tax. Please add applicable state and local taxes.

CODE: 2A719

Mail Order Form To

SLACK Incorporated
Professional Book Division
6900 Grove Road
Thorofare, NJ 08086-9864

OR

Call 800-257-8290 or 856-848-1000
Fax 856-853-5991
Email Orders@slackinc.com

Visit Our World Wide Web: www.slackbooks.com